Succession Planning for Small and Family Businesses

Who will lead your organization into the future? Have you created the systems to properly implement required succession transitions? Have you put the financial tools in place to fund the transition? Do you want a plan that connects with your personal and company core values? When do you include timely planning related to strategy and talent issues? What are the appropriate communication strategies for sharing your plan? What legal issues need consideration related to strategy, financial, and people aspects of succession?

So, what is preventing you from starting this effort tomorrow? Small and family businesses are the bedrock of all businesses. More people are employed by small and family-owned businesses than by all multinational companies combined. Yet the research on small and family businesses is bleak: fewer than one-third of small business owners in the United States can afford to retire. Only 40% of small businesses have a workable disaster plan in case of the sudden death or disability of the owner, and only 42% of small businesses in the United States have a succession plan. Fewer than 11% of family-owned businesses make it to the third generation beyond the founder. Lack of succession planning is the second most common reason for small business failure.

Many organizations often wonder where to start and what to do. *Succession Planning for Small and Family Businesses: Navigating Successful Transitions* provides a comprehensive approach in guiding such efforts.

Small and family-owned businesses rarely employ first-rate, well-qualified talent in human resources. More typically, business owners must be jacks-of-all-trades and serve as their own accountants, lawyers, business consultants, marketing experts, and HR wizards. Unfortunately, that does not always work well when business owners embark on planning for retirement or business exits. To help business owners avert problems, this book advises on some of the management, tax and financial, legal, and psychological issues that should be considered when planning retirement or other exits from the business. This comprehensive approach is unique when compared to the books, articles, and other literature that currently exist on the market. This book takes on a bold and integrated approach. Relevant research combined with the rich experiences of the authors brings this comprehensive, evidence-based approach to action-based approaches for the reader.

Succession Planning for Small and Family Businesses

Navigating Successful Transitions

Edited by
William J. Rothwell & Robert K. Prescott

Routledge
Taylor & Francis Group
A PRODUCTIVITY PRESS BOOK

First published 2023
by Routledge
605 Third Avenue, New York, NY 10158

and by Routledge
4 Park Square, Milton Park, Abingdon, Oxon, OX14 4RN

Routledge is an imprint of the Taylor & Francis Group, an informa business

ISBN: 9781032249889 (hbk)
ISBN: 9781032249872 (pbk)
ISBN: 9781003281054 (ebk)

DOI: 10.4324/9781003281054

Typeset in Garamond
by Deanta Global Publishing Services, Chennai, India

William J. Rothwell dedicates this book to his wife *Marcelina*, his daughter *Candice*, his son *Froilan*, his grandsons *Aden* and *Gabriel*, and his granddaughters *Freya* and *Lina*.

Robert K. Prescott dedicates this book to his wife *Yvonne*, his daughter *Heather*, his granddaughter *Emilie*, and his grandson *Kirin*.

Contents

Preface

Who will lead your organization into the future? Have you created the processes and systems to properly implement required succession transitions? Have you put the financial tools in place to fund the transition? Do you want a plan that connects with your personal and company core values? When do you include timely planning related to strategy and talent issues? What are the appropriate communication strategies for sharing your plan? What legal issues need consideration related to strategy, financial, and people aspects of succession?

So, what is preventing you from starting this effort tomorrow? Small and family businesses are the bedrock of all businesses. More people are employed by small and family-owned businesses than by all multinational companies combined. Yet the research on small and family businesses is bleak: less than one-third of small business owners in the United States can afford to retire. Only 40% of small businesses have a workable disaster plan if the sudden death or disability of the owner occurs, and only 42% of small businesses in the United States have a succession plan. Just 11% of family-owned businesses make it to the third generation beyond the founder (Businessweek.com 2010). Lack of succession planning is the second most common reason for small business failure.

Many organizations often wonder where to start and what to do. *Succession Planning for Sustainable Small and Family Businesses: Navigating Successful Transitions* provides a comprehensive approach in guiding such efforts.

The Purpose of the Book

Small and family-owned businesses rarely employ a comprehensive set of first-rate, well-qualified talent in human resources. More typically, business owners must be jacks-of-all-trades and serve as their own accountants, lawyers, business consultants, marketing experts, and HR wizards. Unfortunately, that does not always work well when business owners embark on planning for retirement or business exits. To help business owners avert problems, this book offers limited advice on the management, tax and financial, legal, and psychological issues that should be considered when planning retirement or other exits from the business. This comprehensive approach is unique when compared to the books, articles, and other literature that exist on the market. This book takes on a bold and integrated approach. Relevant, practical research combined with the rich experiences of the authors bring this comprehensive, evidence-based book to the reader.

The Target Audience for the Book

This book is written for anyone interested in succession planning for small and/or family businesses. That includes business owners, family members with a stake in family businesses, and those interested in offering services to small and family businesses.

The Organization of the Book

This book opens with a dedication, a table of contents, acknowledgments to those who helped with the book, the biosketches of the editors and contributing authors, and an advance organizer that makes it easy to jump to chapters based on the reader's immediate needs.

The book, organized in three major parts, opens with **Part I: Deciding What to Do: Life and Career Planning for Small Business Owners and Family Leaders**. This part addresses an important first step, which involves business owners deciding what they want to do with their lives and their businesses. **Chapter 1** is entitled "Considering Your Choices." The chapter addresses a key question: What do small business or family business owners want to do? What are common choices—such as sell the business, turn the business over to a partner, make the business employee owned, and others. Small and family business handoffs start with the business owners or family leaders deciding what they want to do and then pondering it with key stakeholders (such as spouses, key employees, family members, and even key customers). Business owners must decide what they want to do with their lives and careers after the business before they can plan for the business. An important issue for owners to consider is how much, if at all, they wish to remain involved with the business after they "step down" or "retire." (There are degrees of how much to exit.) In family businesses, special issues emerge around how much or whether to transfer the business to a family member and/or to those who married into the family.

Part II: Planning for Succession in Small and Family Business consists of two chapters.

Chapter 2 is called "Strategic Planning for Succession Sustainability." In this chapter, authors Timothy Ullmann and Shanna Ullmann review what is needed in a strategic succession plan. A strategic succession plan results from a deliberate and considered process for defining the future direction of a company when the owner retires. Through a precise and well-articulated plan, this document facilitates a change in ownership with continued operations or the liquidation of the business. This chapter discusses factors to consider when transferring, selling, or liquidating a business using a time-sensitive strategic plan. The chapter also discusses why it's important to create a strategic succession plan and the consequences of not doing so. It also offers practical and measurable strategic methods for creating a successful succession plan. Finally, a Strategic Succession Plan Roadmap outlines a step-by-step procedure for developing and implementing an effective succession plan. A smooth transition, sale, or liquidation of the company could be achieved.

Chapter 3 is called "Recruiting a Successor from Inside, Outside, or Utilizing Other Options for the Organization." In this chapter, authors Kay Turner, Deborah M. Adwokat, and Robert K. Prescott examine options for a succession. Good successors can be sought both internally and externally. Recruiting an internal successor will assist small organizations, particularly those with a distinct company culture. Recruiting a leader from within a company with a strong or dominating culture has shown to be a cultural "fit" in multiple settings. When "critical leadership abilities in companies are insufficient for satisfying (its) current and future needs," according to the Center for Creative Leadership, external talent can be a critical component in a small business succession plan.

Part III: Special Issues in Small and Family Business Succession Planning is the heart of the book. It consists of Chapters 4 through 10.

Chapter 4 is called "Family-Owned Business Dynamics and Politics." Small and family business owners face special political issues that may be of less concern to large, publicly traded companies or to government agencies.

As the chapter dramatically illustrates, it is not for the faint of heart to navigate the dynamics and politics of a family-owned firm. Issues they encounter, regardless of industry, may be of little interest to large corporations or government organizations. Family members who are invested in the company's success must help the CEO and other members of the leadership team build long-term business practices. They might begin by ensuring that their ethics and values are in sync. Although competencies are critical, particularly in family-member executive jobs, the ability of the Board and leadership to assess candidate motivation during the selection process is also critical. Both can have long-term consequences for the family and the company. It's also critical to define, build, and sustain a desired company culture that guides how individuals should behave in the workplace.

Chapter 5 is called "What Psychological Challenges Affect Small and Family Business Succession?" Small and family firms face psychological challenges with succession planning. The patterns of interaction among relatives, their roles and relationships, and the numerous elements that impact their interactions were defined in this chapter. Family members are one of the key sources of relationship security or stress since they rely on each other for emotional, physical, and financial support. Family dynamics are crucial in succession planning for small family businesses because they can influence how successors are chosen, who they are chosen for, and the impact that decision has on the organization.

The idea known as the *Sequel Fallacy* is based on the assumption that the second generation of a family will naturally acquire the business. "Many well-intentioned family company successions are constructed around the concept that next-generation leaders can simply walk into the huge shoes of their predecessors and run the business (and the family) just as their father or mother would have done," says Taylor Law. However, this ignores that each new generation of leaders will have different abilities and interests, and the fact that company circumstances and demands will undoubtedly change. When a family firm assumes that the next generation can simply take over without evaluating the CEO's job description, governance, or succession planning, they are making a mistake.

As this chapter demonstrates, identity is linked to the family company and the family that owns it. What effect does one have on the other, and are they distinct? Consider the question, "Who am I?" Who are we, exactly? Many entrepreneurs spend years, if not decades, establishing their company from the ground up, much like raising a child, and many entrepreneurs feel the same emotional bonds, sacrificial pain, and beaming pride toward their firm as they would a child. This brings with it a slew of psychological issues that must be addressed as you would with your own children.

Chapter 6 is entitled "Questions and Answers about Legal Issues in Small and Family Business Succession." This chapter answers some of the most prevalent legal questions that small and family business owners have about succession planning, and provides practical ideas and tools that can help key stakeholders come up with actual answers to crucial questions. Usually you'll discover there isn't a clear answer, rather a framework for determining the greatest decision for your business and succession goals after reading this chapter.

The subjects covered in this chapter may fill a book on their own. The chapter is not intended to provide complete legal guidance. Instead, it provides a road map for common legal techniques and considerations that will lead you to the legal partnerships, planning, and papers you must build for the business legacy you want.

Chapter 7, called "Valuing the Small and Family Business for Succession Planning," focuses on the common tax and accounting issues that may be of less concern to large, publicly traded companies or to government agencies. This chapter presents a bird's-eye view of small and family business valuations. On this subject, volumes have been written. Many professionals make a living by offering appraisal services. The business valuation has been presumed to be for inheritance and gift tax purposes, and that the business being assessed is a going concern. Due to space constraints, this chapter does not prepare the reader to fight the Internal Revenue Service. It is therefore suggested that anyone who needs a valuation for estate and gift tax purposes hire a business appraiser qualified to work with the IRS. Organizations such as the American Institute of CPAs and the American Society of Appraisers, among others, certify these professions.

Chapter 8, called Questions and Answers about Financial Planning Issues in Small and Family Business Succession, is about financial planning for small business and family business owners. Small and family business owners face many financial planning issues that may be of less concern to large, publicly traded companies or to government agencies. Succession planning is a methodical procedure. To put all the parts together, it takes time, a willing business owner, and a determined team of professionals. Because so many other aspects of the plan depend on it, the financial planning component of the picture must be addressed early on. The financial plan should urge business owners to consider their current and future financial needs and objectives to construct a road map. The financial plan will reveal flaws, possibilities, and places for improvement, forcing the business owner to think and plan for both the short and long term.

Chapter 9 is entitled Talent Management in Small and Family Businesses and centers on talent management questions that can bedevil small and family business owners. Obtaining, engaging, deploying, assessing or rating, and retaining talent are defined in this chapter as talent management. How the term "talent" is interpreted is a critical problem. Developing people for additional or different responsibilities was termed succession planning. If talent management is taken to mean, in the most basic sense, attempts to attract, develop, and retain talented people, small and family business owners have unique obstacles. With all human resource difficulties, some challenges have long existed for small and family businesses; other, fresh challenges have been sparked by the epidemic and its aftereffects.

Chapter 10, the last chapter, is "Transitioning the Business and Executing the Succession Plan." This chapter presents intriguing tales that depict various scenarios that could arise when a business is transitioning from one owner or manager to another. Individual Development Plan (IDP), execution, and transition management were all given key definitions. The chapter includes coaching advice on how to prepare for change. The chapter also looks at common procedures and challenges for hiring a successor from outside the company, promoting a successor from inside the company, and selecting one of the many alternatives to an external recruitment or internal promotion. The chapter includes step-by-step instructions on how to handle hiring a new CEO, GM, or firm owner from the outside, promotions from within, or other options.

The book ends with two appendices. **Appendix I** focuses on frequently asked questions (FAQs). **Appendix II** provides resources about small and family succession to carry the reader on for more information on the topics of each chapter.

William J. Rothwell and Robert K. Prescott

Acknowledgments

The editors appreciate all those who contributed to this project.

William J. Rothwell wants to express his special thanks to Robert K. Prescott for his excellent ability to herd cats. Bob put the project plan together and was mindful of deadlines and publisher requirements while also shouldering the responsibilities of writing his chapters. Rothwell would also like to thank Aileen Zaballero for reviewing the book while in draft and Farhan Sadique, his graduate assistant, for his help with the resource guide in the appendix to this book.

Robert K. Prescott wants to convey his continued appreciation to William J. Rothwell for his exceptional guidance and wisdom in book publication. Bill taught this author how to write books to maximize reader comprehension and learning. Prescott would also like to thank the co-authors of this book and Denise Anderson for their significant contributions and friendship.

William J. Rothwell
State College, Pennsylvania
March 2022

Robert K. Prescott
Pine Mountain, Georgia
March 2022

About the Editors and Contributing Authors

Editors

William J. Rothwell, PhD, SPHR, SHRM-SCP, RODC, CPTD Fellow, is President of Rothwell and Associates, Inc., a full-service consulting company that specializes in succession planning. He is also a Distinguished Professor of Education in the Workforce Education and Development program, Department of Learning and Performance Systems, in the College of Education at The Pennsylvania State University, University Park campus. In that capacity, he leads a top-ranked graduate program in learning and performance and in Organization Development. He has authored, co-authored, edited, or co-edited 300 books, book chapters, and articles—including 154 books. Before arriving at Penn State in 1993, he had 20 years of work experience as a Training Director in government and in business. As a consultant, he has worked with over 50 multinational corporations—including Motorola, General Motors, Ford, and others. In 2004, he earned the Graduate Faculty Teaching Award at Pennsylvania State University, a single award given to the best graduate faculty member on the 23 campuses of the Penn State system. His train-the-trainers programs have won global awards and, in 2022, he was given the 2022 Advancing a Global Penn State Lifetime Achievement Award to recognize his sustained lifetime commitment to international training, education, research, service, and consulting. In 2022 he was also given the Lifetime Achievement Award by the Organization Development Network.

His recent books include *High-Performance Coaching for Managers* (Routledge, 2022); *Rethinking Organizational Diversity, Equity, and Inclusion* (Routledge, 2022); *Organization Development Interventions:*

Executing Effective Organizational Change (Routledge, 2021); *Virtual Coaching to Improve Group Relationships* (Routledge, 2021); *The Essential HR Guide for Small Business and Start Ups* (Society for Human Resource Management, 2020); *Increasing Learning and Development's Impact Through Accreditation* (Palgrave, 2020); *Workforce Development: Guidelines for Community College Professionals*, 2nd ed. (Rowman-Littlefield, 2020); *Adult Learning Basics*, 2nd ed. (ATD Press, 2020); *Human Performance Improvement: Building Practitioner Performance,* 3rd ed. (Routledge, 2018); *Innovation Leadership* (Routledge, 2018); *Evaluating Organization Development: How to Ensure and Sustain the Successful Transformation* (CRC Press, 2017), *Marketing Organization Development Consulting: A How-To Guide for OD Consultants* (CRC Press, 2017), *Assessment and Diagnosis for Organization Development: Powerful Tools and Perspectives for the OD practitioner* (CRC Press, 2017); *Community College Leaders on Workforce Development* (Rowman & Littlefield, 2017); *Organization Development in Practice* (ODNetwork, 2016); *Mastering the Instructional Design Process*, 5th ed. (Wiley, 2016); *Practicing Organization Development*, 4th ed. (Wiley, 2015); *Effective Succession Planning*, 5th ed. (Amacom, 2015); *The Competency Toolkit*, 2 vols., 2nd ed. (HRD Press, 2015); *Beyond Training and Development*, 3rd ed. (HRD Press, 2015); *The Leader's Daily Role in Talent Management* (McGraw-Hill, 2015); *Organization Development Fundamentals* (ATD Press, 2015); *Creating Engaged Employees: It's Worth the Investment* (ATD Press, 2014); *The Leader's Daily Role in Talent Management* (Institute for Training and Development [Malaysia], 2014); *Optimizing Talent in the Federal Workforce* (Management Concepts, 2014), *Performance Consulting* (Wiley, 2014); the *ASTD Competency Study: The Training and Development Profession Redefined* (ASTD, 2013); *Becoming An Effective Mentoring Leader: Proven Strategies for Building Excellence in Your Organization* (McGraw-Hill, 2013); *Talent Management: A Step-by-Step Action-Oriented Approach Based on Best Practice* (HRD Press, 2012); the edited three-volume *Encyclopedia of Human Resource Management* (Wiley, 2012); *Lean But Agile: Rethink Workforce Planning and Gain a True Competitive Advantage* (Amacom, 2012); *Invaluable Knowledge: Securing Your Company's Technical Expertise-Recruiting and Retaining Top Talent, Transferring Technical Knowledge, Engaging High Performers* (Amacom, 2011); *Competency-Based Training Basics* (ASTD Press, 2010); *Practicing Organization Development*, 3rd ed. (Pfeiffer, 2009); *Basics of Adult Learning* (ASTD, 2009); *HR Transformation* (Davies-Black, 2008); *Working Longer* (Amacom, 2008); and *Cases in Government Succession Planning: Action-Oriented Strategies for*

Public-Sector Human Capital Management, Workforce Planning, Succession Planning, and Talent Management (HRD Press, 2008).

Robert K. Prescott, PhD, SPHR, SHRM-SCP, has spent 20 years in industry and 22 years in teaching and consulting positions. Included in Bob's rich experiences is work in Corporate Engagement at the College of Continuing Studies at the University of Alabama, Graduate Faculty of Management at the Crummer Graduate School of Business at Rollins College in Winter Park, Florida, Director of Executive Education at Penn State and Director of Human Resources for BellSouth Communications, Inc.

His consulting initiatives have placed him in advising and teaching positions with such organizations as AAA, ARAMARK, Deloitte, Delphi Automotive Systems, Estee Lauder, Internal Revenue Service (IRS), Lockheed Martin EIS, the National Basketball Association (NBA), Olive Garden Restaurants, Pitney Bowes, Scholastic Book Fairs, The Social Security Administration, T Mobile, UNICEF, Walt Disney World, and the US Army. His extensive international work has been with companies such as Corporación Elite, Ecuador, Grupo Industrial de Monclova, Mexico, Mavesa de Venezuela, Minerven, Mota-Engil, Portugal, and the Bermuda Employers Council.

In both corporate and academic settings, Bob has taught graduate level courses in the Executive Doctorate, MBA, and Master of Human Resources (MHR) programs and business application training in the areas of strategic leadership, agile leadership, organization behavior, influence strategies, human resource management, supervision, and enterprise consulting. He is a native of Birmingham, Alabama, holds a BS in marketing from the University of Alabama and a PhD in workforce education and development from the Pennsylvania State University. Bob co-authored the books *The Strategic Human Resource Leader: How to Prepare Your Organization for the 6 Key Trends Shaping the Future* (Davies-Black, 1998); *HR Transformation: Demonstrating Leadership in the Face of Future Trends* (Davies-Black/SHRM, 2009); and the *Encyclopedia of Human Resource Management – Volume One* (Wiley, 2012).

Contributing Authors

Shirley Adams, MBA, SPHR, SHRM-SCP, is a proven HR professional and trainer with over 30 progressive years of hands-on operations and strategic leadership experience. Working with organizations has given her a well-rounded knowledge of HR and has directly managed functions to include safety and environmental, payroll and benefits, employee relations, recruitment, selection and retention, and various operations functions.

Believing that people are the key to success, Shirley has a passion for helping organizations work toward aligning their human capital resources with the corporate strategic plan and mission to maximize efficiency and profit.

Education and certifications include:

■ Executive MBA from the University of Central Florida
■ BA in organizational management from Palm Beach Atlantic University
■ SPHR designation from HRCI
■ SCP designation from the Society for Human Resource Management (SHRM)
■ Certified MBTI Facilitator
■ Certified Dave Ramsey Facilitator

Community service activities include:

■ Past board chairwoman for The Grove Counseling Center
■ Past member for the WSIA Scholarship Committee
■ Treasurer for Marine Industry Technical Education Council – MITEC
■ Society of Human Resources member
■ Board member of American Boat Builders and Repairers Association—ABBRA

Deborah M. Adwokat, SHRM-SCP, is the Senior Manager, Talent Management at Fordham University. She partners and supports the Fordham Community in the hiring and promotion process ensuring adherence to the University's diversity, equity, and inclusion initiatives.

■ Deborah serves as the Human Resources Adviser for recruitment strategies across all areas and divisions of the University, guiding best practices. She manages talent acquisition for the institution from position requisition development to onboarding to exit interviews. She supports managers in the recruitment, interviewing, and offer process, and ensures I-9 federal compliance.
■ Deborah helped to implement Fordham's first electronic applicant tracking system, including launching software, and training managers. To

increase employee retention, she led the Human Resources project to select, develop, and institute an electronic exit interview survey.

■ Before her 17 years in higher education, Deborah began her career as a counselor and spent 20 years working as the corporate director of human resources in a family-owned business.

■ During her tenure at the family-owned business, she was responsible for the human resources function nationwide, including benefits, talent acquisition/management, and employment/labor issues. In addition, she opened new locations and closed others, hired senior executives, developed manager training programs, and successfully managed EEOC claims.

■ Deborah holds a BA in psychology and an MS in counseling in education from Herbert H. Lehman College, City University of New York.

Larry Baldwin, SPHR, SHRM-SCP, MBA, proudly serves as the Director of the Alabama Human Resource Institute and as a Human Resource Management Clinical Instructor for the Culverhouse College of Business at the University of Alabama. He is the Angus R. and David J. Cooper Faculty Fellow. Having served in his role since January 2014, Larry brings a comprehensive working background of 30 years as a human resource executive and practitioner to the classroom and to his work in the institute on projects with the business, government, and labor community. His successful career also includes progressive experience in general sales, and risk management in various industries and environments such as manufacturing, nonprofit, health care, maritime, and wireless communications. This experience is used to tirelessly prepare his students to begin their career journey in the human resource and business career fields. His passion for his students and the career field are critical in his work in human capital management. He also serves as an instructor for HR practitioners and executives preparing for the SHRM-CP and SCP certification exams.

Larry holds a BS in industrial relations and an MBA in general management from the University of South Alabama. He also holds these certifications: Senior Professional in Human Resource (SPHR) and SHRM-SCP from the Society of Human Resource Management. He has also completed the University of Alabama On-Line Instructor Certification Course and served as an Arbitrator for the Better Business Bureau.

His strong background in academics and business provides a unique perspective to people, business, and strategic issues facing all organizations today.

Larry has also served as an Adjunct Professor, focusing on HR management, leadership, business ethics, and negotiation classes at the University of South Alabama, Samford University, and the University of Alabama-Birmingham. He and his wife are natives of Mobile, Alabama. Larry is also a veteran of the US Air Force and holds an FCC Amateur Radio Ham License.

Jacqueline "Jackie" T. Brito, founder and CEO, is a highly credentialed evidence-based HR strategist, executive coach, and speaker.

Included in Jackie's diverse experiences is work in recruitment, marketing, and career development at Rollins College Crummer Graduate School of Business in Winter Park, Florida, and as an HR consultant (HR business partner) at the Chicago Tribune's *Orlando Sentinel*, a multimedia communications company.

In both academic and industry conference settings, she has facilitated graduate-level courses in executive education, MBA and Master of Human Resources programs and business-application training.

Jackie also founded a coaching and consulting practice built on the belief that: *Every experience matters – even the ones you regret.* By incorporating her customized The Balanced-Life Perspective tool—an introspective coaching assessment—her clients are equipped to develop strategies for success in a range of personal and professional areas. She has helped C-suite professionals, emerging leaders, entrepreneurs (advanced and startups), attorneys, and a host of others reposition themselves by transforming their thinking to allow opportunities to emerge.

Her proven coaching methodology has been used to establish effective partnerships with individuals and teams as they navigate some of their toughest transitions in life and business.

She is a native of Dothan, Alabama, and lives in Orlando.

Kelsey Lovett, CFP®, works with a Benefit Compensation Group based in Auburn, Alabama. Her goal as a Certified Financial Planner® is to help create and sustain healthy family organizations and businesses that will steward wealth and long run family goals. She looks to cultivate family legacies through succession planning, wealth management, and intergenerational collaboration. Kelsey believes that a focus on family politics, within the financial planning framework, is essential for success and expansion.

Kelsey's passion for working with family-owned and operated businesses comes from her own family's story. Her grandfather bought an independent pharmacy in 1962, and the family continues to own and operate it today. She knows, first-hand, the importance of succession planning for businesses and families. Her goal is to help clients address their current financial objectives, but also plan strategically for multiple generations.

Kelsey has worked in the financial planning industry since 2006. She graduated from Auburn University with her BS in Finance and has continued her educational pursuits through the American College of Financial Planning.

Kyle S. Meyer, PhD, is the Executive-in-Residence for Accounting at the Rollins College Crummer Graduate School of Business. Before coming to Rollins, Kyle served as President of Pineloch Management Corporation, a family-owned business in Central Florida. He also served as Chief Financial Officer in a variety of industries including large-scale real estate developers such as The Ginn Company and Terrabrook. Kyle spent five years on audit staff of Arthur Andersen & Co. at the beginning of his career.

Kyle's areas of expertise include auditing, financial accounting, managerial accounting, and cost accounting. He has advised closely held businesses with succession planning strategies and asset valuations. Kyle has experience with valuing closely held businesses in connection with succession planning and shareholder buyouts.

Kyle holds a BS from Florida State University, an MBA from Rollins College, and PhD from Florida State University.

Ashley Ridgeway-Washington, JD, became a member of the CHRISTUS Health in 2014 and serves as the System Interim Vice President of Human Resources where she provides strategic HR leadership to the Corporate, Northeast Texas region, and Continuing Care organizations. In her role, she collaborates closely with leaders to align HR strategy with business strategies to achieve organizational goals and act as a culture steward for the organization.

Besides her full-time role at CHRISTUS, Ashley serves as adjunct faculty in the College of Management at the University of Texas, Arlington, where she taught human resource management courses. Ashley continues to pursue excellence through entrepreneurship as her passion manifests to help others be their best selves. Ashley is the Founder and CEO of Hoop Shots for Kids (www.hoopshots.org). Through Hoop Shots programs, her company brings basketball fundamentals, sportsmanship, character development, and fitness to North Texas child development centers as a full-service basketball and character development ancillary program serving children ages 2 to 10. In addition, Ashley continues to operate the Law Offices of Ashley Ridgeway-Washington as a practicing attorney in Florida focusing on creating HR compliance solutions and consulting for small businesses.

Although Ashley continues to build her brand as a HR strategist, engagement influencer, thought leader and trusted partner in the corporate human resources space, she heralds her greatest charge and sense of accomplishment as her impact in her role as "mom" to Aniyah (age 17) and Robert (age 8).

Farhan Sadique is a recognized student leader and a PhD student in Workforce Education & Development program at Penn State University. He received an MS from Pittsburg State University. Farhan is a globally experienced, value-driven professional with years of experience in management with a successful record of creating a better workplace. He is passionate about studying innovative organization development and change management approaches and applying that knowledge to retail organization transformation. Even though his research interest primarily focuses on the sustainability and development of retail organizations, he has successfully contributed to related research projects, including an open-source model for OD application, OD career assessment tools, evaluation capacity development, employee career hopefulness, and job satisfaction. He can be contacted at fvs5201@psu.edu.

Kay Turner serves as Vice President for Human Resources at Fordham University since September 2017. In this role, the certified senior professional in human resources and attorney is charged with spearheading state-of-the-art strategies and programs to recruit, hire, develop, and retain diverse and talented faculty, administrators, and staff.

In her brief time at Fordham, Turner has led the HR team in developing and implementing innovative solutions that enhance delivery of HR services, including benefits design and administration, professional development initiatives, labor and employee relations, and HR information systems that ensure compliance at the local, state, and federal levels. Turner provides strategic and organizational guidance, and advice and support to senior leaders and the entire University Community regarding human resources issues and administration.

Turner has an extensive background in human resources and employment law at higher education, nonprofit, and government institutions including multilocation, multistate operations in the tri-state area. Besides her role at Fordham, Turner shares her experience in the classroom, teaching ethics, governance, and accountability at York College. She also taught business law, and human resource training and development.

Before Fordham, Turner served four years as Vice President of Human Resources at the New Jersey Institute of Technology (NJIT), where she functioned as an adviser to the board of trustees and university president on executive compensation considerations, secured three years of funding to advance technology within HR, and also launched a successful internal HR marketing campaign that led to a widely published cadre of HR services and solutions.

Before making her move into higher education, Turner was Vice President of Human Resources at JCCA, formerly known as the Jewish Child Care Association; the Director of Employee Relations at the nationally recognized Hackensack University Medical Center, a 900-bed nonprofit, research, and teaching hospital in Hackensack, New Jersey; and the Director of Employee Relations and Diversity at the MTA Metro-North Railroad, the second largest commuter railroad in the country with 6,000 employees on three shifts and 18 collective bargaining agreements.

In the 1990s, she held several law positions including attorney and assessment liaison for the New York City Board of Education; assistant district attorney at the Kings County District Attorney's Office in Brooklyn, New York; and attorney and mediator for the US Equal Employment Opportunity Commission.

Turner holds a bachelor's degree in economics from the City University of New York—York College and a juris doctor degree from St. John's University School of Law. Additionally, she has credentials in SPHR (Senior Professional in Human Resources) and SHRM-SCP (Society for Human Resource Management Senior Certified Professional). Turner and her family reside in the Bronx, New York.

Shanna L. Ullmann, PhD, is the founding partner of Transformation Partners, offering specialized consulting and employee learning and development programs empowering clients to be more successful in all aspects of their business engagements. She has worked with a wide range of professionals teaching them the art and practice of effective interactions and communications with clients and between colleagues.

Shanna has over 25 years of hands-on human relations, executive education, and corporate training experience advising global corporations, universities, the US military and US federal government organizations on agile leadership development, strategic planning, constituent engagement, cross-cultural communications, professional etiquette and protocol, business communications, diversity, and mediation and workplace conflict resolution. She holds a Dun & Bradstreet Open Ratings Past Performance Review of 100% satisfaction from clients. She has experience as an adjunct instructor with the University of Alabama, Auburn University, Rollins College, USAF Air University, and Fordham University.

Shanna is a graduate of the Protocol School of Washington in Washington, DC, and is certified as a Master Trainer in Business Communications, Professional Business Etiquette and Protocol, and International Protocol. She is a certified Master Trainer by the American Society of Training and Development. In addition, Ms. Ullmann holds certification as a Cross-Cultural and Diversity specialist through the Interchange Institute in Cambridge, Massachusetts. She is also a certified Workplace Conflict Resolution trainer through Mediation Training Institute International, and holds triple certification as a Professional Mediator in Workplace Conflict through Mediation Training Institute International, the Pulse Institute of Canada, and the Justice Center of Atlanta. Ms. Ullmann holds a degree in commerce and business administration/human resources management from the University of Alabama.

Timothy T. Ullmann, PhD, EdD, is an organizational management and strategic operations professional with extensive national and international experience. He has advised US military services, foreign national militaries, US embassies, nongovernmental and philanthropic organizations, corporate and higher education leaders as well as serving as a Pentagon liaison to Capitol Hill and the White House. He led cross-cultural teams in Europe, the Middle East, Central Asia, Africa, the Republic of South Korea, Japan, and Guantanamo Bay, Cuba. In addition, he taught cross-cultural awareness in the Middle East, Asia, Europe, Guantanamo Bay, Cuba, and the United States. He has also worked with a variety of US industries and the US Air Force providing organizational assessments, leadership and management skills, strategic planning, leadership development, public speaking and business communications, conflict resolution, and mediation training. In addition, he has written organizational policies, procedures and guidance, change management guidance, leadership development, and cross-cultural manuals.

He holds an EdD in higher education administration from the University of Alabama, Tuscaloosa, Alabama, and a PhD in diplomacy and international affairs from Euclid University, Washington, DC. In addition, he holds an MA in organizational management, the George Washington University, Washington, DC; an MS in operational science, Air Command and Staff College, Air University, Montgomery, Alabama; and a BS in education from the University of Colorado, Boulder, Colorado. He also holds certifications in senior leadership development and business operations; budgets and funds management; policy and guidance development; critical thinking development; workplace mediation and conflict resolution; cross-cultural engagement; and business communications.

Advance Organizer

Complete the following organizer before you read the book. Use it as a diag-nostic tool to help you assess what you most want to know about succession planning in small and family businesses—and where you can find it in this book *fast*.

The Organizer

Directions

Read each item in the organizer below. Spend about ten minutes on the organizer. Be honest! Think of succession planning in small and/or family businesses as you would like it to be. Then indicate whether you would like to learn more about succession planning efforts to develop yourself profes-sionally. For each item in the center column, indicate with a *Y* (for Yes), *N/A* (for Not Applicable), or *N* (for No) in the left column whether you would like to develop yourself. When you finish, score and interpret the results using the instructions appearing at the end of the organizer. Then be prepared to share your responses with others you know to help you think about what you most want to learn about succession planning in small and family busi-nesses. To learn more about one item below, refer to the number in the right column to find the chapter on that topic.

The Questions

Circle your response for each item below:	***I would like to develop myself to:***

Chapter in the book in which the topic is covered:

Y N/A N 1.   Explore career options about departing from
ownership of a small or family business.   **1**

Y N/A N 2.   Learn a systematic approach to exiting from a
small or family business.   **2**

Y N/A N 3.   Consider what to look for in a successor.   **3**

Y N/A N 4.   Navigate political (power) issues in succession planning   **4**
for small or family business.

Y N/A N 5.   Address the psychological issues that can complicate   **5**
succession planning for small or family business.

Y N/A N 6.   Reflect on ways to deal with the legal issues that may   **6**
come up when planning for small or family succession.

Y N/A N 7.   Consider tax and accounting issues that may arise during   **7**
succession planning for small and/or family business.

Y N/A N 8.   Review options for financial planning in the wake of   **8**
decisions about small and family business succession
planning.

Y N/A N 9.   Contemplate a range of talent management issues that   **9**
confront those who conduct succession planning
for small and/or family business.

Y N/A N 10. Plan for a smooth and efficient exit from a small or family   **10**
business.

Y N/A N 11. Answer quickly important questions about succession planning **Appendix I**
in small or family business.

Y N/A N 12. Find additional resources quickly on small and family business **Appendix II**
succession planning.

_____ **Total**

Scoring and Interpreting the Organizer

Give yourself *1 point for each Y* and a *0 for each N or N/A* listed above. Total the points from the *Y* column and place the sum in the line opposite to the word **TOTAL** above. Then interpret your score:

Score

***12–11* = points**	Congratulations! This book is just what you need. Read about the issue(s) you marked *Y.*
***10–9* = points**	You have great skills in small and/or family business already, but you also have areas where you could develop professionally. Read those chapters marked *Y.*
***8–5* = points**	You have skills in small and/or family business already, but you could still benefit to build skills in selected areas.
***4–0* = points**	You believe you need little development in planning, implementing, and evaluating succession planning in small and/or family business.

Good luck!
The Editors, William J. Rothwell and Robert K. Prescott

DECIDING WHAT TO DO: LIFE AND CAREER PLANNING FOR SMALL BUSINESS OWNERS AND FAMILY LEADERS

1

This part addresses an important first step. That involves business owners deciding what they want to do with their lives and their businesses. Experience demonstrates that succession planning is pointless if the goals are unclear.

Chapter 1 is entitled "Considering Your Choices." The chapter addresses a key question: *What do small business or family business owners want to do?* What are common choices—such as sell the business, turn the business over to a partner, make the business employee owned, and others? Small and family business handoffs start with the business owners or family leaders deciding what they want to do and then pondering it with key stakeholders (such as spouses, key employees, family members, and even key customers). Business owners must decide what they want to do with their lives and careers after the business before they can plan for the business. A critical issue for owners to consider is how much, if at all, they wish to remain involved with the business after they "step down" or "retire." (There are degrees of how much to exit.) In family businesses, special issues emerge around how much or whether to transfer the business to a family member and/or to those who married into the family.

DOI: 10.4324/9781003281054-1

Chapter 1

Considering Your Choices

William J. Rothwell

Contents

DOI: 10.4324/9781003281054-2

1.1 Decisions Start with You

Owners of small businesses and/or family businesses should typically consider succession planning as part of life planning. They (the business owners) must know what they want out of their lives before they decide about their careers and business issues related to their lives and careers. Succession planning for small and/or family business owners is thus part of a bigger picture that includes life plans, career plans, and even what to do after they pass their businesses on to others.

Consider such questions as these: (1) what do you want to do with the rest of your life (regardless of your age)? (2) when, if ever, do you want to retire? (3) what would happen, and who would handle your business, if you were suddenly and unexpectedly incapacitated due to illness for an extended time span? (4) have major or minor events—such as health concerns about yourself or your significant others, regulatory concerns in your industry, or other matters (such as fights with family or in-laws)—recently prompted you to consider passing business responsibilities on to someone else?

How have you been handling succession so far? According to a 2014 study by ChiefLearningOfficer.com (Kalman 2014), fewer than 40% of US firms with fewer than 10,000 employees have a working succession plan—even to handle short-term emergencies, let alone handle permanent replacements of key job holders.

1.2 What Is the Situation in Your Business?

Read these vignettes and, on a separate note-taking sheet, describe how you would solve the problem in each vignette. If you can offer an effective solution to all the problems in the vignettes, then your organization may already have an effective succession effort in place; if not, your organization may urgently need more attention devoted to succession.

Vignette 1

George Smith, a licensed personal care home administrator, owns and operates a personal care home for the elderly. Not to be confused with a nursing home, this business cares for older people who would rather live in a residential community but can walk on their own. This business was valued at US$5,000,000 in 2010, and it employs 27 full-time and part-time workers. The mortgage on the business is US$1,000,000. Most of the business value centers on the single building that houses the elderly, which was newly constructed in 1997. The business is licensed to house 54 elderly people in a homelike environment.

It is a family business. George hired his daughter-in-law as one manager for the company. His son occasionally works in the business, though the son is a nurse at a local hospital. In 2015, local state government regulations affecting personal care homes grew more restrictive due to elder abuse widely reported in mass media outlets. Inspectors would often arrive at the facility and, when they did, felt obligated to make up problems even if they found no problems otherwise.

George grew tired of dealing with the onerous state regulations. He also grew tired of dealing with his daughter-in-law, who expected to receive special treatment due to her status as an in-law. George sold the business. That was easy to do because a profitable business in a growing market often has many eager buyers. The business was sold outright, and George learned, to his dismay, that federal and state taxes took about half of the business value during the sale.

Vignette 2

Mary Patterson owns a small dry-cleaning business. It is in the suburb of a big city, and its location is ideal at the crossroads of two major roads. Mary's company employs 12 full-time and part-time workers. The business, while facing much local competition from chain dry-cleaning outlets, has done well over the years. Unfortunately, Mary suffered a sudden stroke and was hospitalized. She had to close her business while she was hospitalized because she had no employees she could trust to run it, and she had no living relatives. Eventually, the business assets had to be liquidated to help Mary pay her medical bills, which were staggering.

Vignette 3

Morton Wiles owned a small factory in a small town. His company manufactured cosmetics—mostly pancake makeup—from local corn available in the fields surrounding the town. Morton inherited the business from his father, the founder. The factory employed 93 full-time and part-time people who come from the community. Several years ago, Morton's business fell on hard times because many large beauty product companies purchased their pancake makeup from foreign markets that could sell at much lower costs. Morton was compelled to take a partner. Morton knew Greg Larson from the community, and he had great respect for Greg's track record as the manager of a local Walmart store. In their discussions over beers, Morton learned that Greg had doubled the sales of the local Walmart store while he was manager. That sounded impressive to Morton. Both Morton and Greg were married. Morton had a college-age son and a high-school-age daughter, and Greg had a four-year-old daughter. Morton asked Greg if he would like to give up his day job at Walmart and join the factory as a General Manager with an initial investment of US$1,000,000. With that cash infusion, Morton's business could expand into other product lines and use the manufacturing facilities for some goods other than cosmetics. Greg agreed. But Greg insisted on a written partnership agreement. As soon as Greg joined the company and provided the cash investment, Morton had a sudden heart attack and passed away. That left the business in Greg's hands. But he knew little about manufacturing and about cosmetics.

Vignette 4

Marietta Diaz is single but wealthy. At age 65, she retired as manager of the small hotel she owns. She does not want to sell the business but hand it over to someone to manage for her while she pursues her lifelong dream to become a rock singer. The hotel has only 20 rooms, but it has done well in the local community. Its occupancy rate is often over 70%, an enviable record for a small hotel in the inner city of a major metro area. Marietta realizes that she could sell the business and make a handsome profit since real estate downtown is worth a fortune. But Marietta inherited the business from her parents, and it has sentimental value to her. She wants to keep it but also wants to experience the dream of her youth, traveling the world as a singer. Marietta looks for a successor and finds one in Janet Long. Janet, 20 years younger than Marietta, has long worked in hotels and knows how to make them work. Marietta hires Janet as her second-in-command and promptly trains her to be a successor. Marietta is very direct about it, making no secret she plans to make Janet the hotel manager if she can make the business pay. The hotel has no debt and is owned outright by Marietta. As Marietta plans to train her successor, she realizes she is not too sure of the best way to do it.

Vignette 5

Rhonda Larson runs a small business on a street corner. She owns a small pushcart that sells hot dogs. While Rhonda has never been rich, she has made a decent living from her pushcart over the years. That pushcart provided the funding for her to raise her family of two children as a single parent. But as Rhonda ages—she is now 68—she dreams of retirement. Her children are grown and have no interest in continuing the pushcart business. So, Rhonda thinks about what comes next in her life. She puts the pushcart business up for sale. A willing buyer, Ronald Ronson, surfaces almost immediately. But Ronson knows little about pushcarts. Rhonda wonders how she can ethically transition the business to him if he does not know how to run it. She asks some other former pushcart owners about their experiences in transitioning their businesses, and she learns more than she expects about the challenges of doing that.

Vignette 6

Linda Childress manages a convenience store. She owns the store and has no family or investors. But one day Linda gets in her car and, while driving to work, has an accident and is killed. She has made no provision for such an emergency. Her workers—and she employs about ten people in the store—are put out of work suddenly. The store is shuttered and closed. When her will is read, Linda surprised everyone by leaving the value of her estate to her church. The estate is sold, and the cash is given to her church. Her employees are left without employment until they can find something else.

1.3 Defining Terms

Consider the meanings of some common terms:

- **Replacement planning**: It is short-term planning for a replacement to do the job while a suitable full-time successor to fill a position is found. It should not be confused with succession planning because those asked to step up to their boss's jobs temporarily are not necessarily selected as the permanent successor. But those temporary backups are asked to do the job of their boss until a well-qualified candidate can be recruited and can start work (Rothwell 2011).
- **Succession planning**: It is the process of systematically preparing people for more responsibility by a promotion to a higher level on the organization chart (vertical promotion) or to a higher level of expertise by a promotion to a higher level of technical ability (horizontal promotion). Not all organizations use horizontal promotions, but they are possible in dual-career-path organizations. Succession planning requires employee development because it is assumed that work at higher levels of responsibility or technical expertise requires preparation or development. Work experience at one level is no guarantee of job success at higher levels of responsibility or of technical expertise (Rothwell 2015).
- **Talent**: A popular term, talent has more than one meaning. It can mean "ability to perform a job." It can mean "potential for promotion to higher levels of responsibility or expertise." It can mean both "ability to perform a job and potential for promotion." The term can also have other meanings, such as: (1) personal strengths; (2) inborn gifts; (3) specialized knowledge or expertise; (4) special ability to innovate; (5) special friendships or affiliations with those who matter to the organization; and (6) other meanings (Rothwell, Stopper & Zaballero 2015).
- **Talent management**: While this term can have various definitions depending on how the word "talent" is defined, it often means attracting, developing, and retaining people (Rothwell, Jones, Kirby & Loomis 2016).
- **Talent acquisition**: The process of systematically recruiting and selecting talented people.
- **Talent development**: The process of systematically developing people.
- **Talent engagement**: Inspiring passion, commitment, and productivity among people (Rothwell, Alzhahmi, Baumgardner, Buchko, Kim, Myers & Sherwani 2014).

▪ **Talent retention**: Retaining people.
▪ **Transition management**: In the most general sense, transition management refers to the systematic process of transitioning from one to another. That can mean one executive or CEO or business owner to another—or it can refer to the transition from one entire senior leadership team to another. If business owners sell their businesses, they begin a process of transition. If it is planned, then it is usually more effective than if it is handled in sudden stop-and-go jolts. Transition management can refer to more than succession-related issues. When an organization's leaders shift from one business model (way to make money) to another, then the business begins a transition process. If a business converts from a single owner to an employee-owned organization, it begins a transition process, too.

1.4 Differences and Similarities between Small Businesses and Family Businesses

Although this book is about the unique challenges in succession planning that face small business owners and family business owners, they are different business organizations. Many small businesses are family businesses. But not all family businesses are small. Consider family-dominated companies that are huge. Examples that spring to mind include DuPont, Ford, and Walmart—to name just a few.

Small businesses include sole proprietorships, partnerships, and so-called S corporations. These organizations are special case situations. They also pose special-case issues in succession planning.

The biggest difference between small businesses and family businesses is simply how many and what kind of people are involved in business transfers of ownership. A small business has no family members who may expect to inherit. A family business does.

1.5 Facts and Figures about Succession Planning in Small and Family Businesses

According to Eido Walny (cited in Gran 2021), "statistics bear out that 60-70 percent of small business owners wish to pass along their businesses to the next generation of family members, yet only about 15 percent ever do that."

The reason for this gap between intention and action, between the ideal and the actual, stems from poor succession planning. Much can happen to a business owner. Among them are disability, sudden death, divorce, or family estrangement. Each event, and others, can shape the direction that business transfer takes. That can include dissolution (liquidation) of the business and/or outright sale.

Consider:

■ "58% of small business owners have no succession plan, according to a study of 200 privately held businesses by Wilmington Trust" (Kline 2018).

■ "47% of those over the age of 65 did not have a specific transition plan" (Massimo 2019).

■ Most small businesses without a succession plan (78%) gave the reason that they enjoyed "managing their company too much to start thinking about a future transition," while 42% said they were too busy to plan, and 44% felt that succession was "too far in the future" to need to establish a plan now" (Kline 2018).

■ Only 70% of small business owners have a sense of what their businesses are worth, and they need updated valuations (Massimo 2019).

■ A mere 7% of company leaders say that COVID-19 has not affected succession planning for their organizations ("30+ Succession Planning Statistics" no date).

■ "40% of new CEOs fail to meet performance expectations in the first 18 months" (Harrell 2016).

■ "Only about 30% of family businesses even make it to the second generation. 10-15% make it to the third, and 3-5% make it to the fourth" ("Family Succession Planning" no date).

■ "According to the Conway Center for Family Business, 40.3% of family business owners expect to retire at some point. But of those planning to retire in less than 5 years, less than half have selected a successor" ("Family Succession Planning" no date).

What conclusions can be reached after reviewing the summary above? It would seem logical to conclude that succession planning is important to small and family businesses but is not always done. One important reason is nobody likes to think about their death, disability, or business failure. These topics are not pleasant ones on which to dwell and are about as welcome as contemplating the purchase of a burial plot or arranging for one's own cremation.

Still, it is needed for the business. And it is also needed to ensure the continued well-being of loyal employees who worked for the business and for those who depend on the business for their well-being such as family members and even customers, suppliers, dealers/distributors of organizational products, and members of the community of which the business is part of the tax base.

1.6 Life and Career Planning for Yourself

The first step in transitioning from business owner to something else— whether that something else means full-time retirement, part-time retirement, reliving a dream from youth, selling all you have and moving to some exotic offshore location (Buford 1994), or some other option—is to decide what you want to do. All planning begins with getting clear (1) where you are now and (2) where you want to go. Yet many business leaders, when they contemplate the future, are stunned by the dizzying array of options that may confront them. See the following list of options. Think about them. Scan the list and identify the top 1 to 3 options you may find of interest:

- Sell the business outright.
- Liquidate the business for cash.
- Sell part of the business.
- Sell the business gradually through a phased sale (like a contract for deed for a property).
- Sell one or more locations of a business with multiple locations.
- Sell the business outright to a relative/spouse/ex-spouse/child/or in-law.
- Sell the business outright to a partner or partners.
- Sell the business outright to a supplier.
- Sell the business outright to a distributor.
- Sell the business outright to a competitor.
- Sell the business outright to an unrelated business.
- Sell the business to an adjacent business (like next-door neighbor).
- Sell to someone you hire and groom and then retire and become a silent partner.
- Sell to an employee.
- Sell part of the business to an employee.
- Sell to all your employees (ESOP).
- Promote an employee and then retire full time or part time.

- Promote a group of employees to run the business and then retire full time or part time.
- Give the business away to another organization.
- Give the business away to charity.
- Give the business away to the government deliberately.
- Deliberately allow your business to be dissolved and sold off for back taxes.
- Have your business managed by a bank or other property manager.
- Leave your business in your will (or without a will) to your spouse or significant other.
- Leave part of your business in your will (or without a will) to your spouse and part to one or more of your children.
- Leave your business in your will to a relative.
- Leave your business in your will to a business partner.
- Leave your business in your will to your child or children.
- Leave your business in your will to one child but exclude spouse and/or other children.
- Leave your business in your will to a supplier.
- Leave your business in your will to a distributor.
- Leave your business in your will to a competitor.
- Leave your business in your will to a customer or customers.
- Leave your business in your will *deliberately* to the government.
- Leave your business in your will by default to the government.
- Leave your business in your will to your estate, order it to be liquidated, and have assets distributed to others.
- Leave your business in your will to a trust, have it managed, and have profits (if any) distributed to spouse, children, and/or others.

Life planning and career planning for you begin in the same way that planning for your business begins. A modified version of the well-known strategic planning process is an excellent starting point (Rothwell, Jackson, Ressler & Jones 2015).

Consider these steps in a modified version of the business planning process that should work for career planning:

- *Step 1*: Decide what you most want out of life and out of your future work.
- *Step 2*: Formulate a vision of a successful or desirable future.
- *Step 3*: Set your initial targets.

- *Step 4*: Scan the external environment to determine what changes may affect the achievement of your targets.
- *Step 5*: Identify your own strengths and areas for improvement (weaknesses).
- *Step 6*: Conduct a strengths, weaknesses, opportunities, and threats (SWOT) analysis.
- *Step 7*: Consider the range of choices.
- *Step 8*: Select the most desirable choice.
- *Step 9*: Create action/transition plans.
- *Step 10*: Implement the plans over time, making modifications as conditions warrant.
- *Step 11*: Evaluate results against targets (step 2).
- *Step 12*: Make corrections to the action plans as needed.

These steps are described below. Use the tool at the end of this chapter to help you brainstorm on how to carry out these steps as you read the following explanation of each step.

1.6.1 Step 1: *Decide What You Want*

Business planning begins by deciding the mission (purpose) of the organization. It sets forth the philosophy of the business and indicates how the business will be better and different from its competitors. Who will be served by the business? How will they be served? What will be done to make the answers to those questions a reality?

Likewise, career planning—at any stage of life—begins with self-reflection (that is, some soul-searching) about what you most want from life, why you want that, what you will do to get what you want from life, how you will interact with others (such as family, friends, and business associates) to achieve your results, and what strengths you have that may give you a competitive advantage in achieving your results.

A good place to begin soul-searching is with an assessment of your values. A good tool for that is the Rokeach Value Survey (Rokeach 1973). A value means "what you care about most." A value means "what you want" or "what you regard as important." Rokeach distinguished between instrumental values and terminal values. A *terminal value* is what you want from life. An *instrumental value* refers to the means you will use primarily to achieve that terminal value.

Rokeach's terminal values are these:

- A world at peace: free of war and conflict.
- Family security: taking care of loved ones.
- Freedom: independence; free choice.
- Equality: brotherhood; equal opportunity for all.
- Self-respect: self-esteem.
- Happiness: contentedness.
- Wisdom: a mature understanding of life.
- National security: protection from attack.
- Salvation: saved; eternal life.
- True friendship: close companionship.
- A sense of accomplishment: a lasting contribution.
- Inner harmony: freedom from inner conflict.
- A comfortable life: a prosperous life.
- Mature love: sexual and spiritual intimacy.
- A world of beauty: beauty of nature and the arts.
- Pleasure: an enjoyable, leisurely life.
- Social recognition: respect; admiration.
- An exciting life: a stimulating, active life.

Rokeach's instrumental values are these:

- Cheerfulness.
- Ambition.
- Love.
- Cleanliness.
- Self-Control.
- Capability.
- Courage.
- Politeness.
- Honesty.
- Imagination.
- Independence.
- Intellect.
- Broad-Mindedness.
- Logic.
- Obedience.
- Helpfulness.
- Responsibility.
- Forgiveness.

What do you find as your most important meaning in life? Consult the list of terminal values. List your priorities where 1=Most important. Then examine the list of instrumental values to identify the priorities of how you would pursue those terminal values. Consult the list of instrumental values. List your priorities where 1=Most important.

There are other good tools. One is strengths-finders (Rath 2007). Many people find instruments helpful.

Once you have clarified your direction in life, you are positioned to think about a vision for the future.

1.6.2 Step 2: Formulate a Vision of the Future

What is your dream? What do you most want to do with the rest of your life? By answering these questions, you are charting a destination. The clearer your vision of an ideal future, the more likely you are to achieve it. But those who do not know what they want will not know if they have realized their dreams.

Visualize yourself doing what you most want to do. What is that exactly? Do you know?

I know business owners—and other professionals—who have trouble envisioning themselves doing anything than the daily grind they have done for many years. But pause a moment and think about YOU. What do you most enjoy doing? Do you prefer being by yourself, being with other people, being with family, being in exotic locales, or doing something else?

Until you have a vision of what you want, it is difficult to set a direction for the future and pick one of the many options available to you. If you are stumped and not sure what you want, then talk to friends, family, and those whose opinions you value. They can shed light on the future. Then talk to people who are retired full time, those retired part time but working occasionally, and those doing something else. If you do not know how to find such people, consider posting on social media to source them. Consider Nextdoor.com, Friendmatch.com, and similar sites.

1.6.3 Step 3: Set Your Targets

Once you clear the hurdle of formulating a vision, then you are ready to set targets. Decide what you will need to get where you want to go.

For instance, if you are making a career shift, then consider if you will need additional education or licenses to realize your dream. If you plan to retire, where will you retire? What steps are needed to make your dream come true, and what are the targets to be achieved to carry out those steps?

Try to make your targets measurable. Set the ultimate target and then work backward to set milestones and targets to achieve by each milestone date or milestone accomplishments.

1.6.4 Step 4: *Scan the External Environment*

The difference between long-range planning and strategic planning is what assumptions are made about the future. Long-range planning assumes the future will be a logical continuation of the past. But strategic planning assumes that future events may unfold in ways different from that logical continuation based on changes in economic conditions, legal/competitive conditions, technological change, social change, geographical movements, demographic change, and much more.

Environmental scanning is necessary to consider how events outside of your control may influence your decisions about leaving your business, achieving your dream, and meeting your measurable targets toward realizing your dream.

Consider: what assumptions can you safely make about the future? How will unfolding trends affect your goals? What threats will external environmental trends pose toward your goal achievement? What opportunities may changing events present that may make it easier for you to realize your goals and dreams?

1.6.5 Step 5: *Identify Your Strengths and Weaknesses*

What are your present strengths and weaknesses? What do you do well now? What should you do well to realize your dreams?

This step, more than others, requires clear-headed soul-searching. Some people cannot do this analysis on their own. They may need input from their closest friends. They may need input from family—and others who know them best, such as significant others. In addition, they may need professional counseling or even therapy.

List what you think you do well. List areas where you think you do not do so well. Then share those lists with family, friends, and others.

1.6.6 Step 6: *Conduct a SWOT Analysis*

Using the results of Steps 4 and 5, you should be well equipped to conduct a SWOT analysis about yourself and how you can make your dream of a future after your business life come true.

SWOT analysis is not as direct as working on a mathematical problem; rather, it usually involves applying a level of intuition. Would it work best in pursuing your dream to overcome your weaknesses, build on your strengths, take advantage of future opportunities, or avoid future threats? What action plans do overcoming weaknesses imply? Building on strengths? Seizing opportunities? Averting threats?

1.6.7 Step 7: Consider the Range of Choices

Now do some brainstorming. What are the ways you could realize your dream? Do you have enough money to pursue your dream now? Could you have enough money if you sold your business or eased out of it slowly? Will your family, friends, and significant other support you in making your dream come true? What options do they suggest in realizing your dream?

1.6.8 Step 8: Select the Most Desirable Choice

What choice, from those identified in Step 7, seems most realistic and achievable? Do you have enough time, money, and support to implement your choice? Consider limitations on your choices and pick one or more that seem realistic to you with the time, money, and support available.

1.6.9 Step 9: Create Action/Transition Plans

Now turn your choice from Step 8 into an action plan. As a businessperson, you should know how to do that. Decide on the action steps. Decide what you will need to do to carry out those steps. Apply Project Management 101 and identify what to do, how to do it, what you will need to do to make each step happen, how much money you will need, and when the steps should be achieved. Share the plan with other people to get their opinion on how realistic it is.

Also consider plans for what you are leaving behind and what you are working toward. For instance, if you are retiring from your business, you will need to have a transition plan for the exit and an action plan for achieving your dream for life after the business.

1.6.10 Step 10: Implement the Plans

Implement means simply execute the plan. That may take an extended time. How long will it take to transfer your business to a new owner, for instance?

How is the transition period managed? How is the implementation tracked against the action plan?

1.6.11 Step 11: *Evaluate Results against Targets*

Review your plan implementation periodically against targets. Do so regularly. Celebrate, even if by yourself, successes, and reconsider what to do if your conditions change.

1.6.12 Step 12: *Make Corrections to the Action Plans as Needed*

If unexpected situations or external environmental conditions arise—such as the impact of future "black swan events" like the COVID-19 virus—consider whether the targets need to be changed or else the dream changed.

1.7 Succession Planning after Life and Career Decisions

Once you decide you have made your choices about what you want to do, you are well positioned to consider the next steps regarding the business transition. Among the options—but by no means the only options—are to sell the business, pass the business on to a relative if you own a family business, promote an existing employee, phase out your active involvement, or hire someone from outside and groom that person to take your place as a business leader while you pursue other interests. Those are not the only choices as the list earlier in the chapter dramatically illustrated. But they are some.

If you do pass on the business to an employee or hire someone to take your place, you will need to prepare that person for the job. Even if your employee or new hire has an exemplary track record of previous job performance, that does not mean he or she is well equipped to handle more responsibility. Developing the person may require a detailed plan and daily efforts to prepare the person (see Rothwell, Chee & Oi 2015).

Succession planning in small and family-owned businesses differs from succession in major corporations or in government (Rothwell 2015). In large organizations much time—and money—can be devoted to clarifying the work duties of successors, pinning down necessary competencies required, assessing present job performance and future promotion potential, and implementing many methods by which to prepare the person. But in small and family businesses, succession planning looks more like planned on-the-job training or structured coaching.

A good place to begin is by writing your own job description. Make it detailed. Try to make it reflect your daily responsibilities. Keep a log of what you do every half hour and then use that log to create a detailed job description. That can be the start of a roadmap to use to assess what your prospective successor needs to learn—and demonstrate.

But as you embark on this planning, also consider these questions:

■ Who expects to be your successor, and how will he or she greet the news you have chosen someone to prepare for the job? (Do not assume you can hide your decision because it will quickly become apparent as you have someone shadowing you.) Have you conversed with that person about what you plan to do and how he or she may factor into that? Will disappointed people who expected to be considered for promotion leave the business or cause you trouble in other ways? What can you do to head off that trouble?

■ If you are in a family business, how will the family react to news of your pending move? How will you make the announcement?

■ If you have made decisions in your will, have you tried to avoid problems after you pass away? Have you tried to anticipate how other people will respond to your will? What are the chances they may try to challenge your will in due course and endanger the viability of the business through legal action that could even lead to a liquidation? (One problem: you leave a controlling share of the business to the oldest child, but other children consider that unfair and challenge your decisions after you are dead. Another problem: you leave your business to your spouse or significant other, but he or she does not know enough about the business and must turn to other people for help to run it.) Head off family conflicts and conflicts among your workers before you leave the business—or leave this life.

■ Have you given thought to your employees? Loyal people who have served you over the years deserve to be treated fairly. Have you tried to do that as you make your choices for the future?

■ Have you given thought to the legal requirements if you sell the business or pass it on before death (as a gift) or after death (in a will)?

Read a later chapter about legal issues. Seek the advice of a competent attorney.

■ Have you given thought to the tax implications if you sell the business or pass it on before death (as a gift) or after death (in a will)? Read a later chapter about tax issues. Seek the advice of a competent accountant familiar with your type of business and local/state/federal issues affecting sales, gifts, or estates.

■ Have you given thought to the psychological implications to your workers, customers, suppliers, and dealer/distributors (if any) that might result from the news of you leaving the business to retirement or to pursue other interests? How will people react? What steps can you take to avoid trouble you might leave in your wake as you leave the business?

■ Have you given thought to the financial implications to yourself when you leave the business? If you sell the business, will that give you enough money once all debts and taxes are paid? Read a later chapter about financial advice. Seek the advice of a competent financial advisor familiar with your type of business and local/state/federal issues affecting investments decisions for the future.

■ What else might have been forgotten? Think about it.

Plan for the transition. See the last chapter for more information about transition planning (Table 1.1).

1.8 Chapter Summary

Planning for succession is only one choice confronting a small business or family business owner when considering next steps in life—or succession after death. This chapter guided you, the reader, through a consideration of the issues you face when planning to give up your business and move on. The chapter listed choices to make for the next steps for you and provided a step-by-step model to consider for career and succession planning. Once the decision is made to leave the business, you will need a plan about how to do so. You will also need competent management, legal, tax, financial, and other advice relevant to your business, your family, your workers and customers, and others who depend on you.

Table 1.1   A Tool for Career Planning

Directions: For each step shown in the left column below, brainstorm your own ideas about how to carry out that step in the right column below. After you take your own notes, feel free to share this tool with your significant other, family, friends, or others who may give you useful advice. Consider also sharing your thoughts with competent legal, accounting, financial advising, psychological, and management advisors. There are no right or wrong answers in any absolute sense because the answer depends on you.	
Steps to Take in Career Planning for Your Future	**Your Notes about the Steps**
Step 1: Decide what you most want out of life and out of your future work.	
Step 2: Formulate a vision of a successful or desirable future.	
Step 3: Set your initial targets.	
Step 4: Scan the external environment to determine what changes may affect achievement of your targets.	
Step 5: Identify your own strengths and areas for improvement (weaknesses).	
Step 6: Conduct a strengths, weaknesses, opportunities, and threats (SWOT) analysis.	
Step 7: Consider the range of choices.	
Step 8: Select the most desirable choice.	
Step 9: Create action/transition plans.	
Step 10: Implement the plans over time, making modifications as conditions warrant.	
Step 11: Evaluate results against targets (Step 2).	
Step 12: Make corrections to the action plans as needed.	

Works Cited

Buford, Bob. 1994. *Half-Time: Moving from Success to Significance*. New York: Harper-Collins.

"Family Succession Planning: 3 Best Practices and A Review of the Statistics." n.d. *Above the Canopy*. Accessed March 12, 2022. https://www.abovethecanopy.us/family-business-succession-planning/

Gran, Benjamin. 2021. "All You Need to Know About Small Business Succession Planning." *PNC Insights*. May 28, 2021. https://www.pnc.com/insights/small-business/business-planning/all-you-need-to-know-about-small-business-succession-planning.html.

Harrell, Eben. 2016. "Succession Planning: What the Research Says." *Harvard Business Review*. December 1, 2016. https://hbr.org/2016/12/succession-planning-what-the-research-says.

Kalman, F. 2014. "Organizations Work to Bridge Succession Planning Gap." *Chief Learning Officer*. April 18, 2014. https://www.chieflearningofficer.com/2014/04/18/organizations-work-to-bridge-succession-planning-gap__trashed/#:~:text=According%20to%20the%20survey%2C%20about%2085%20percent%20of,don%E2%80%99t%20have%20any%20succession%20plan%2C%20the%20survey%20found.

Kline, Daniel B. 2018. "Most Small Business Owners Lack a Succession Plan." *The Motley Fool*. August 3, 2018. https://www.fool.com/careers/2018/08/03/most-small-business-owners-lack-a-succession-plan.aspx

Massimo, Charles. 2019. "Council Post: Business Owners, What's Your Succession Plan?" *Forbes*. June 5, 2019. https://www.forbes.com/sites/forbesnycouncil/2019/06/05/business-owners-whats-your-succession-plan/

Rath, Tom. 2007. *Strengths-finder 2.0*. Washington, DC: The Gallup Press.

Rokeach, Milton. 1973. *The Nature of Human Values*. New York: The Free Press.

Rothwell, W. 2015. *Effective Succession Planning: Ensuring Leadership Continuity and Building Talent from Within*. 5th ed. New York: Amacom.

Rothwell, W., P. Chee, and J. Ooi. 2015a. *The Leader's Daily Role in Talent Management Maximizing Results, Engagement, and Retention*. Singapore: McGraw-Hill Education Asia Collection.

Rothwell, W., Angela Stopper, and Aileen Zaballero. 2015b. *Building A Talent Development Structure Without Borders*. Alexandria, VA: ATD Press.

Rothwell, William J. 2011. "Replacement Planning: A Starting Point for Succession Planning and Talent Management." *International Journal of Training and Development* 15(1): 87–99. https://doi.org/10.1111/j.1468-2419.2010.00370.x.

Rothwell, William J. 2014. *Creating Engaged Employees: It's Worth the Investment*. Alexandria, VA: Association for Talent Development.

Rothwell, William J., Robert D. Jackson, Cami L. Ressler, Maureen Connelly Jones, and Meg Brower. 2015d. *Career Planning and Succession Management: Developing Your Organization's Talent: For Today and Tomorrow*. 2nd ed. Santa Barbara: Praeger.

Rothwell, William J., Maureen C. Jones, Maria T. Kirby, and Frederick D. Loomis. 2016. *Talent Management: A Step-by-Step Action-Oriented Guide Based on Best Practice.* Amherst, MA: HRD Press, Inc.

Shortlister. "30+ Succession Planning Statistics." January 12, 2020. https://www.myshortlister.com/insights/succession-planning-statistics.

PLANNING FOR SUCCESSION IN SMALL AND FAMILY BUSINESS

Part II: Planning for Succession in Small and Family Business consists of two chapters.

Chapter 2 is about *strategic succession planning*, defined as a deliberate and considered process for defining the future direction of a company when the owner retires. Through a precise and well-articulated plan, this document facilitates a change in ownership with continued operations or the liquidation of the business. This chapter discusses factors to consider when transferring, selling, or liquidating a business using a time-sensitive strategic plan. The chapter also discusses why it's important to create a strategic succession plan and the consequences of not doing so. It also offers practical and measurable strategic methods for creating a successful succession plan. Finally, a Strategic Succession Plan Roadmap outlines a step-by-step procedure for developing and implementing an effective succession plan. As a result, a smooth transition, sale, or liquidation of the company will be achieved.

Chapter 3 is entitled "Recruiting a Successor from Inside, Outside, or Utilizing Other Options for the Organization." As noted by chapter authors Kay Turner, Deborah M. Adwokat, and Robert K. Prescott good successors for the firm can be sought both internally and externally. Recruiting an internal successor will assist small organizations, particularly those with a distinctive company culture. Recruiting a leader from within a company with a strong or dominating culture has shown to be a cultural "fit" multiple times. When "critical leadership abilities in companies are insufficient for satisfying (its) current and future needs," according to the Center for Creative Leadership, external talent can be a critical component in a small business succession plan.

DOI: 10.4324/9781003281054-3

Chapter 2

Strategic Planning for Succession Sustainability

Timothy T. Ullmann and Shanna L. Ullmann

Contents

DOI: 10.4324/9781003281054-4

Warren's family was known throughout the region as superb cabinet makers. Mr. Jenkins, a master craftsman, started a small business, employed a handful of local men and women, produced well-made cabinets, and made a moderate income. Although Warren grew up and worked in all aspects of the family business, his life's goal was to be an architect. He wanted to design grand structures, stately buildings, and epic monuments. He even earned his undergraduate degree in architecture. However, the unwritten and undiscussed expectation was for Warren to take over and run the family business.

Newly married and anticipating a bright career in an architectural firm, Warren was blindsided at a family dinner when his father announced him as the successor of the business. The terms were simple: assume the leadership role over the next six months. However, Warren did not know the additional terms. These unfolded as he unwillingly stepped into leadership: refit and update a small, outdated shop, generate new business (no new orders were on the books), pay off a US$300,000 small business loan, and pay his father his usual annual salary and benefits throughout his retirement. Warren reluctantly assumed the leadership role with its terms and spent the next three decades salvaging and expanding the business.

Today, the would-be architect runs a state-of-the-art cabinet business with 50 employees which is renowned as the premier high-end cabinet maker across the United States. And as Warren nears retirement, he is perplexed about the future. His children have no interest in running the business, and there does not appear to be an employee able to take over the business. What Warren needs is a strategic succession plan that allows him to exit the business on favorable terms and in a timeframe of his choosing.

Small business is the nation's CPU (central processing unit). It spurs innovation, local job creation, and entrepreneurship among wide portions of the population that energize local, state, and national economies. These essential businesses utilize leadership, management, and daily operation plans to ensure success. However, most small businesses do not go beyond these day-to-day plans. If the business is to succeed in the future, it needs a thoughtful and implementable plan for its ongoing viability once the business owner exits. Enter in Strategic Planning for Succession Sustainability. Also known as a Strategic Succession Plan, this plan helps ensure small business succession by positioning the leadership to maximize its current and future operations leading to innovation and economic sustainability once the owner exits.

2.1 What Is a Strategic Succession Plan?

The first thing to understand about a Strategic Succession Plan is that it is *strategic*. This means taking a long view of the desired future end state. The process: begin with the end in mind, gather information, and craft the plan to achieve the end state. Typically, the business owner drives this process by identifying long-term aims and interests and the ways of achieving them. The business owner determines the future desired state of the business once he or she departs and how to make it happen. And at the discretion of the owner, he or she may solicit the assistance of trusted agents to function as key advisors in creating the plan.

At its core, a *succession plan* is a strategy for passing on the role of leadership. Therefore, the owner thoughtfully works to identify and articulate how the future end state will be achieved and sustained through new leadership (again, key advisors may provide valuable insights). Thus, a strategic succession plan is an intentional and thoughtful process for determining the future course of a business as the owner exits—leadership, management, and operations. This document will guide a change in ownership (internal succession or sale of the business) with sustained operations, or the liquidation of the business, through a detailed, well-articulated, and time-/date-driven plan.

Recent studies show that about 30% of family businesses make it to the second generation. Only 10–15% make it to the third generation, and 3–5% make it to the fourth. These numbers sound low, but they are only counting businesses run by families' younger generations. Many businesses are sold or merged, which is not a failure. The numbers bear out—intentional succession planning is necessary for success.

Strategic succession planning means establishing and documenting the direction of a business as the owner anticipates his or her exit. First things first. The owner must decide his or her personal desires: Is it to remain connected to the business? Is it to transfer leadership to a chosen successor? Is it to sell the business assets and prepare employees for transition into another business? Or is it to liquidate the business? What is the end goal?

Next, the owner, along with key advisors, assesses where the business is, where it is going, and how to position leadership and operations for the desired goal. For example, Mike wants his roofing company to continue. Will leadership come from within the business, or will it be external? What leadership qualifications are needed to ensure a smooth transition and seamless operations? Danny wants to sell his plumbing business, but to whom? A relative, a partner, an employee, or a third party? Janet wants to liquidate her floral shop. So, how will assets be sold, and employees transitioned within the industry?

A strategic succession plan provides a written record of the business mission (purpose/reason for existence), the owner's vision of the business future as they exit, and long-term goals with specific, time-sensitive action plans utilized to reach and achieve the intended end state. In addition, this plan informs business leadership how best to respond to opportunities and challenges that inevitably arise. Therefore, a well-written strategic succession plan is key and essential to achieving the goal of the owner as he or she anticipates exiting the business.

2.2 What a Strategic Succession Plan Is Not

What a Strategic Succession Plan is not is a haphazard wishful wag (wild-ass guess) about what the business owner hopes will happen. Hope is not a strategy. Nor is it ignoring the inevitable as every business owner will leave their business at some point whether voluntarily or involuntarily (that is, illness, disability, or death). Many small business owners succumb to the *Ponce de Leon Syndrome*—the Fountain of Youth. These owners refuse to accept the possibility of their own mortality. They think medical advances will allow them to live indefinitely. Illustrating this mindset, one study found that 58% of small business owners surveyed did not have a succession plan. And of those businesses without a succession plan, 47% of owners thought a succession plan was unnecessary (Thienel 2020). Such thinking leaves a small business in peril. A strategic succession plan can mitigate an unfortunate and untimely demise of the business.

2.3 Why Strategic Planning for Succession Sustainability Is Important for Small Businesses

Small business strategic succession planning is important for a variety of reasons. The primary advantage is that it benefits the owner, the company, employees, and successors. It also benefits customers and clients by ensuring the company will undergo a stable transition enabling it to seamlessly provide the goods and services customers rely upon; or, in the event of liquidating the business, provide customers and employees with viable alternatives for the future. And the bottom line: *having a succession plan in place can increase the value of your business.*

Some benefits of a small business strategic succession plan include:

■ Puts the business owner in the driver's seat—he or she chooses how to exit the business. (This may include creating one or more roles for the owner to continue working for the company if transferring the company to a new owner.)
■ Intentional plan to transfer or liquidate the company.
■ Maximize the value the owner receives for the company if transferred to a third party or liquidated.
■ Stable, predictable, and smooth transition of the company.
■ Choose and train a successor.
■ Identify key employees and develop a plan to retain them after the transfer.
■ Prepare to handle unexpected events.
■ Plan for the incapacitation of the owner or key employees.
■ Identify company weaknesses and develop a plan to mediate the issues.
■ Determine the legal documents and financial tools necessary to carry out the strategic succession plan.
■ Create roles for family members within the company.
■ Provide for the future financial stability of the owner's family.
■ Maintain the owner's lifestyle during retirement.

2.4 Myopia and Wishful Thinking— Failing to Think Strategically

Notwithstanding the benefits of strategic succession planning, too many business owners focus solely on the here and now. They experience the stress to grow their business and keep it financially solvent. Others assume strategic succession planning is too expensive and time consuming when leading a thriving company. This is myopic.

Some business owners enjoy running their business so much they do not think about a time when they will exit the company. They think of succession planning much like a will—both should be avoided. They neglect strategic succession planning because it forces them to consider giving up their company. Many simply assume a family member or valued employee will take over the reins. This is wishful thinking.

Regardless of the reason a business owner claims for failing to develop a strategic succession plan, the owner is giving up a valuable opportunity to ensure the legacy and success of the business even after the owner steps aside by failing to develop a strategic succession plan. Early planning gives the owner more flexibility to tailor a succession plan that allows the owner to remain with the company in a capacity he or she chooses for as long as he or she desires.

2.5 Organizing and Implementing a Strategic Succession Plan

Formal strategy planning was developed by the US military during World War II. Noting the advantages to large and small organizations, strategic planning was developed in large companies and business schools. Most models of strategy planning today reflect those beginnings and reinforce the widespread notion that planning is a big, complicated process. This could not be further from the truth. Like most management processes, it should be lean, structured, and thorough.

Strategy is based on answering a few basic questions. Therefore, the shape of a strategic succession plan will depend on how specific questions are answered:

1. *What is the goal of the business owner?* Understanding the business owner's goal will shape the scope or "strategic focus" of the business. Is the goal to pass the business on to a successor, sell the business, or liquidate it? Once this goal is determined, the strategic focus is further refined. For example, what specific products and/or services will the company continue to provide? What specific markets or customers will it serve?
2. *How will leadership and operations transfer?* This question seeks to identify the sustainable basis for a competitive advantage. This is the Strategic Competency of the business (the unique niche of the business in the industry).
3. *What are the owner's exit options?* This question identifies what the owner seeks to gain upon leaving the business. Does he or she want a cash out? A retirement plan? A combination of the two? Are there other desired options?
4. *What is the exit timeframe?* This places a time constraint on the process. When will the succession planning begin? What are the key objectives to be achieved by the given dates? When will the business transfer be completed?

Answering these questions will allow the business owner to control the transition process and exit on favorable terms.

Ideally, strategy succession planning is a process whereby a management team produces answers to these questions that enables a seamless transition for ongoing leadership and optimal operations. The steps in the process include:

- A situation analysis (Where are we today?).
- Strategy formulation (Where do we want to go?).
- Implementation planning (How do we get there?).
- Provision of resources for implementation (time and money).
- Schedule for monitoring, assessment, feedback, and updates (ongoing evaluation).

2.5.1 What Is the Business Owner's Goal?

This decision is fundamental for the business owner. The business owner should have a clear personal vision and a vision for the future of the business. Will the business continue offering niche goods and services to its customers? If so, this will inform decisions about succession and operations, owner exit options, and an optimal transition timeframe. If the business ceases upon the owner's exit, this will inform owner exit options (that is, cash out), and an optimal timeframe to wrap up the business.

Goal 1: Continue the business into the future. The first consideration is to determine a chosen successor. This requires the owner to make an informed and practical decision about who will take on the business leadership—a family member, an employee, or a new leadership hire. Making this decision means the owner and his or her trusted agents evaluate and determine who is best qualified to lead the business successfully into the future. Once this decision is made, the terms of transition (this may include a payout and/ or retirement for the owner), the process of transition, training the successor, and the timeframe are to be articulated ensuring a smooth transition. For example, the owner of a dairy enterprise skipped a generation and determined his grandson would take over the business. The owner worked with key employees to establish a transition, a process to mentor his grandson for two years, determined an owner-financed loan to his grandson, and established a personal retirement schedule upon his exit.

Goal 2: Sell the business. If a purchase is involved, the sale price, purchase terms, and timeframe are to be outlined which relieves stress for

the owner and his or her family. As an example, the owner of a remark-
ably successful athletic apparel company sold her business to a third party.
In the transition terms were the purchase price, timeframe, and a bonus
for employees—US$10,000 and two first-class airline tickets to a destina-
tion of choice. Be specific about the goals—personal, business future, and
employees.

Goal 3: Cease business operations. Typically, this involves liquidating the
company. While this sounds straightforward, closing the business has its
own considerations. First, terms, conditions, and timelines maximize capital gains for the owner and employees. For example, during two years, the
owner of a business equipment manufacturer sold his inventory to a distributor, sold his equipment to a competitor, facilitated the hire of employees to
similar businesses, and leased his buildings to create a monthly income.

2.5.2 Leadership and Operations Options

If the business owner's goal is to continue operations into the future, it is
essential to select the most qualified candidate who can move the business successfully into the future. The business owner will be wise to solicit
assistance from trusted agents organic to the business and those outside
the business such as key suppliers, trusted clients, and industry experts.
This succession planning team can draw from its collective expertise to
ensure the optimal candidate is chosen for succession leadership—one who
understands and is competent in both business leadership and operational
demands. The team can look internally for candidates within the business
(for example, a high potential family member or employee) or externally for
candidates. The succession aim is to select a candidate who can fulfill and
expand leadership and operational business demands into the future.

2.5.3 Business Owner Exit Options

Whether a business owner's goal is to continue the business into the future
or cease operations, he or she will want to plan his or her exit options.
Why? These allow the owner to exit the business on their own terms. Here
are strategic considerations: obtain a payout, provide a retirement income,
determine the level and nature of business engagement by the owner after
the transition, provide for the employees, and/or eliminate debt.

The number of exit options is as vast and unique as each business. So,
each business owner should determine what they realistically need from

the business as they exit. Some considerations: level and type of business involvement (if any), payout based on business valuation, stock options (if available), retirement plan, benefits plan, etc. While it may be tempting to trust new leadership to "do the right thing" for the exiting owner, a detailed and binding agreement must benefit all parties. Therefore, in determining exit options, it is highly recommended to consult a business attorney, an accountant, and the owner's financial planner. Employing the services of these professionals will help to ensure the owner can optimize their exit options.

2.5.4 *Owner Exit Timeframe*

Typically, a business owner has an estimate of an exit timeframe. But is it realistic? For too many owners, the exit timeframe begins the moment he or she wants to exit and ends at some indeterminate time. Regrettably, this is short sighted and may not consider all the decisions, positioning, and intricacies needed for a smooth or desirable exit.

An exit timeframe is a planned and timed process to move the owner and the business to the desired final goal. An optimal exit timeframe is approximately five years; however, a shortened or protracted timeframe can be employed depending on unique circumstances. It is helpful to note that the longer the timeframe, the greater likelihood of achieving the owner's goal.

The exit timeframe is the process where the strategic succession plan is implemented in an intentional manner. Owners working with their strategic succession planning team will determine a time-sensitive phased approach to execute the business goal. This means establishing a realistic timeframe that begins with the end in mind. Start with the time (a determined date) the owner exits the business for the last time and work backward to the beginning of the process. This will help determine the time needed to complete each part of the transfer or cessation of business leadership and operations. Therefore, the strategic succession planning team assigns specific time-sensitive "gates" leading to completing the business goal.

One example from a large landscape design-build business determined the owner wanted to exit on December 31 in five years. After assessing the business position, the strategic succession planning team allotted one year to determine a successor. Next, they planned two years of owner mentorship for the successor. Year three saw the successor taking on measured leadership and operations oversight. Year four increased successor responsibilities and the decrease in owner engagement. Year five determined valuation of the business, payout to the owner and a retirement and benefits package, and complete transition of business leadership and operations to the successor. The owner exited on December 31 with a handsome payout and a retirement and benefits package. He exited on his own terms.

Thus, the aim of a thoughtful and well-articulated strategic succession plan is to benefit the interests of all parties—the departing owner, family members, employees, potential successor (if applicable), suppliers, and clients.

2.6 How Long Will It Take?

Ideally the strategic succession planning team will set aside one day per month for strategic planning. There will also be some research and preparation between meetings for some of the team members. There will also be a great deal of work in implementing the resulting strategic initiatives. Next to running the business, this is job number one and an ongoing work-in-progress that never ends.

A note of caution: A quest for perfection will doom the planning process. The business owner and team members may regard the choices to be made as so monumental that they must find perfect answers or risk losing the business. This attitude can lengthen the information-gathering phase indefinitely. **Solution**: Practice the 80% rule. Gather much information, knowing there will not be an initial 100% solution because there are unforeseen unknowns. But do not stop; keep moving. Once there is an 80% solution, begin the planning process and then, implement. As current information arises, adjust the plan and implementation until a near 100% solution is achieved. Do not get caught up in paralysis by analysis—move forward with known information and adjust as new information becomes available.

Also, do not do the entire strategic succession plan in a few consecutive days. Establish a schedule that allows for time between meetings to reflect on the discussions, dig up additional data, and build consensus.

Typically, the requirement will be to invest 2–4% of the team's time in the process, including the planning meetings, preparation, and research. As the succession strategy becomes clear, implementing the plan becomes a normal part of running the business, helping the business achieve stronger results and greater efficiency in the transfer.

Realistically, to develop a strategic succession plan will take approximately one year with dedicated teamwork. Implementing the plan can last between three and five years.

2.7 How Frequently Should the Plan Be Updated?

The short answer—Continually! Too many small business owners and their teams think of strategic succession planning as a once-and-done event. History tells us the inflexibility of plans leads to frustrations and dead ends. This is not the model to follow when transferring the business.

Some business owners and their teams have long time horizons because they want to continually expand the business. While this is admirable, remember the primary goal—transfer of leadership and operations. Therefore, the succession planning team needs to focus on transition to maximize operations. This will require the team to remember rapid changes in market needs and preferences, technologies, competition, regulations, and economics which have shorter time horizons accomplished through greater speed and agility.

One day per month is an appropriate target for strategic succession planning. This will provide ample time for monitoring progress, reviewing and revising the strategy, and developing new objectives, budgets, action plans, and time schedules. And it does not interfere with everyday business.

2.8 Necessary Preparations

A strategic succession plan will succeed only if the owner and other key team members believe in it and openly support it. This may seem like common sense, but it is all too common for companies to start the planning process before the leaders have agreed to adhere to the outcome. **Caution**: The planning effort will be half-hearted if the team doing it senses they lack staunch support by the owner and that their decisions may be challenged or even overturned.

The business owner and team members must do more than approve the process. They must be active participants. In some small businesses, the owner tries to delegate the plan to a committee. This usually results in extreme frustration for both the team members and the owner if the plan does not measure up to the owner's expectations and he or she is forced to modify it.

By widening the succession planning team, creative synergies among members will increase the range of skills and talents that go into the plan (see above Leadership and Operations Options). This also builds a sense of ownership and commitment to the succession plan that emerges. However, team-based processes do have limits. The team can get so large there is too much discussion and too little decision-making. Research studies show that a team size of six to ten people is optimal.

The composition of the strategic succession planning team is important. The best team consists of those who will be responsible for the plan's execution. Team members should be colleagues who can discuss openly and frankly any issue that arises. They should represent a spectrum of perspectives, functional disciplines, business backgrounds, and experience within the business and industry. One person should be appointed as the process leader. This individual takes care of the agenda and minutes, pays attention to procedural details, and channels the discussion so the other participants may focus on strategy and content. Teams will be wise to avoid the temptation to let the owner fill this role. He or she needs to be engaged in strategizing, not managing the discussion, watching the clock, or negotiating disputes.

Some businesses will recruit outside of the company to find a person with the right mix of skills and experience to lead the strategic succession planning process. If an outside consultant is selected, be sure he or she is competent in strategic succession strategy and the intended process. It is also essential to remember not to delegate strategic decisions to an outsider. Assisting with the strategic process and research is fine; however, be sure that the owner, team members, and the outside consultant understand the consultant's role is to help the team make crucial decisions and not to decide for them.

2.9 Ensuring Anticipated Results Are Achieved

It is a challenge to create a strategic succession plan for a small business, but it is even more challenging to follow it and achieve the desired results. All too often, many plans become the object of "document worship" rather than a management tool. To the detriment of the business, a strategic succession planning team that rarely reviews or consults it will set the business adrift as they grapple to make the difficult choices.

A strategic succession plan that does not help a business anticipate changes, make tough choices, and exploit new opportunities is obviously a waste of time and effort. What can be done? Plan the process and follow the process! Businesses that do an excellent job of implementing their strategy can expect to achieve 80–90% of their objectives.

2.10 Three Tools Vital for Implementation Success

Action plans. For each objective in the overall strategic succession plan, the team should develop an action plan that spells out the steps taken to:

- Achieve the objective.
- The time and resources needed.
- The team member who will see that each is carried out.

The overall strategic succession plan that emerges should have a few objectives—typically ten or fewer. Each should be focused on the near term. If it will be a long-term objective, such as the final exit of the owner, it should become a Goal with shorter-term objectives, such as determining the owner's desired exit options.

Table 2.1   A "To Do List" to Consider for the Business Transition

Step	Questions to Answer	Completed: Yes/No	Decision
Step 1	What is the business owner's personal vision?		
	How does he or she see their life and lifestyle once they exit the business?		
Step 2	What is the business owner's vision for the business after they exit? (i.e., transfer leadership, sell, or liquidate)		
Step 3	Who, specifically, will be members of the succession planning team?		
Step 4	How and when will employees be informed of the transition and its timeframe?		

Table 2.2   A "To Do List" to Consider for Business Transfer

		Completed: Yes/No	Decision
Step	*Questions to Answer*		
Step 5	What is the timeframe from start to final owner exit?		
Step 6	What leadership and operational competencies are required of a successor?		
Step 7	Who are likely succession candidates? (Internal or external— assign specific names)		
Step 8	What type of training is needed for the successor?		
	What duration?		
	Why (for both)?		
	Training decision:		
	Duration decision:		
Step 9	How will successor training be conducted and by whom?		(Two decisions here)
Step 10	How and when will employees be informed of the successor and his or her qualifications?		
Step 11	How will operations proceed during the transition? (i.e., maintain, expand, or decrease operations)		
Step 12	What are the specific time-sensitive gates for leadership and operations transfer?		
	Gate 1: Leadership start date: End date: (Add more as appropriate)		
	Gate 2: Operations start date: End date: (Add more as appropriate)		

If transferring the business:

Table 2.2 (Continued) A "To Do List" to Consider for Business Transfer

	If transferring the business:		
Step	*Questions to Answer*	*Completed: Yes/No*	*Decision*
Step 13	How and when will employees be informed of the time-sensitive gates?		
Step 14	What is the valuation of the business?		
Step 15	What are the business owner's exit options? (Payout and/or retirement package)		
Step 16	When will the business owner exercise his or her exit options? (i.e., specific date)		
Step 17	When will the owner exit the business?		

Budgets. A meaningful cash flow budget is necessary. This will allocate funds on a prioritized basis to action plans. This may be a limiting factor in scheduling the action plans.

Scheduling managers' time. Most businesses run out of time before they run out of money. While most companies do detailed financial budgets, they frequently don't assess or plan the time top managers will need to devote to implementing action plans. Top management's time is a precious resource for any business. It is critical to determine how much time top managers must spend each month on implementing action plans. Therefore, delegation of Action Plans is essential. Time availability is crucial in scheduling the start and completion of action steps and in achieving timely completion.

Tables 2.1, 2.2, 2.3, and 2.4 provide business owners with some "to do lists" to guide them in their thinking if they should choose different options for business transfer.

2.11 Chapter Summary

Strategic Succession Planning is an intentional and thoughtful process for determining the future course of a business once the owner exits. This

Table 2.3 A "To Do List" to Consider for Selling the Business

	If selling the business:		
Step	*Questions to Answer*	*Completed: Yes/No*	*Decision*
Step 5	What is the timeframe from start to final owner exit?		
Step 6	What leadership and operational competencies are required of a buyer?		
Step 7	Who are likely purchaser candidates? (Internal or external—assign specific names)		
Step 8	What type of training is needed for the purchaser (if any)?		
	What duration?		
	Why (for both)?		
Step 9	How will purchaser training be conducted and by whom?		(Two decisions)
Step 10	How and when will employees be informed of the purchaser and their qualifications?		
Step 11	How will operations proceed during the transition? (i.e., maintain, expand, or decrease operations)		
Step 12	What are the specific time-sensitive gates for leadership and operations transfer?		
	Gate 1: Leadership start date: End date: (Add more as appropriate)		
	Gate 2: Operations start date: End date: (Add more as appropriate)		
Step 13	How and when will employees be informed of the time-sensitive gates?		
Step 14	What is the valuation of the business?		
Step 15	What are the business owner's exit options? (Payout and/or retirement package)		
Step 16	When will the business owner exercise his or her exit options? (i.e., specific date)		
Step 17	When will the owner sell the business and exit?		

Table 2.4   A "To Do List" to Consider for Liquidating the Business

Step	Questions to Answer	Completed: Yes/No	Decision
If liquidating the business:			
Step 5	What is the timeframe from start to final owner exit?		
Step 6	What leadership and operational competencies are required of a buyer(s)?		
Step 7	Who are likely purchaser candidates? (Internal or external—assign specific names)		
Step 8	What type of training is needed for the purchaser(s) (if any)?		
	What duration?		
	Why (for both)?		
Step 9	How will purchaser(s) training be conducted and by whom?		(Two decisions)
Step 10	How and when will employees be informed of the purchaser(s) and their qualifications?		
Step 11	How will operations proceed during the transition? (i.e., maintain, expand, or decrease operations)		
Step 12	What are the specific time-sensitive gates for leadership and operations transfer?		
	Gate 1: Leadership start date: End date: (Add more as appropriate)		
	Gate 2: Operations start date: End date: (Add more as appropriate)		
Step 13	How and when will employees be informed of the time-sensitive gates?		
Step 14	What is the valuation of the business?		
Step 15	What are the business owner's exit options? (Payout and/or retirement package)		
Step 16	When will the business owner exercise his or her exit options? (i.e., specific date)		
Step 17	When will the owner liquidate the business and exit?		

document guides a change in ownership with sustained operations or the liquidation of the business through a detailed and well-articulated plan. This chapter provided considerations for business owners to transfer, sell, or liquidate the business by following a time-sensitive strategic plan. The chapter also identified reasons to develop a strategic succession plan and the pitfalls of neglecting such a plan. It also provided practical and tangible strategic processes to develop a successful succession plan. Finally, a Strategic Succession Plan Roadmap provided a step-by-step process to develop and implement a viable succession plan. Therefore, the successful transition, sale, or liquidation of the business will hinge on the successful implementation of the plan by the business owner and his or her team. The benefit of this strategic plan will benefit the business owner, his or her family, employees, suppliers, and the clients served.

Works Cited

Above the Canopy. n.d. Retrieved from https://www.abovethecanopy.us/family-business-succession-planning

Bledsoe, G. 2021. "Family Succession Planning: 3 Best Practice & A Review of the Statistics." *Above the Canopy*. Accessed March 18, 2022. business/succession-planning-for-small-businesses.html.

Carlson J. M. 2021. *Surge in Succession Planning*. Jersey City: Forbes. Retrieved from https://www.forbes.com/sites/juliacarlson/2021/04/26/surge-in-succession-planning/?sh=1af29129479a

Cyr, Chris. 2020. "Council Post: How To Tackle Succession Planning For Your Small Business." *Forbes*. March 4, 2020. https://www.forbes.com/sites/forbesbusinesscouncil/2020/03/04/how-to-tackle-succession-planning-for-your-small-business/

Executive Headhunters. 2019. "9 Steps to Effective Succession Planning for Small Business Owners." London, England: EMA Partners. October 25, 2019. Retrieved from https://insights.executiveheadhunters.co.uk/blog/effective-small-business-succession-planning

Farrell, P.E. 2020. *Your Business Needs a Success Plan: Here Are the Basics*. New York: Kiplinger. Retrieved from https://www.kiplinger.com/business/small-business/601698/your-business-needs-a-succession-plan-here-are-the-basics.

FindLaw's Team. 2016. *Succession Planning for Small Business*. Eagan, MN: Thomson.

Kenton, Will 2020a. *Succession Planning*. New York: Investopedia.

Kenton, Will. 2020b. "Understanding Succession Planning." *Investopedia*. December 6, 2020. https://www.investopedia.com/terms/s/succession-planning.asp.

Monte, Jill. 2018. "5 Get-Started Steps for Your Small Business Succession Plan." *EDSI*. September 17, 2018. https://www.edsisolutions.com/blog/5-get-started-steps-for-your-small-business-succession-plan.

Newcomer-Dyer, Robert. 2019. "Business Succession Planning: 5 Ways to Transfer Ownership Of Your Business." *Fit Small Business*. October 11, 2019. https://fitsmallbusiness.com/business-succession-planning/.

"Succession Planning for Small Businesses." 2016. *Findlaw*. June 20, 2016. https://www.findlaw.com/smallbusiness/closing-a-business/succession-planning-for-small-businesses.html

Thienel, S. 2020. *Small Business Succession Planning Survey*. Columbia: Wilmington Trust.

Chapter 3

Recruiting a Successor from Inside, Outside, or Utilizing Other Options for the Organization

Kay Turner, Deborah M. Adwokat, and Robert K. Prescott

Contents

3.1 Introduction

Darren Dahl emphasizes the importance of putting a succession plan in place by sharing the cautionary tale of a small family business owner in Delaware who failed to develop a succession plan and lost the business in his article "Succession Stories: The Good, the Bad, and the Ugly"

(Dahl 2011). He recounts the story of Brad Winton, a financial planner, whose family owned a small business since the mid-1940s.

He explains the business began as a

> popular dinner theater, which was founded by his grandfather and his grandfather's brother in the mid-1940s. Winton's mother was one of nine children in the second generation who gradually took over the theater's operations, which seated 1,000 and employed a total of 300 workers, as the founders, who had been circus acrobats in their youth, got on in years.

Unfortunately, issues arose because of poor succession planning. Among them, the aging founders refused to relinquish any decision-making or control and were reluctant to change or accommodate societal influences that affected the success of the business. The business "came to a screeching halt in 2008" (Dahl 2011).

"After 30-plus years of working her tail off, my mother walked away with nothing," says Winton, adding that "because they had worked for the family business their whole lives, his mother, aunts, and uncles had specialized skills that made finding new jobs a challenge." Winton added that "it makes everyone sad to think that the business didn't work out because they didn't do the proper planning" (Dahl 2011).

3.2 Importance of Succession Planning

What is succession planning? "Succession Planning is essentially planning for and executing smooth transitions of leadership" and key positions in a business ("What is Succession Planning and Why Is It Important?" 2018). It anticipates for planned or unplanned separations of an incumbent and prepares for the successful transition of a new leader.

Succession planning is especially important for small and family-owned businesses to continue effective operations in anticipation of the departure of one or more key individuals or key position incumbents. There are many reasons key leaders may leave business operations—including retirement, divorce, untimely illness, incapacitation, death, or several other unplanned circumstances. Making succession arrangements or choosing a successor well in advance reduces the disruptive impact that an abrupt, unplanned departure may have on business operations and company culture.

Table 3.1 Example of Small Business Size Standards Set by the US Small Business Association

Industry	Not to Exceed
Wind Electric Power Generation	250 employees
Libraries & Archives	US$16.5 million average annual revenue
Couriers & Express Delivery Services	1,500 employees
Farm Management Services	US$8 million average annual revenue
Wineries	1,000 employees
Family Clothing Stores	US$41.5 million average annual revenue
Machine Shops	500 employees

Source: US Small Business Association, Table of Small Business Size Standards Matched to North American Industry Classification System Codes, August 19, 2019.

The American Society for Quality (ASQ) defines a small business as "a privately-owned corporation, partnership, or sole proprietorship that has fewer employees and less annual revenue than a corporation or regular-sized business" (American Society for Quality 2022). The US Small Business Association (SBA) defines small businesses by a set of standards matched to certain industries either by the number of employees or average maximum annual receipts (Table 3.1).

A complete list of size standards for small businesses can be found on the website of the National Archive Code of Federal Regulations, Title 13, §121.201 "What size standards has SBA identified by North American Industry Classification Codes" (Code of Federal Regulations 2022).

The definition of a family-owned business, the oldest form of business organizations, differs slightly. Inc. defines these companies "as any business in which two or more family members are involved and most of the ownership or control lies within a family" ("Family-Owned Business" 2021).

In their article "A Small Business Is Not a Little Big Business," John A. Welsh and Jerry F. White describe the unique challenges that small businesses face; and while failing to have a good succession plan can be devastating to any business, the consequences can be catastrophic to a small or family-owned enterprise (Welsh and White 1981).

The Corporate Finance Institute adds that a good "succession plan guarantees an organization that there are employees waiting and ready to take over key management and leadership roles" ("Succession Planning" n.d.).

Have a well-defined succession plan for both small and family-owned businesses. Succession planning:

■ Arranges for transferring ownership or leadership because it identifies potential candidates to run the business at the appropriate time, reducing uncertainty internally and externally.
■ Reduces business risk and costs because the business has a plan in place for the future.
■ Builds a responsive business flexible to adapt to change.
■ Prepares the business to handle unexpected events, for example, an untimely illness or death of the leader.
■ Helps to identify skill and competency gaps within the business to maintain a competitive advantage.
■ Keeps up with the changing business environment if the succession plan is reviewed periodically.
■ Ensures the success of the business.
■ Offers family-owned businesses the ability to:
  – Transition and continue to maintain ownership.
  – Minimize costs including recruitment, taxes, and development/training.
  – Maximize the value of the business.
  – Maintain a legacy for future generations.

Last, it is critical for all small businesses to review their succession plans annually, at the minimum, to ensure that adjustments are made as employees, products/services, customers, markets, and the business environment change.

To ensure that the selection of a family-owned or small business successor is carefully planned and meets the challenges of the business, this chapter will discuss:

1. The process to determine if the successor should be selected from inside the business or recruited from outside the business.
2. Alternative options other than promoting internally or recruiting externally.
3. How to effectively handle the recruitment and transition processes.
4. The nuances of succession planning in family-owned small businesses.

3.3 Selecting a Successor from Within or Outside the Business

Good successors may be found internally or externally for the business. Although there are no fixed rules to deciding, there are some especially important points to consider when recruiting from within or from outside of the company. Sigma Assessment Systems, a leader in succession planning for over 50 years, explains that a well-run small business should have a good succession sense of the positions that can be filled by its personnel and when an external source needs to be recruited ("External Candidates and Succession" n.d.).

Small businesses, especially those with a unique or specific company culture, will undoubtedly benefit from recruiting an internal successor. In the article "Organizational Culture and Impact on Opportunities for Professional Advancement," published in the *Journal of Business and Economic Studies*, Phoebe Massimino and Kay Turner state, "Knowledge of business etiquette and business culture has been shown to be a determinant of success in the workplace" (Massimino and Turner 2018).

Often, a leader recruited from within a company with a strong or dominant culture has been proven to be a cultural "fit." Theoretically, this individual already understands the construct of unwritten rules, values, customs, and traditions that support the company's ethos and thus stands a better chance of gaining trust and acceptance by their colleagues to lead the organization into its next phase.

Recruiting an internal candidate has major advantages in companies that require an understanding of very specialized or complex industry or trade processes or practices. The downtime or lost productivity experienced during the recruitment, onboarding, and assimilation process of an externally recruited leader can be significant. These costs are further amplified in small business settings where resources may be limited. Significant savings can be realized simply by recruiting an internal candidate for the succession arrangement. Internal candidates also bring an understanding of organization-specific business processes and methodologies. The overall work environment allows these individuals to hit the ground running in their new roles much faster than potential external counterparts.

A good succession plan engages in due diligence to ensure that the designated internal candidate is the best suited for the position. This can be challenging in small and family-owned businesses with few or no formal succession planning policies in place. "There is nothing more detrimental" to the success of the plan "than overlooking qualified candidates or choosing" an internal candidate that angers your employees, customers, and/or vendors. "Without an objective, justifiable process, you risk picking the wrong people, or the selected individuals turn out to be not ready" to move into key leadership positions (Yvanovich 2019).

For small businesses where cost containment may be a priority, the cost associated with employee turnover can affect the bottom line. Succession plans that favor the development and selection of internal successors, especially for key leadership positions, have been found to promote employee retention and reduces costs associated with employee turnover. The Society for Human Resource Management (SHRM) reports it costs an average of half to three-quarters of an employee's salary to replace that individual which can cost even more for key positions ("The Cost of Employee Turnover for a Small Business" 2021).

Successors recruited from outside the business can add exponential value and should be considered when the company will benefit from a new and innovative perspective. External successors are also a viable option when companies are prioritizing growth as a component of their business strategy. Airswift, an international workforce solution provider, explains that new talent can be more adaptable and open to new ways of working even though it can be more comfortable to choose an internal successor familiar with the company's values, customs, and standard way of operating; however, taking a chance on an external candidate may add more value eventually as this could lead to innovative changes that will grow the business ("Innovative Hiring: The Benefits of Recruiting from outside Your Sector" 2020).

External talent is a vital component in a small business succession plan when "crucial leadership skills in organizations are *insufficient* for meeting (its) current and future needs," according to the Center for Creative Leadership. External successors should be considered when "expertise … is lacking in your organization, and it is not something that can be readily developed from within your existing talent pool," to prepare the business for continued and future success ("External Candidates and Succession" n.d.).

Businesses intent on making a cultural shift for competitive advantage should recruit externally as part of their succession planning strategy. Naviga, a recruiting and executive search firm, posits that hiring external talent is strongly recommended "if your company is trying to go in a different direction culturally or is trying to shake things up. Changing the leadership is a great way to change to solidify this shift" ("How Hiring Outside Leadership Can Benefit Your Company" n.d.).

Professor Stephen Ferris, director of the Financial Research Institute at the University of Missouri Robert J. Trulaske, Sr. College of Business, along with researchers from the Georgia Institute of Technology and California State University at Fullerton, studied succession patterns of the 2,524 CEO turnovers. Ferris believes, "If a company currently is either mired in mediocrity or performing poorly and it announces the hiring of an external CEO, it could be a signal that … (they are) serious about fixing problems." Ferris, who has been studying this area of practice for over 60 years adds, "Change clearly is needed in those situations, so it makes sense to look outside the company for someone to rejuvenate the firm" (Phys. 2015) (Table 3.2).

3.4 Additional Options for Selecting a Successor

Interim successors are a practical, intermediate alternative to recruiting an internal or external successor, especially with the unexpected loss or unavailability of a key individual. Naming a temporary successor who immediately provides the guidance and stability to the business affords the organization the latitude to engage in a thoughtful deliberative, succession planning exercise.

According to "Succession Planning in Times of Crisis" utilizing an interim or temporary successor with the express understanding that "there is no expectation that such person will continue in that role on a long-term basis" is a much better alternative to "putting a promising talent in a role too early and in a time of crisis." Such circumstances "may create a very challenging experience that could result in a loss of a promising (future) leader in the organization. Where there is no "ready now" (internal or external successor), we recommend placing a more seasoned interim successor in the role." Internal or external retired small business leaders "in a similar industry (or who have experience leading businesses of) comparable levels of complexity and size" make ideal interim successors. These retired interims "can also serve as a mentor to the eventual long-term successor" (Sherman and Sterling 2020).

The US Small Business Administration (SBA) and SCORE, the nation's largest network of volunteer expert business mentors, provide comprehensive resources to assist small business owners and leaders to develop a

Table 3.2   Pros and Cons of Selecting Internal and External Successors

Successor	Pros	Cons
Internal	Proven cultural fit therefore a better chance of gaining trust and acceptance by the individual's colleagues. For family-owned businesses— understands the intricacies of the organization including relationships, roles, and responsibilities between/among family members.	Choosing the wrong internal candidate can anger employees, customers, vendors, etc. The selected individual is not ready or prepared to move into the key leadership position. Employees are familiar with the successor and have a perception of the individual's competencies and skills which may be negative.
	Reduces downtime and lost productivity during the recruitment, onboarding, and assimilation process.	
	Understands organization-specific business processes, methodologies, and overall work environment that allows the internal candidate to hit the ground running.	Comfortable and content with the culture, employees, and business as it stands which can stall innovation and fresh ideas.
	Promotes employee retention and reduces the costs associated with employee turnover, as well as demonstrates that employees have an opportunity to develop and grow in the business.	
External	Opportunity for fresh ideas, thoughts, and innovation, as well as brings a new perspective to the business.	Longer transition time to learn the intricacies of the business, as well as increased downtime and lost productivity during the recruitment, onboarding, and assimilation processes.
	Can be open to new ways of working and adaptable to change.	

(Continued)

Table 3.2 (Continued)   Pros and Cons of Selecting Internal and External Successors

Successor	Pros	Cons
	Current internal potential candidates have insufficient crucial leadership skills for meeting current and future business needs.	
	Organizational expertise is lacking from the current internal candidate pool.	
	Business is intent on making a cultural shift that cannot be accomplished with an internal candidate; an external successor is required to make the necessary changes.	

robust succession plan right for them. In addition, SBA and SCORE can also help small business leaders and owners determine if selling their business is a viable option.

SCORE, in partnership with MassMutual, developed "The Small Business Owner's Guide to Succession Planning" that explains four steps to develop a succession plan ("The Small Business Owner's Guide to Succession Planning" 2019):

1. Decide How to Exit the Business
   a. Transfer the business to an heir
   b. Sell the business to a business partner
   c. Sell the business to a key employee
   d. Sell the business to an outside buyer
2. Conduct a Business Evaluation – Assets, Income, Market Value
3. Prepare for the Transition
4. Review the Succession Plan Regularly

3.5 Succession Planning Best Practices and Tools

The fundamentals of a succession plan apply to both large corporations and small businesses. For a corporation, these plans can be very comprehensive.

For a small business, they may be more narrowly defined. Regardless of the breadth of the succession plan, best practices should always be executed.

Genvieve Roberts' article "Top 10 Best Practices for Succession Planning Make Certain Your 'Who's Ready Next' List Is Solid" explains the challenge that businesses of all sizes face when posed with the question of who is ready to take over the leadership position (Roberts 2022).

Roberts provides a list of the ten best practices to guide the succession planning process:

1. Start With The End In Mind (include the roles to fill, requirements, core competencies, skills, and any additional criteria relevant to the position)
2. Be Clear About The Roles That Will Be Included (and not)—(identify the roles and those involved in the process to help alleviate employees' angst)
3. Engage All Stakeholders Who Will Be Impacted In The Process (ensure the process is driven by business leaders soliciting feedback from stakeholders via interviews, surveys, focus groups, etc.)
4. Look Ahead 1-3-5 Years (provides continuity and forecasts future workforce needs)
5. Incent and Recognize Leaders Who Develop Others (developing employees is a skill that should be recognized)
6. Use Technology (make the investment in talent management software to track performance, i.e., a Human Resources Information System)
7. Conduct Talent Assessments At Least Annually (succession planning is fluid, utilize assessment tools to assist in this process)
8. Facilitate The Creation Of Employed-Owned Development Plans (the plan is pathway for the employee to reach their goals, and a way for the business to evaluate talent)
9. Regularly Engage In 2-Way Feedback (honest, open two-way feedback helps to eliminate any misconceptions of where the employee fits within the business)
10. Communicate Communicate Communicate (transparency builds trust; this helps to retain potential leaders)

With these steps, it is critical to utilize reliable, valid assessment tools to evaluate talent. Jill Hauwiller, in her *Forbes* article "Successful Succession Planning: Managing Transparency and Risk," states,

> Assessments like TALENTx7 Learning Agility can be incredibly useful in determining potential, which for the purposes of succession

planning is defined as the interest and ability to take on bigger or broader roles. The nine box grid is another commonly used tool that maps talent by performance and potential.

(Hauwiller 2021)

The Talentx7 Assessment tool measures seven facets of learning agility (https://thetalentx7.com/talentx7-assessment-learning-agility/, retrieved 2022):

1. Interpersonal Acumen
2. Cognitive Perspective
3. Environmental Mindfulness
4. Drive to Excel
5. Self-Insight
6. Change Alacrity
7. Feedback Responsiveness

Academy to Innovate HR (AIHR) developed the "The 9 Box Grid: A Practitioner's Guide" for talent management and succession planning ("The 9 Box Grid: A Practitioner's Guide," Updated December 2021). This tool divides employees into nine categories based on their performance and potential (Table 3.3).

The 9 Box Grid is a versatile, easy-to-use tool that takes a holistic approach to identifying talent.

3.6 Effectively Recruiting and Transitioning a Successor

Once a decision to retain the business has been made, a well-crafted succession plan that allows for a smooth transition should be developed.

A good succession plan identifies and prepares new leaders to replace leaders when they leave. It has been "described as having the right people in the right place at the right time" (Atwood 2007).

Positions needing succession planning are critical to the continued success of the business and vulnerable if knowledge loss occurs. Once these critical positions have been identified, a position profile with performance expectations will assist in determining whether anyone within the organization has the skills, abilities, and/or experience to take over the successor role. Once this process has been completed, the successor recruitment process may begin.

Table 3.3   AIHR 9 Box Grid Talent Assessment and Succession Planning Tool

9 BOX GRID

POTENTIAL

DYSFUNC-TIONAL GENIUSES	HIGH POTENTIALS	STARS
UP OR OUT DILEMMAS	CORE PLAYERS	HIGH PERFORMERS
BAD HIRES	UP OR OUT GRINDERS	WORKHORSES

PERFORMANCE

Source: https://www.aihr.com/blog/9-box-grid/, updated December 2021.

The recruitment process begins by identifying potential successor talent in the small business. Internal candidates in positions most similarly aligned in function, task, and competencies to the vacated or vacating successor ideally are well poised for development or nomination into the successor role. Mining these positions and other closely related jobs is a natural starting point for identifying internal successor talent. Where no well-suited internal candidates can be identified or developed, successor qualifications should be incorporated into an external recruitment strategy to fill the successor role with a permanent or interim candidate from outside of the small or family-owned business.

Transition planning is a critical component of a good succession plan. A transition plan is a proactive way to capture and document the essence of an incumbent's role—including the position's core functions, the associated day-to-day responsibilities, customary professional networks, assigned budget, inventory, etc. A well-developed transition plan ensures continuity of the vacated position's responsibilities and secures the position's assigned resources if a planned or unplanned departure occurs. The plan incorporates all items and business matters to be permanently or temporarily transferred upon the incumbent's departure.

Effective transition management also provides opportunities for transferring "legacy knowledge" critical elements and information not necessarily documented in a traditional format. Utilizing transition interviews with vacating incumbents allows for honoring and preserving the knowledge, work experience, and accomplishments that have contributed to the success of the business. These interviews provide an opportunity for a meaningful exchange of professional experiences, lessons learned, valuable insights, tips, tactics, and knowledge that contributed to the vacating incumbent's success in the role ("Transition Planning Interview Guide" n.d.).

Besides effectively transitioning the successor, a key component for implementing a small business succession plan is communicating key leader changes. Unlike large publicly traded companies, small businesses have no legal obligation to publicly disclose changes in leadership. Notwithstanding, small businesses still have compelling incentives to communicate a well-developed transition plan to the company's community of employees, customers, suppliers, and distributors. Transition plans should be shared to inform these stakeholders of the key leader changeover to prevent leaks, rumors, and damaging misinformation.

Jane Pettit, Director of Programming in Organizational Learning at the University of Michigan, suggests that when transitioning staff during periods of change, constituents should be advised of "what is changing, what is not changing, who will be impacted, how we will be impacted" (Pettit n.d.). The message should be communicated first to employees, then to additional constituents, and through multiple channels based on the audience—town halls, face-to-face, memos, and emails. Pettit further explains, *"not everyone is ready* to hear the news at the same time. Therefore, it is important to convey your message in several different modes and many times" (Pettit n.d.).

Unfortunately, even the best succession arrangements do not always go as planned.

Rick Yvanovich outlines the unintended consequences of a poorly crafted, socialized, and communicated succession plan in "Succession Planning: 5 Common Mistakes and How to Avoid Them" (Yvanovich 2019). The five common mistakes include:

1. Playing Favorites
2. Lack of an Objective Process for Spotting Successors
3. Do not Address Disappointment
4. Process Becomes a Competition
5. The Succession Planning Process is a Kept Secret

Succession plans falter when transparency is not promoted in the process and the work is not done to develop and execute a well-thought-through implementation plan. Mike Kappel, in his *Forbes* article "Transparency in Business: 5 Ways to Build Trust," defines business transparency as "the process of being open, honest, and straightforward about various company operations … because transparency in business leads to trust" (Kappel 2019) (Table 3.4).

Table 3.4 Checklist for Selecting a Family Member Successor

To attain a smooth transition, the potential successor, whether a family member or relative through marriage, must be qualified to handle the responsibilities of becoming the family business leader. However, more importantly, the individual must be motivated and want to succeed at this leadership level. If the successor is "forced" to take the lead role, this has the potential to place the person and business on a path to failure.
Family Member Successor Checklist
• Decide who in the family is a viable candidate to become the successor. There may be more than one candidate. Also, refrain from assuming that the potential candidate(s) is interested and motivated to embrace the position. • Speak with the family member(s) who has the potential to be the successor to ensure the individual(s) envisions this career path. • Evaluate the candidate(s) based upon skills, competencies, demure, and needs of the business. This point in the process is a good time to engage advisers in and outside of the business to assist in the evaluation process. An outside third party can facilitate the evaluation process to ensure consistency and fairness. • Once the candidate is selected, prepare a professional development and training plan for the successor before the family member takes on the leadership role to ensure the selected individual understands all facets of the business from products/services to managing employees to operations to finances. This plan must be thorough and prepared thoughtfully. In addition to on-the-job training and position rotation, the succession plan should include external professional development education. • Be methodical in announcing the new successor by having a clear, concise communication plan in place. The choice of a predecessor should not be a surprise to the family or company employees. When appropriate in the process, leadership should inform family members and employees that a transition in leadership will be taking place. It is critical to the health of the business that everyone is on board and supportive of the selected successor. If the succession planning is done appropriately, this will not be an issue. • Ensure enough time is planned for the transition process, if possible. Don't underestimate the value of the former leader supporting the new leader in taking the reins.
It is only appropriate to recruit a family member to be the successor if there is an individual who has been mentored, as well as has the experience, skills, desire, and passion to effectively run the business.

However, transparency is not a one-size-fits-all situation. There can be disadvantages to succession planning transparency:

1. Providing too much information to employees.
2. Employees not happy with the information fosters negativity in the workplace.
3. Employees separating from the business.

To avoid pitfalls, when sharing information with employees about succession planning, ask these questions:

1. Who should be told?
2. How much information should be shared?
3. Who should tell them?
4. How should they be told?
5. How do we manage disappointment?

Hauwiller adds,

> A highly talented employee may feel misunderstood or undervalued if they are identified for a role that doesn't align with their career goals. This gives the organization time to identify a better successor and it creates an opportunity to reassess and support a more desirable career path for the original successor.
>
> **(Hauwiller 2021)**

The appearance of inappropriate favoritism in the successor candidate selection can destroy the credibility of the succession plan and cause valued talent to leave the company. As Yvanovich explains, "favoritism can cloud your judgment when selecting potential candidates for your succession plan and hence derail the entire process. Your favorite employees may not possess the critical skills required, or to simply put, they lack the potential factors" (Yvanovich 2019).

This can be a thorny issue in small and family-owned business settings where employees are few and can easily interact and communicate informally. Even with the best communicated and published succession plans, there will be talented and valued employees who believe that they should have been a chosen successor.

Yvanovich states,

> Everyone deserves an explanation as to why they are (or) not on
> your list of potential candidates. A part of achieving transparency
> in succession planning is to ensure the employees understand why
> certain people are on your list while others are not. Having an
> honest discussion about what those employees lack can help sub-
> due disappointment, making it easier for people to swallow.
>
> **(Yvanovich 2019)**

It also provides an opportunity to further invest in those employees' development to address performance gaps which can result in greater benefits for
the employee and the business.

> Letting employees know that their skills and experience are val-
> ued dissuades top performers from leaving, according to David
> Leonard, executive director of the executive development program
> at the University of North Carolina. He recommends providing top
> performers with leadership development opportunities to drive
> engagement and satisfaction.
>
> **(LaMarche and Ruyle 2015)**

Marie LaMarche and Kim E. Ruyle in "Point-Counterpoint: Should You Tell
Employees They're Part of a Succession Plan?" point out that discussing an
employee's career goals helps to gauge the individual's interest in opportunities within the business because the employee's skills may not match their
ambitions (LaMarche and Ruyle 2015).

All the above are proven strategies to retain valued employees who were
not selected for a successor role.

3.7 Nuances of a Family-Owned Business

A strong organization prepares to keep itself alive for future generations—no
different for small or family-owned businesses. That is why succession planning is critical. Family-owned businesses face unique challenges. However,
if succession planning is done thoughtfully, methodically, and transparently,
family-owned businesses can thrive.

PwC's "Family Business Survey 2021" states, "Every business should have a near-term business continuity plan and long-term succession plan … only one-third of North American family business leaders say they have a robust, documented and communicated succession plan in place" (PwC 2021).

What is the resistance to succession planning in family-owned businesses?

The Family Business Survey PwC 2021 explains there are long-established reasons for this plight:

- Leaders and founders find it hard to envision not controlling the business.
- Leaders and founders are not ready to cede responsibilities to others.
- It is challenging to determine who is willing, able, and capable to take over the business and even more daunting to seamlessly transition the new leader.
- Issues with levels of authority—Who starts the conversation to plan?

Although North American family business leaders want the next generation to become majority stakeholders, they are not properly planning for the future (PwC 2021).

Francois Botha's *Forbes* article "Family Business Challenges: The 3 Issues Families Can't Ignore" posits that the more interconnected a family is, the greater potential for family members to feel entitled to benefits that exceed their contributions, to encounter sibling rivalry, and to argue over employing spouses (Botha 2020).

In addition, family-owned businesses face the challenges of employee accusations of nepotism; the emotional issue of separating business from personal feelings; managing generational differences regarding operations and growth; and family members encountering the pressure to stay in a business of no interest to them.

It also should be noted there is an inaccurate perception that family-owned businesses are small. In 2011, there were 5.5 million family-owned businesses in the United States, contributing 57% of the GDP and employing 63% of the workforce (Family Enterprise USA 2011).

In the article "Succession Planning in a Family Business: Benefits, Challenges, and Guiding Principles," Davis Tremaine states,

> Succession planning is key to achieving a long-term legacy in a family business by, among other things, defining when family members may work in the business, how profits should be

distributed, who may serve on the board, how to plan for future leadership, and other matters such as taxes, liability, estate planning, ownership stakes, and voting rights.

(Tremaine 2021)

The benefits of a thoughtful and thorough succession plan for family-owned businesses include the ability to:

- Evaluate the skills of the family members to determine the individual who fits into the leadership role.
- Mentor the family successor over time so the individual is prepared for the new role.
- Evoke transparency within the business so those family members not chosen for the leadership role can make informed decisions about their future.

However, family-owned business succession planning is not without its challenges, which include:

- Selecting the most suitable family member.
- Repercussions from those family members not selected.
- Lack of interest from younger family members to lead the business.

The statistics confirm why it is imperative to have a succession plan for a family-owned business:

- It is estimated that 40.3% of family business owners expect to retire, creating a significant transition of ownership in the United States. Less than half of those expecting to retire in five years have selected a successor ("Family Business Facts" n.d.).
- Nearly half of family business owners (43%) have no succession plan in place (Family Business Survey PwC 2021).
- Even though nearly 70% of family businesses want to pass their business on to the next generation, only 30% will succeed at transitioning to the next generation ("Family Business Facts" n.d.).

There are unique common threads and challenges faced by all family-owned businesses, regardless of size. Typically, in a non-family business, succession planning is based on the skills, abilities, and interests of the employees.

However, when family dynamics and relationships are added to the mix, another layer of potential issues arise.

In a *BW Businessworld* article entitled "The Importance of Succession Planning for Business Families," author Rajmohan Krishnan states,

> statistics prove that 70% of family-owned businesses globally are sold before the second generation gets a chance to take over, and only 10% of family businesses survive till the third generation. When we analyze this statistic, the reasons for the low survival rate of family-owned businesses are the limited or lack of succession planning.

Succession planning is critical for family-owned businesses to be successfully "handed down" to the next generation (Krishnan 2020) (Table 3.5).

However, if the internal candidates demonstrate that they lack the skills and foresight to lead the business, it may be time to recruit a successor from outside the family business. That is why succession planning should begin early and be reviewed periodically to ensure the potential family member successor remains the viable candidate.

Part of the learning process should include assigning family members to fewer senior roles while they are learning the business. In addition, the leader should periodically meet individually and collectively with the family members to discuss goals, strategy, successes, and improvements.

Table 3.5   Benefits of Transparency in Succession Planning

• Increases employee retention because employees are informed and feel valued.
• Encourages employees to discuss potential future positions in the business.
• Helps small businesses retain top performers by creating an environment of trust.
• Demonstrates business stability by letting employees know the company is planning for the future.
• Minimizes rumors, politics, and innuendos.
• Encourages a workplace environment that values open communication.
• Keeps employees apprised of any significant changes that might occur in the future—leadership, compensation, benefit changes, etc.
• Expands employees' comfort level to share ideas.
• Builds employees' trust and loyalty.
• Keeps employees informed about the financial health of the business.

Selecting a successor takes time, patience, and planning. It is an iterative process because business needs change. Therefore, when evaluating the strengths and weaknesses of each family member, avoid basing decisions on false assumptions, including birth order, emotional connection, or outstanding performance in one facet of the business. The successor decision should be based on the ability of the successor to lead, perform, and adapt.

Conflict may arise when family members are not chosen as the successor or not selected for a position they wanted. One best way to handle this challenge is to hire a mediator to assist with the situation. A mediator will facilitate the conversation between family members who disagree by helping the individuals focus on the issue at hand so each can voice their concerns. It is best these conversations remain confidential so each family member can speak openly.

Referral services, local chamber of commerce, local bar association, internet search, family-business associations, and recommendations from colleagues are several ways to find the appropriate mediator. If the conflict is ignored, it could lead to dissent and can affect the efficient functioning of the business. It is critical that the health of the family business is the driving force behind all succession decisions.

Sometimes there are no qualified or interested successors available within the family. When this occurs, family-owned businesses have the options to recruit externally, transfer the business to a family member, or sell the business to an employee, family member, or business partner.

If the decision is to recruit outside the business, the leader of the family business must inform the family members there will be an external search for the successor. The search process will be more effective if the family members understand and agree that recruiting externally is the best option.

External recruitment should begin by hiring an experienced search firm to manage the process. As with any search, a position description must be written clearly, outlining the responsibilities, qualifications, and reporting status. In addition, it would be helpful if the search firm understood the nuances of the family-run business to ensure that the selected successor is flexible to work in this environment.

The Search Committee should comprise a diverse group of individuals, including family members. The search firm should ensure that all members of the committee participate and have an equal voice. Before the process begins, it should be determined how the final decision will be made either through consensus or a majority rule. It should also be decided if the leader makes the final decision. All these decisions should be considered before the interview process begins.

What can be done to incent employees to stay at a family business when those employees believe they should have been chosen as the future leader, but they were not provided the opportunity, but are still considered a valued member of the organization? This is universal in all large or small family-owned businesses.

The key is to be transparent.

1. Explain to the employees, individually, why they were not chosen for the position, letting each know that they are a valuable member of the business, and leadership is committed to help them achieve their career goals. Depending on the employee, this support can include formal education, mentoring, professional development, and management skills.
2. Explain to all company employees the rationale for the external search and the process implemented to hire the successor.
3. Update company employees regularly on the progress of the search. This will quell rumors and misconceptions.
4. As soon as a leader has been selected, make the announcement. First to the family members, then the company employees, then the vendors, distributors, and customers.

The importance of succession planning for small and family-owned businesses should not be underestimated. Whether successors are selected or developed from inside or outside of the enterprise, or whether an interim or temporary successor strategy is deployed, investing the time and resources to safeguard the company's future is a critical component of operating the business.

3.8 Chapter Summary

Good successors may be found internally or externally for the business. Small businesses, especially those with a unique or specific company culture, will undoubtedly benefit from recruiting an internal successor. Often, a leader recruited from within a company with a strong or dominant culture has been proven to be a cultural "fit." External talent can be a vital component in a small business succession plan when "crucial leadership skills in organizations are *insufficient* for meeting (its) current and future needs," according to the Center for Creative Leadership.

Interim successors are a practical, intermediate alternative to recruiting an internal or external successor, especially with the unexpected loss or unavailability of a key individual. Naming a temporary successor who immediately provides the guidance and stability to the business affords the organization the latitude to engage in a thoughtful deliberative, succession planning exercise.

Once a decision to retain the business has been made, a well-crafted succession plan that allows for smooth transition should be developed. Positions needing succession planning are critical to the continued success of the business that is vulnerable if knowledge loss occurs. Once these critical positions have been identified, a position profile with performance expectations will assist in determining whether anyone within the organization has the skills, abilities, and/or experience to take over the successor role.

The benefits of a thoughtful and thorough succession plan for family-owned businesses include the ability to:

■ Evaluate the skills of the family members to determine the individual who fits into the leadership role.
■ Mentor the family successor over time so the individual is prepared for the new role.
■ Evoke transparency within the business so those family members not chosen for the leadership role can make informed decisions about their future.

But family-owned business succession planning is not without its challenges, which include:

■ Selecting the most suitable family member.
■ Repercussions from those family members not selected.
■ Lack of interest from younger family members to lead the business.

Works Cited

Academy to Innovate HR. 2021. "The 9 Box Grid: A Practitioner's Guide." December 2021. https://www.aihr.com/blog/9-box-grid/

American Society for Quality. n.d. "What is a Small Business." Accessed January 15, 2022. https://asq.org/quality-resources/small-business

Anchin. 2018. "Seven Steps to Choosing a Successor for the Family Business." March 29, 2018. https://www.anchin.com/news/anchin-private-client-center-seven-steps-to-choosing-a-successor-for-the-family-business

Botha, Francois. 2020. "Family Business Challenges; The 3 Issues Families Can't Ignore." *Forbes*. March 31, 2020. https://www.forbes.com/sites/francoisbotha /2020/03/31/family-business-challenges-the-3-issues-families-cant-ignore/?sh =fcbb0103cf46

Center for Creative Leadership. 2020. "Leading Effectively Staff. The Leadership Gap: How to Fix What Your Organization Lacks." December 4, 2020. https:// www.ccl.org/articles/leading-effectively-articles/leadership-gap-what-you-still -need/

CFI. 2021. "Succession Planning." Accessed December 30, 2021. https://corporatefi nanceinstitute.com/resources/knowledge/strategy/succession-planning/

Christee Gabour Atwood. 2007. *Succession Planning Basics*. American Society for Training & Development, Alexandria, VA: ASTD Press.

Christee Gabour Atwood. 2020. *Succession Planning Basics*. 2nd edition. Association for Talent Development. Alexandria, VA: ASTD Press.

Conway Center for Family Business. 2021. "Family Business Facts." Accessed December 12, 2021. https://www.familybusinesscenter.com/resources/family -business-facts/

Dahl, Darren. 2011. "Succession Stories: The Good, the Bad, and the Ugly." *Inc. Com*. March 29, 2011. https://www.inc.com/articles/201103/succession-stories -keeping-the-business-in-the-family.html

Enrich. 2021. "The Cost of Replacing an Employee and the Role of Financial Wellness." Accessed December 28, 2021. https://www.enrich.org/blog/The-true -cost-of-employee-turnover-financial-wellness-enrich

ERC. 2018. "What is Succession Planning and Why Is It Important." *HR Insights Blog*. February 16, 2018. https://www.yourerc.com/blog/post/what-is-succes- sion-planning-and-why-is-it-important

Farm Bureau Financial Services. 2021. "Why Do I Need a Family Business Succession Plan?" November 24, 2021.

GMS. 2021. "The Cost of Employee Turnover for a Small Business." April 8, 2021. https://www.groupmgmt.com/blog/post/the-cost-of-employee-turnover-for-a -small-business/

Hall, Tennille. 2020. "Innovative Hiring: The Benefits of Recruiting from Outside your Sector." *Airswift*. July 22, 2020. https://www.airswift.com/blog/innovative -hiring-recruit-outside-your-sector

Hauwiller, Jill. 2021. "Successful Succession Planning: Managing Transparency and Risk." *Forbes*. October 20, 2021. https://www.forbes.com/sites/forbescoach escouncil/2021/10/20/successful-succession-planning-managing-transparency -and-risk/?sh=18001c282761

Inc.com. 2020. "Family-Owned Businesses." August 11, 2020. https://www.inc.com /encyclopedia/family-owned-businesses.html#:~:text=A%20family%2Downed %20business%20may,control%20lies%20within%20a%20family.&text=Today %20family%20owned%20businesses%20are,participants%20in%20the%20world %20economy

Kappel, Mike. "Transparency in Business: 5 Ways to Build Trust." *Forbes*. April 3, 2019. https://www.forbes.com/sites/mikekappel/2019/04/03/transparency-in -business-5-ways-to-build-trust/?sh=2da5eee96149

Krishnan, Rajmohan. 2020. "Importance of Succession Planning for Business Families." *BusinessWeek*. March 10, 2020. http://www.businessworld.in/article/Importance-Of-Succession-Planning-For-Business-Families-/03-10-2020-326948/

LaMarche, Marie, and Kim E. Ruyle 2015. "Point-Counterpoint: Should You Tell Employees They're Part of a Succession Plan?" *Society for Human Resource Management*. January 7, 2015. https://www.shrm.org/hr-today/news/hr-magazine/pages/010215-sucession-planning.aspx

Massimino, Phoebe, and Kay Turner. "Organizational Culture and Impact on Opportunities for Professional Advancement." *Journal of Business and Economic Studies* 22.1 (2018): 44–66.

Minton-Eversole, Theresa. 2014. "Will They Be Ready to Leave When You're Ready to Leave?" *SHRM*. June 22, 2014. https://www.shrm.org/resourcesandtools/hr-topics/organizational-and-employee-development/pages/succession-planning.aspx

National Institutes of Health Office of Management. 2021. "Succession Planning: A Step-by-Step Guide." March 2021. https://hr.nih.gov/sites/default/files/public/documents/2021-03/Succession_Planning_Step_by_Step_Guide.pdf

Naviga. n.d. "How Hiring Outside Leadership Can Benefit Your Company." Accessed December 28, 2021. https://www.navigarecruiting.com/how-hiring-outside-leadership-can-benefit-your-company/

NYC Office of Administration Trials and Hearings. n.d. "What is Mediation?" Accessed January 2, 2022. https://www1.nyc.gov/site/oath/conflict-resolution/what-is-mediation.page

Personio. n.d. "Effective Succession Planning In 7 Key Steps." Accessed December 12, 2021. https://www.personio.com/hr-lexicon/succession-planning/

Pettit, Jane. n.d. "Ways to Transition Staff Smoothly During Periods of Change." University of Michigan Medical School. Accessed December 29, 2021. https://faculty.medicine.umich.edu/ways-transition-staff-smoothly-during-periods-change

Phys. 2015. "Outside CEOs Could Rejuvenate Struggling Businesses." April 1, 2015. https://phys.org/news/2015-04-ceos-rejuvenate-struggling-businesses.html

PricewaterhouseCoopers. 2021. "Family Business Survey." https://www.pwc.com/gx/en/services/family-business/family-business-survey.html

Roberts, Genvieve. "Top 10 Best Practices for Succession Planning Make Certain Your "Who's Ready Next" List is Sold." Accessed January 15, 2022. https://www.ajg.com/us/news-and-insights/2018/12/top-10-best-practices-for-succession-planning-make-certain-your-whos-ready-next-list-is-solid/

SBA. n.d. "National Archive Code of Federal Regulations, Title 13, §121.201 "What size standards has SBA identified by North American Industry Classification Codes." https://www.ecfr.gov/current/title-13/chapter-I/part-121#121.201

Score. 2019. "The Small Business Owner's Guide to Succession Planning." April 30, 2019. https://www.score.org/resource/small-business-owner-guide-succession-planning#:~:text=It%20helps%20you%20develop%20a,get%20loans%20or%20attract%20investors

Shearman and Sterling. 2020. "Succession Planning in a Time of Crisis." March 2020. https://www.shearman.com/Perspectives/2020/04/Succession-Planning-in -a-Time-of-Crisis

SHRM. 2022. "Engaging in Succession Planning." Accessed January 13, 2022. https:// www.shrm.org/resourcesandtools/tools-and-samples/toolkits/pages/engagin ginsuccessionplanning.aspx

Sigma Assessment Systems. 2021a. "Common Succession Planning Pitfalls and How to Avoid Mistakes." Accessed December 14, 2021. https://www.sigmaassess mentsystems.com/top-10-succession-planning-mistakes/

Sigma Assessment Systems. 2021b. "External Candidates and Succession." Accessed December 13, 2021. https://www.sigmaassessmentsystems.com/external-candi -dates-and-succession/

Talentx7 Assessment. 2021. "The Ultimate Learning Agility Assessment." Accessed December 28, 2021. https://thetalentx7.com/talentx7-assessment-learning -agility/

"The Cost of Employee Turnover for a Small Business." 2021. April 8, 2021. https:// www.groupmgmt.com/blog/post/the-cost-of-employee-turnover-for-a-small -business/.

Tremaine, Davis. 2021. "Succession Planning in a Family Business: Benefits, Challenges, and Guiding Principles." *JDSUPRA*. September 23, 2021. https:// www.jdsupra.com/legalnews/succession-planning-in-a-family-6923024/

United States Small Business Administration. Accessed December 28, 2021. sba.gov

van Vulpen, Erik. 2020. "The 9 Box Grid: A Practitioner's Guide." *AIHR* (blog). July 27, 2020. https://www.aihr.com/blog/9-box-grid/

Welsh and White. 1981. "A Small Business Is Not a Little Big Business." July 1981. https://hbr.org/1981/07/a-small-business-is-not-a-little-big-business

"Why Do I Need a Family Business Succession Plan?" 2021. *Farm Bureau Financial Services*. November 24, 2021. https://www.fbfs.com/learning-center/why-do-i -need-a-business-succession-strategy.

Yvanovich, Rich. 2019. "Succession Planning: 5 Common Mistakes & How to Avoid Them." *TRG International*. July 17, 2019. https://blog.trginternational.com/suc -cession-planning-common-mistakes-and-real-life-case-studies

SPECIAL ISSUES IN SMALL AND FAMILY BUSINESS SUCCESSION PLANNING

Part III: Special Issues in Small and Family Business Succession Planning is the heart of the book. It consists of Chapters 4 through 10.

Chapter 4 is called "Family-Owned Business Dynamics and Politics." Small and family business owners face special political issues that may be of less concern to large, publicly traded companies or to government agencies. As the chapter dramatically illustrates, it is not for the faint of heart to navigate the dynamics and politics of a family-owned firm. Issues they encounter, regardless of industry, may be of little interest to large corporations or government organizations. Family members who are invested in the company's success must help the CEO and other members of the leadership team build long-term business practices. They might begin by ensuring that their ethics and values are in sync. Although competencies are critical, particularly in family-member executive jobs, the ability of the Board and leadership to assess candidate motivation during the selection process is also critical. Both can have long-term consequences for the family and the company. It's also critical to define, build, and sustain a desired company culture that guides how individuals should behave in the workplace.

Chapter 5 is called "What Psychological Challenges Affect Small And Family Business Succession?" Small and family firms face psychological challenges with succession planning. The patterns of interaction among relatives,

DOI: 10.4324/9781003281054-6

their roles and relationships, and the numerous elements that impact their interactions are defined in this chapter. Family members are one of the key sources of relationship security or stress since they rely on each other for emotional, physical, and financial support. Family dynamics are crucial in succession planning for small family businesses because they can influence how successors are chosen, who they are chosen for, and the impact that decision has on the organization.

The idea known as the *Sequel Fallacy* is based on the assumption that the second generation of a family will naturally acquire the business. "Many well-intentioned family company successions are constructed around the concept that next-generation leaders can simply walk into the huge shoes of their predecessors and run the business (and the family) just as their father or mother would have done," says Taylor Law. However, this ignores that each new generation of leaders will have different abilities and interests, and the fact that company circumstances and demands will undoubtedly change. When a family firm assumes that the next generation can simply take over without evaluating the CEO's job description, governance, or succession planning, they are making a mistake.

As this chapter demonstrates, identity is linked to the family company and the family that owns it. What effect does one have on the other, and are they distinct? Consider the question, "Who am I?" Who are we, exactly? Many entrepreneurs spend years, if not decades, establishing their company from the ground up, much like raising a child, and many entrepreneurs feel the same pride, emotional bonds, sacrificial pain, and beaming pride toward their firm as they would a child. This brings with it a slew of psychological issues that must be addressed as you would with your own children.

Chapter 6 is entitled "Questions and Answers about Legal Issues in Small and Family Business Succession." This chapter answers some of the most prevalent legal questions that small and family business owners have about succession planning, and provides practical ideas and tools that can help key stakeholders come up with actual answers to crucial questions. Usually you'll discover there isn't a clear answer, rather a framework for determining the greatest decision for your business and succession goals after reading this chapter.

The subjects covered in this chapter may fill a book on their own. The chapter is not intended to provide complete legal guidance. Instead, Chapter 6 provides a roadmap for common legal techniques and considerations that will lead you to the legal partnerships, planning, and papers you must build the business legacy you want.

Chapter 7, called "Valuing the Small and Family Business for Succession Planning," focuses on the common tax and accounting issues that may be of less concern to large, publicly traded companies or to government agencies.

This chapter presents a bird's-eye view of small and family business valuations. On this subject, volumes have been written. Many professionals make a living by offering appraisal services. The business valuation has been presumed to be for inheritance and gift tax purposes, and that the business being assessed is a going concern. Due to time constraints, this chapter does not prepare the reader to fight the Internal Revenue Service. It is therefore suggested that anyone who needs a valuation for estate and gift tax purposes hire a business appraiser qualified to work with the IRS. Organizations such as the American Institute of CPAs and the American Society of Appraisers, among others, certify these professions.

Chapter 8, called Questions and Answers about Financial Planning Issues in Small and Family Business Succession, is about financial planning for small business and family business owners. Small and family business owners face many financial planning issues that may be of less concern to large, publicly traded companies or to government agencies. Succession planning is a methodical procedure. To put all the parts together, it takes time, a willing business owner, and a determined team of professionals. Because so many other aspects of the plan depend on it, the financial planning component of the picture must be addressed early on. The financial plan should urge business owners to consider their current and future financial needs and objectives to construct a road map. The financial plan will reveal flaws, possibilities, and places for improvement, forcing the business owner to think and plan for both the short and long term.

Chapter 9 is entitled Talent Management in Small and Family Businesses and centers on talent management questions that can bedevil small and family business owners. Obtaining, engaging, deploying, assessing, rating, and retaining talent is defined in this chapter as talent management. How the term "talent" is interpreted is a critical problem. Developing people for additional or different responsibilities was termed as succession planning. If talent management is taken to mean, in the most basic sense, attempts to attract, develop, and retain talented people, small and family business owners have unique obstacles. With all human resource difficulties, some challenges have long existed for small and family businesses; other, fresh challenges have been sparked by the epidemic and its aftereffects.

Chapter 10, the last chapter, is "Transitioning the Business and Executing on the Plan." This chapter presents intriguing tales that depict various scenarios that could arise when a business is transitioning from one owner or manager to another. Individual Development Plan (IDP), execution, and transition management were all given key definitions. The chapter included coaching advice on how to prepare for change. The chapter also looked at common procedures and challenges for hiring a successor from outside the company, promoting a successor from inside the company, and selecting one of the many alternatives to an external recruitment or internal promotion. The chapter included step-by-step instructions on how to handle hiring a new CEO, GM, or firm owner from the outside, promotions from within, or other options.

Chapter 4

Family-Owned Business Dynamics and Politics

Jacqueline T. Brito

Contents

Antonio's tile-laying skills became such an art form that he started his own luxury lifestyle flooring company. After immigrating from Italy to the US with his parents and two younger siblings when he was a teenager, he often dreamed of building a better life for himself and his family, including starting a business. Over 50 years later, three sons and two daughters-in-law,

DOI: 10.4324/9781003281054-7

both siblings and their spouses, and several other family members work in the business—some more diligently than others. As the business has grown and as the number of family members on the payroll has increased, business issues often overflow into external family gatherings. They lost focus on the businesses' founding principles and values, which has resulted in a toxic working environment filled with chaos cascading from family members with executive leadership titles without core competencies or motivation to lead. Quality control has suffered. So has the trust and loyalty of some customers who have been with them since the beginning. The business is no longer profitable, and they are US$3.4 million in debt. The company Antonio founded barely resembles the legacy he envisioned for himself and his family.

Read the additional vignettes below and describe how you would address the issues on a separate sheet of paper. Suppose that you can recommend a viable solution to each situation. In that case, perhaps your family-owned business leaders may have mastered the art of navigating dynamics and politics that plague small and family-owned businesses.

Vignette 1

Jake Bass, III inherited his grandfather's thriving specialty coffee business which has existed for 87 years. His sister, her husband, Jake's late father's youngest sister, and two of her children also work in the family business— all in leadership roles. Since Jake assumed the CEO position following his father's untimely passing, some heirs are grumbling among different family branches stating they deserve dividends. Others are now expecting executive roles and requisite compensation for positions that do not exist and others they are not qualified to hold.

Vignette 2

Zelda McCray and one of her cousins, Sheila Wilson, own a financial advisory company they started with seed money from their fathers, who are also brothers and successful entrepreneurs. Because of the family's extensive connections, they have built an impressive book of business. They employ 11 full-time credentialed professionals—Certified Financial Planners (CFP) and Chartered

Financial Analysts (CFA). Despite uncertainty due to the coronavirus, the business has been doing well. Also, due to the virus and the emotional and philosophical impact it has had on her, Sheila is no longer as enamored with the clients they have been serving. She would like to modify their business strategy to include offering advisory services to people in lower-income brackets. Zelda vehemently opposed the idea and told Sheila it was not an option she would ever consider.

Vignette 3

Juan Carlos owns a small restaurant and catering business specializing in authentic Cuban cuisine. The business rests in the heart of an urban district employing many young finance and technology professionals. There's heavy foot traffic, many parking options, and easy access from a major highway. Juan and his wife, Marianna, have a six-year-old son, Juan, Jr. Besides her responsibilities as a mother, Marianna has a full-time job teaching English in the middle school close to their home.

During the past two years, Juan has been struggling to get all the supplies he needs to fulfill catering requests and provide all the menu items for the restaurant. He has reduced his staff to seven full-time and five part-time employees. He had to use some of the family's savings to make up for the payroll deficit on a couple of occasions. Once school lets out, Marianna takes Juan Jr. to her mother and assists in the restaurant and catering functions since she is not on the payroll.

4.1 Defining Terms

Consider the meaning of some standard terms:

■ **Competency**: The knowledge, skills, abilities, and behaviors that contribute to individual and organizational performance. *Knowledge* is information developed or learned through experience, study, or investigation. *Skill* results from repeatedly applying expertise or ability.

- **Extrinsic motivation**: When external causes stimulate behavior.
- **Family branch**: A group of family members descended from one person.
- **Family coalition**: When two family members form a covert alliance—temporary or permanent, against another member. Coalitions usually form across generational boundaries.
- **Generative family**: This term refers to a successful, long-term family enterprise that creates continuous value across generations (Jaffe 2018).
- **Intrinsic motivation**: Completing an activity simply due to the inherent satisfaction one expects to receive.
- **Legacy**: Core beliefs, values, and attitudes passed down from one generation to the next.
- **Professionalizing** occurs when CEOs and other executive leaders of family-owned businesses behave like a public company in terms of governance with transparency, communication, and separation.

As these vignettes illustrate, entrepreneurship is not for the faint of heart. Small and family-owned business leaders face many unique issues that may be of less concern to large, publicly traded companies or government agencies. When you add family dynamics such as entitlement mindsets, power struggles, rivalries among different family branches, non-qualified family executives, and politics to the mix, some businesses cannot withstand the impact on the environment and the company's bottom line. Legacies are at risk of being destroyed. Relationships become fractured due to actual or perceived lack of care or concern for shareholder voices in business and family matters.

While extensive research on the impact of succession planning on family businesses has been conducted, two authors (Kelly and Powell 2020) found "when succession planning is applied to family businesses, and closely held firms, the level of complexity can increase dramatically. Emotions and sentiments are involved. Operating decisions often impact personal finances, not just the balance sheet" (p. 89).

So, what can CEOs of family-owned businesses do to ensure their ability to navigate family dynamics and politics within their business while leading efforts to sustain their product line, customer base, and family legacy throughout the years? More than you might think. Based on initial research and subsequent interviews with CEOs and innovators, initiatives to demonstrate ethics and values in their operation, assessment of family members' motivation in the succession/selection process, and the ability to define, establish, and maintain a desired organizational culture are critical to sustainable business practices.

4.2 Ethics and Values

Merriam-Webster Dictionary defines ethics as "a set of moral principles; a theory or system of moral values." In a family-owned business, ethics are the compass to help navigate how family and non-family employees, shareholders, and others affiliated with the enterprise engage with each other. Ethics and values do more than complement each other; they go hand in hand.

Cambridge English Dictionary defines values as "the principles that help you to decide what is right and wrong, and how to act in various situations." Practicing ethics and values from all levels of leadership strengthen a shared understanding and commitment to do what is right in fulfillment of obligations to self and others. Plus, these practices provide employees (family and non-family members) with standards and expectations of the leadership team and for themselves. Those who lead with clear ethical guidelines and solid moral values are straightforward in addressing questionable behavior among other family members engaged in the business.

The Family Business Institute (2019) published a Family Business Succession Planning White Paper which included these data:

■ About 30% of family-owned businesses survive into the second generation.
■ 12% are still viable into the third generation.
■ Only about 3% of all family businesses operate into the fourth generation or beyond.

One multi-industry, family-owned business has defied those odds. They have a fourth-generation chief executive officer (CEO) and some fifth-generation cousins working in the business. During an interview with the company's CEO (whom I will call R.J.), he was cautiously optimistic about their progress as a family with a business that bears their name.

A self-proclaimed introvert, R.J. vividly recalled always having a keen interest in the business. "I read the financial page of the newspaper when I was a child." Although a fourth-generation CEO, he was the first in several other areas. For instance, he was the first in his family to earn a graduate degree—accounting and finance. Determined to prove himself, first, he gained external experience in various publicly traded Fortune 500 companies and industries. He pursued a different pathway than his other family members, whose only experience has been in the business. He believed it would be in his best interest and the longevity of his family's enterprise.

4.3 Dynamics and Politics in Selection

Some chief executive officers were more forthright than others in explaining their selection process for the lead position in their respective family businesses. "The kitchen got a little messy at times; hard to keep a clean apron as this was going on," one person commented. He further explained that some of his family thought "so and so" would automatically get the job. He referred to members from that family branch as having an "old school mindset." They held strong convictions that a specific family member (based on birthright) would be selected and not him. His predecessor did not place him at the top of the list of viable candidates, either.

R.J. was refreshingly candid about his family business dynamics and the politics that affected his CEO selection process. He discussed how the board of directors (six family members and four outside individuals) decided on a deliberate approach to the milestone transition from third- to fourth-generation CEO. Absent a succession plan, they hired an outside family business consulting firm to ensure professionalism and transparency in the selection process. The firm's model included an objective set of criteria and a scoring system instead of allowing family politics to decide which child to put into the role. Their approach was methodical, so anyone in the family who wanted to apply for the CEO position could. Those interested in being considered had to submit a resume and cover letter explaining why they thought they were qualified. Along with six family members and three external non-family members, he applied and was interviewed.

Business dynamics and politics are not isolated events unique only to CEO selection. They occur when members from different branches of the family "decide" it is time to join the business, as one CEO recalled when faced with this scenario. His late father's sister, a significant shareholder, told him that her eldest grandson would join their family's business—under no uncertain terms. He was about to graduate with an MBA and expected a prominent position after that. Although the young man was not qualified for the management position his grandmother wanted for him, there was a clear expectation it was a done deal.

He added that because of the sibling rivalry between his aunt's two grandsons and the shared family belief that the firstborn was the favorite, there was a stronger expectation he would be hired in the desired role commensurate with compensation—regardless of his lack of experience and competencies.

One easily overlooked group is the in-laws when planning for family succession and selection. Rob Lachenauer, partner and CEO of Banyan Global and co-author of *Harvard Business Review: Family Business Handbook* (Mazzella 2021), estimates that "about 10% of family businesses include an in-law."

Research shows two primary philosophies on navigating the role of in-laws in family businesses. The first provides them with the same opportunities bestowed upon those descendants of the founder(s). The second philosophy supports exclusion at all costs through a "no in-law" hiring policy.

One former CEO added that his predecessor-father and founder, at the strong encouragement of his wife, created a "no in-law" policy to prevent a new, disapproved daughter-in-law from being hired into the business. Unfortunately, "it was too bad that the policy wasn't in place the other times we failed to hire in-laws based on merit but under duress," he noted. The family leadership was known for biased selection practices, which included hiring certain in-laws but not others based on the branch of the family tree they joined and the in-laws' approval rating.

4.4 Attempted Coup in Selection

Despite carefully orchestrated strategic efforts to ensure integrity throughout his CEO selection process, R.J. commented how things still spun out of control. "I'm ashamed to say that family board members were lobbying each other outside the boardroom. They attempted to form family coalitions to back their preferred candidate," he openly yet quietly shared while reliving the experience. Trust had been broken, along with damage to relationships. Fortunately, R.J.'s fate didn't depend solely on the select family board members whose agendas did not align with the best interest of their family's business. "I have the confidence of knowing that someone didn't just give me the job; I had to earn it," he said.

Once the process was complete, the four independent non-family board members "strongly recommended" to him, their newly elected CEO, that they develop a written Board Code of Conduct. They positioned it as a tool to help mitigate further damages and future risk from the behavior they had just witnessed. He took their advice, and the Code has worked well in reinforcing clear standards of professionalism, ethics, and board behavior.

4.5 Planning Ahead

After transitioning into his new role, R.J. also implemented long-term succession planning for all management positions, including in-laws joining the business. Primarily influenced by his own experiences, he emphasized the importance of starting early and being more deliberate and transparent with executive succession. He now views it as a strategy much easier to articulate than it is to execute when the biased family is involved in the decision-making process. He explained that "the further up the organization chart you go, the more family emotion gets involved."

CEOs of other family-owned businesses shared similar feedback. Regarding planning for the next leader of the family enterprise, no one reported knowing who was in line to become the successor. Instead, as is widespread practice with other family-owned businesses (small, medium, or large), it is up to their board of directors to decide. However, each noted that they would provide their opinion on the perceived strengths and weaknesses of the potential candidates (family and non-family members).

4.6 Understanding Motivations

One of the top priorities of a board of directors should be to plan for the chief executive officer's succession. Although some may not have direct experience or knowledge on the topic, they can begin the process by becoming familiar with the top management of the family business, as some will be considered potential candidates. The board and the incumbent should discuss CEO succession openly. A strategic, multi-year approach would provide the much-needed time to objectively identify a qualified individual for the job and not automatically default to selection based on bloodline.

While assessing a candidate's competencies—abilities to perform the essential functions of a job—is necessary, some established CEOs countered that uncovering their motivation for the job is equally important. The board needs to understand how a CEO candidate's past behavior (performance) may affect the organization's success.

What is motivation? According to the American Psychological Association's *Dictionary of Psychology* (2020), motivation is "the impetus that gives purpose or direction to behavior and operates in humans at a conscious or unconscious level." During the series of structured interviews and informal conversations throughout the selection process, it will be incumbent on each board member to intentionally assess candidates' motivation—intrinsic and extrinsic.

When evaluating each candidate's response, be mindful of factors most significant to the individual selected for the position and organizational outcomes. Listen intently and redirect if a candidate is too ambiguous in their response(s). The main objective is to identify the individual who wants the position for reasons that will benefit themselves and the interests of the family's business.

Suppose founders/presidents/CEOs do not have an established board of directors to lead this initiative. In that case, each executive must accept that leadership change is inevitable for any business—whether it is voluntary or involuntary—no exception. Why opt-in and settle for an exit or transition when the need arises versus a carefully planned CEO succession strategy? It will be worth the investment of time and other valuable resources to determine the best approach (and, the best person) with minimal disruption to family and business relationships. Both matter. Last, you are more likely to see a higher return on investment when you plan. A family-owned business should provide tools to support effective outcomes.

See Table 4.1 for an example of a behavior-based interview guide for assessing motivational fit.

4.7 Organizational Culture

Wong (2020) notes that "organizational culture is the collection of values, expectations, and practices that guide and inform the actions of all team members." Regardless of size, every organization has a unique, definable culture simply because it employs people. Culture is essential to a family business when perceived as an asset to internal and external stakeholders and shareholders. It promotes a productive environment that results in fewer misunderstandings, establishes trust between employees and leaders, elevated levels of engagement, and mutual respect. While culture is everyone's

Table 4.1 Behavior-Based Interview Guide for Assessing Motivational Fit

Directions: Use this qualitative risk assessment tool to solicit a genuine response from candidates about their intrinsic and extrinsic motivation. Avoid asking leading questions that will prompt popular yet disingenuous feedback and the wrong hiring decision.

Questions	Detailed Responses
1. Why have you pursued this opportunity?	
2. What led to your decision to pursue your current position? The one before that?	
3. Based on your experience, should a CEO have an exit strategy, or should they plan to remain in the position indefinitely? What is the basis of your response?	
4. What has been the biggest obstacle you've encountered in your professional career? Why was it an obstacle? What was the outcome?	
5. What has been your most notable professional achievement? What contributed to the success?	
6. Describe the most significant sacrifice you've ever made in your professional career? How was it a sacrifice? What would you do differently? Why?	
7. How have you consistently influenced the culture where you work? Provide a detailed example of one key outcome of your efforts.	
8. When working with your most productive and least productive employees, walk us through your approach and subsequent outcomes from each group.	
9. Tell us about a time when you faced competing priorities at work. At what point did you realize that you could not deliver by the the agreed-upon deadline? How was the situation handled? What was the outcome?	
10. Think back to a time when you knew of unintended consequences resulting from an initiative you led, or one led by someone else. How was it handled? What was the outcome?	
11. Walk us through a strategy you recommended that resulted in a positive outcome for the business.	

(Continued)

Table 4.1 (Continued)   Behavior-Based Interview Guide for Assessing Motivational Fit

Questions	Detailed Responses
12. Tell us about a time when you identified a problem with a process/procedure at work. How was it addressed? How did it improve the business?	
13. Provide a detailed example of one idea you suggested to your leader or board within the last 12 months. Where did the idea originate? Was it approved, and if so, what is the status?	
14. Describe a time when you went beyond your leader or board's expectations to accomplish a challenging task. What influenced your decision to follow the approach you took? What has been the impact on the business?	
15. Think of one example when a department or the company you led reached an impasse. What were the situation and outcome? What was the impact on those involved?	
16. Describe the work environment in which you are most productive. How does it impact your productivity?	
17. Think about a specific position that satisfied you the most. What about the least? Why was one position more satisfying than the other? What was the impact on your performance?	
18. When has an organization failed you?	
19. If selected for this position, where do you want it to take you next? How will this role inform the future you see for yourself?	
20. If an offer were extended to and accepted by another candidate, would you consider reapplying for this position? Why or why not?	

Source: H.R. Asset Partners LLC Motivation Risk Assessment Tool© 2020.

responsibility (Yohn 2021), Groysberg, Lee, and Cheng (2018) note that "for better *and* worse, culture and leadership are inextricably linked. Founders and influential leaders often set new cultures in motion and imprint values and assumptions that persist for decades."

Whether actions lead to functional or dysfunctional behaviors, they align with the values, expectations, and practices of leaders responsible for understanding and self-regulating emotions that set the stage for the work environment.

4.8 Peaceful Transition of Power

Since 1801, the loser of each US presidential election has known there is an expectation to peacefully surrender power to the winner, despite whatever personal animosity or political divisions might exist (Pruitt 2020). Leaders who have fulfilled that expectation established a critical precedent that should transcend Pennsylvania Avenue. Imagine the culture and climate in a family-owned business when a peaceful transition of power is the established norm during each president/CEO transition.

When his former president/CEO uncle committed questionable business practices that compromised their product line and customer trust, the board of directors mandated that he step down. While this course of action provided the opportunity for his candidacy and subsequent promotion, R.J. was confident he would encounter unmerited hostility from certain family members.

> Probably the most awkward day of my life was the day after being announced the new chief executive officer. I had to start immediately building bridges with family members who didn't get the job, reassuring them that I would not be an authoritarian like my predecessor.

His situation was worsened by the failed political maneuvers of family board members who attempted to push their agendas to prevent him from becoming the successor. He was mindful of the negative, raw emotions they were holding.

He added,

> the individual selected to run the family business had the immediate challenge of persuading those who weren't to work together as a team. It is a daunting task to organize a team of rivals. The best CEOs know this and use their emotional intelligence to act accordingly.

While transitioning as the company's new leader, R.J. knew it was his responsibility to end the chaos threatening to destroy 90-plus years' hard work, brand, and family legacy.

Regardless of their industry, emotionally intelligent leaders understand the significance of patience to allow others time to trust a process that initially they may not understand nor want to embrace. Qualitative research supports the benefit of being CEO-elect for a year, then actual CEO for another year before making "big changes" in the business. "I had to get things done through influence and persuasion rather than brute force," one commented. The latter was a leadership behavior commonly attributed to his predecessor, which he did not want to emulate. Instead, he decided that a critical success marker had the family members initially against him eventually come around to trust and accept him as "their" CEO of the family business.

So, why is a peaceful transition of power important? Simply because disruptive changes do not discriminate. They impact both family and non-family members. The family-owned business ecosystem—their network of organizations—including bankers, potential investors, employees, suppliers, customers, competitors, and so on—can affect the company's product or service. Albeit more transactional than relational for some, each has a personal stake in the sustainability of the next generation of leadership.

4.9 Non-Qualified Family Executives

Regardless of the size of their business, CEOs shared that they often feel the political pressure to promote unqualified family employees. Prior expectations were clear. Predecessors established a precedent to prioritize birthright over competence when stepping into an executive role with increasing responsibilities. "Family employees get fixated on title and authority, and the additional money that comes from being in charge, instead of the responsibilities that come with the promotion," said the CEO of an established multi-generation family-owned real estate development company.

He has experienced how some parents "push" for promotions for their children. "If their kid gets to be a vice president, then so does mine," he was told by one family member. Regardless of the position, they will unapologetically voice their sentiment to support their offspring's advancement. "This has been the behavior of more than one parent whose child works in our business," he said. He further added how those individuals who otherwise handled themselves in a logical and reserved manner became highly charged and unreasonable due to their motivations.

R.J. shared that during his selection process to become *CEO*, one family board member "nakedly pushed" his child's candidacy for the position even though that individual, his first cousin, was the lowest-ranked final candidate.

During this research, leaders in other family-owned businesses acknowledged that their predecessors promoted or agreed to promotions even if family members were not qualified. R.J. admitted that several family members in his company were elevated to positions "above their heads" and how awkward it is when they fail at their job.

According to Iqbal, Pendergrast, and Herrera (2020),

> this is one of the thorniest problems [to] deal with, but there are ways to nip it in the bud. Ideally, family members in the business should report to non-family bosses who get the reinforcement they need to provide honest assessments. Non-family supervisors of family employees are in a sensitive position, so should be given clear direction on how to support and evaluate them.

There is a level of difficulty in terminating or demoting a family employee due to unpredictable behaviors from their parents. Some leaders reported that they either created a de facto organization beneath them or whittled their jobs down to what they could handle.

Whether a business is family or non-family-owned, small, medium, or large, each decision has unintended consequences. When considering who to promote or hire, one visionary CEO said, "You have to think about what the company's biggest challenges are and be brutally honest about which person is best equipped to solve them."

R.J. noted that some family executives hired or promoted into positions they did not possess the competencies for developed self-esteem issues in his family business. Deep down, they knew they were not performing in their respective roles. Instead of "failing forward" in humility and with some shred of vulnerability, they adopted an authoritarian management style to soothe their deflated egos. Although learning and development options were provided, none of his underperforming family executives addressed the core competencies needed to improve their performance.

As Rüsen, Groth, and Schlippe (2021) point out, "for managerial succession, members of the next generation should always exhibit a level of competence comparable to that of a potential external manager." Competence should always precede birthright.

See Table 4.2 for assistance in evaluating the competencies of family leaders before they join the family business.

Table 4.2   Worksheet for Evaluating Competency over Birthright in Family Selection Practices

Directions: Use this worksheet to evaluate family-member candidates' knowledge and skills, behavioral attributes for specific roles in the family business, and preparation for next-generation family leaders.		
Questions	**Responses**	**Actions**
Which position-specific core competencies (i.e., abilities and behavioral characteristics) are required for someone to succeed in this position?		
Which position-specific core competencies would be required of non-family leaders?		
Which organizational competencies (i.e., qualities and attributes) that characterize success across the organization are required?		
Which organizational competencies would be required of non-family leaders?		
Does the identified internal successor (family employee) possess personal authority and competence in fulfilling their role and responsibilities for the next generation of family leaders?		
Does the identified internal successor know the business well enough to perform competently?		
Would the family employee be considered a competent successor if s/he were not a relative?		
Is the family employee competent to envision next-generation family interest in working in the business and creating experiential learning opportunities for them to one day pursue those interests?		
What could prevent assessing next-generation family members' leadership style and motivations if they are interested in joining the family business?		
Who can serve as an unbiased expert about the core competencies and experience requirements?		

(Continued)

Table 4.2 (Continued)   Worksheet for Evaluating Competency over Birthright in Family Selection Practices

Questions	Responses	Actions
What could prevent the family from agreeing on an in-depth, neutral assessment process?		
What are the characteristics of the family's existing mental model?		
Does the support for change exist?		

Source: Adapted from *10 Golden Principles to Guide Your Succession Planning* (Rüsen, Groth, and Schlippe, 2021).

4.10 A Lifetime Mindset

Whether serving in the faculty capacity or leadership in higher education, the concept of tenure is inescapable. When faculty have earned tenure at their respective academic institution, in some sense, they "have a job for life." According to *Indeed.com* (2021), however, in the world of business, the term *tenure* has evolved to refer to someone's duration on a job—no longer exclusive to college professors. Some chief executive officers of family-owned businesses covet their position with a lifetime mindset, although never intended to be a lifetime appointment.

R.J. notes that a founder differs greatly from a family member three, four, or five generations into the business. For instance, a first-generation president/CEO who founded and still owns the company sees her- or himself as the company after a prolonged period. "I know this business better than anybody" is often their mindset, he said. The business becomes their identity and letting go is a profound loss, making it difficult to imagine no longer being in control.

This mentality, researched and reported on in earlier works, supports the theory that "an entrepreneur's business is simultaneously his 'baby,' and his mistress. Those who work with him and for him are characteristically his instruments in the process of shaping the organization" (Levinson 1971).

Existing quantitative research suggests that because founders invest so much of their personal (and sometimes financial) resources into organizations when they conceive and launch them, their identities are connected to that organization so much they might relate it to the birth of a child (Rouse 2016).

Because of their deeply embedded emotional connection to the business, they hold a strong resentment to "being replaced" and even stronger emotions toward family or non-family board members brave enough to broach the subject of succession planning as a strategic business imperative.

Fortunately, based on qualitative feedback from former and current CEOs who succeeded their founder, there is a recommended treatment plan:

- Meet founders where they are in respecting their identity connected to the business.
- Solicit support from an advocate the founder trusts and respects to start the succession conversation.
- Engage the founder in developing and operationalizing a succession plan supporting the family business legacy and growth model for the next generation of family leaders.
- Identify accountability advocates to ensure key metrics for the plan are met and adjust swiftly and methodically when needed.
- Ensure clear and transparent timely communication to shareholders and stakeholders regularly.

4.11 Governance

Decisions about the path forward, with family values as the foundation, are important and complex. At their heart, family governance structures should be seen as critical tools to help families communicate, solve problems, and make decisions such as this about how the family will affect the business, and the business will affect the family.

(Pelligana 2017)

This business philosophy reigns true for R.J., who noted that when his predecessor-uncle took over the family business, for years, he served as CEO and chairman of the board, a model that did not go over well with the family. They questioned how a CEO could hold himself accountable if he were also chairman of the board? And how would the board of directors ensure accountability with the management team if the business were not performing well? There were a few seats of governance available; therefore, it seemed like the same "handful of characters," as he referred to them, made all the crucial decisions. He added,

> The same old men would decide on everything … who would get promoted, how much money they made, diversification of product lines, etc., at the board level. The board made too many decisions, and not many people on the board making them.

By professionalizing their practices, CEOs and other executive leaders of family-owned businesses can behave like a public company in terms of governance with transparency, communication, and separation. They can place themselves in a position to be an employee of the company with personal and public accountability.

R.J., like other CEOs, established family governance and board governance, management teams, policies, and practices to include an age limit for CEOs and their board of directors. He believes that without age limits, some would expect to serve well beyond their "shelf life." They wrote family governance bylaws to prohibit CEOs from being a member of the voting governance of the family council.

One small family-owned produce and packing company CEO said it best:

> a CEO, just like any other employee has a shelf life. There is a reason we have term limits for U.S. Presidents. You should not expect always to be the leader of your family's business. Stability does not mean you are pushing the boundaries. One person who is a great leader in one era does not mean they will remain the best leader forever. As circumstances change, there may be someone else who can be more effective in the role.

That is a healthy dose of reality. He added that it was difficult for some of the previous generation CEOs in his family business to accept when it is their time to let go, turn the business over to their successor, and move on.

The most successful family businesses have leaders who understand that their family's legacy and the resiliency of the business depend on their ability to shift their roles at an opportune time to mentor and support the creation of a new generation of leadership. They realize that if they stay on too long as leaders, they may miss the opportunity to install an effective new generation. This was a shared perception by many who provided feedback. Carefully established governance structures allow family relationships and family-owned business decisions to coexist more peacefully while mitigating conflict.

4.12 In-Law Effect

Then some families and businesses have endured the dynamics and politics of the in-law effect. If an in-law comes in and says, for example, "I don't know why this or that …," and goes home at night and discusses their opinions with their spouse, who is the shareholder, their opinion may weaken the bond this person has with their cousin. It can affect family dynamics. The more people you bring into the discussion—who come from outside the family circle and don't espouse the family values—the in-laws' outsized opinions sometimes carry more weight by the third generation.

> Values and points of view diverge, influenced by the spouses that the siblings brought into the family and ultimately by the cousin's own spouses. Diversity and loosening family ties in the cousin generation pose two major challenges: How to build shareholders' voluntary commitment to the family enterprise? and How to hold the family together?
>
> **(Aronoff and Ward, n.d.)**

R.J. described the relational shift between the first two generations,

> a healthy sibling relationship that rivals the kind of relationship you have with your spouse. It is a powerful bond. By the time you get to the third generation, you are dealing with cousins. So, your biological family connection is often not as strong as your connection with your spouse. In-laws begin to take on an excessive amount of influence once you transition into a third generation.

Once that "impenetrable" family bond breaks, it is far less likely to exist among the future generations who work in the family business.

Research shows that only about 3% of all family business operates into the fourth generation or beyond (Family Business Institute 2019). Each chief executive officer interviewed who had not reached that milestone agreed that if they make it that far, the third generation is where family businesses typically go off the rails because cousins are replacing second-generation siblings.

Dennis Jaffe, PhD, conducted the 100-Year Family Enterprise research project. He reports that researchers interviewed family leaders from nearly 100 families who had maintained their family identity and other success factors beyond three generations.

> We refer to these successful, long-term family enterprises as "generative families" because they create continuous value across generations. And the value they create is not just financial, but also comes from developing capable and committed young people in each new generation, and from how both the family and business contribute to the community.
>
> **(Jaffe 2018)**

Insights gained from interviews with current and former CEOs, direct observations, and journal and article research revealed seven consistent principles to close the generational divide among families of family businesses. They are a code of ethics built, strengthened, and passed down to each generation and a standard of conduct for all stakeholders. Consider these recommendations:

1. **Ensure Value-Alignment**. Relationships among family members are influenced by individual personalities with shared values and purposes. Make sharing family values a priority by openly acknowledging when demonstrated. This intentional behavior can affect family members' perceptions and strengthen their connection to the family, mission, and business.
2. **Develop an Ownership Mindset**. A culture that fosters a personal and collective accountability mindset promotes a sense of shared responsibilities. It requires proactive steps to nurture the potential in others to make recommendations and decisions for the long-term care of the family enterprise.
3. **Demonstrate Cohesion**. A family that plays together stays together. Develop meaningful connections through family rituals that become established traditions. The outcomes—positive memories that transcend generational boundaries.
4. **Be Transparent**. "Assumptions degrade trust and disenfranchise family members, potentially causing them to withdraw from the family. Good

questions, on the other hand, build trust, engage family members and seek diverse perspectives" (Nacht and Pitcairn 2016).

The recommendation is that family leaders ask their stakeholders: why, what, and how to gain insights to strengthen multi-generational relationships among family members.

5. **Cross-Generational Engagement and Collaboration**. According to Jaffe (2018),

> in generative families, a shared sense of purpose and a commitment to work together in a cooperative and respectful manner did emerge. Sometimes conflict led branches or individual family members to leave the family enterprise. Those remaining had to renew trust, respect, and cooperation to enable them to make tough decisions.

6. **Overly Communicate**. Meet family members "where they are" by understanding and respecting their specific, unique needs and goals. The absence of communication can lead to conflict among families and exacerbate already fractured relationships.

7. **Demonstrate Fair Treatment**. Ensure consistent and fair treatment of all family members (and non-family employees). Avoid favoritism at all costs (i.e., hiring, promotion, compensation, and acknowledgments).

These principles are not multiple choice—pick what you prefer and ignore the rest. They are all or none.

Intentional efforts to establish and maintain healthy, personal relationships with controlling shareholders while shepherding others fortify the family's identity with each generation. Focus on building a strong culture that supports shared family values will be critical to family and business success and their impact on the community.

4.13 Generational and Mindset Differences

According to a Pew Research Center analysis of US Census Bureau data, "more than one in three American labor force participants (35%) are Millennials, making them the largest generation in the U.S. labor force. Generation X (33%), Baby Boomers (25%), Generation Z (5%), and Traditionalists (2%) make up the rest" (Fry 2018). When considering this distribution mix, family-owned businesses must address tensions between the different generations, their different values, and visions and determine the purpose of the family wealth and its use (Jaffe 2020). Leaders need to understand the importance of bridging generational gaps.

As noted by Hayes (2021),

> a generation gap refers to the chasm that separates the beliefs and behaviors belonging to members of two different generations. More specifically, a generation gap can describe the differences in thoughts, actions, and tastes exhibited by members of younger generations versus older ones.

Acknowledging and addressing these gaps could help break barriers to a healthy organizational culture.

"It's tough even for a public company to remain in business past 100 years, to last that many generations. Keeping your business and product lines relevant and your customers served can be overwhelming at times. Even public companies have a hard time doing it," said the CEO of a small family-owned regional produce company.

R.J. added,

> you don't have to wonder why so many family businesses get sold to bigger conglomerates when you layer in family dynamics. Especially the one that says, "I don't want to work in the business and would like to take my inheritance and go elsewhere."

Several of the more prominent brands "snap up" small companies because eventually, the family dynamic says, "OK, we've finally had enough." The only way to get liquidity is to sell the whole thing. It is problematic to have most people who want to keep the business going but a sizable minority who don't. How do you divide up an operating business? It does not lend itself to that.

Some distant relatives may feel ill-prepared, emotionally disconnected, or simply not interested in a business they did not start? Although they have and continue to benefit from company profits, they may not possess the vision, values, or the same level of grit as those who invested their sweat equity for the harvest they now get to reap.

There is no-one-size-fits-all model for family business engagement. Instead, this generational shift in the labor force will require a different leadership behavior. Ideally, it encourages high commitment, communication, and transparency between family business leaders and their emerging generation family members. A curated organizational culture is needed now more than ever before, and viewing the generational mix is an opportunity to gain different perspectives while strengthening the family and business legacy.

When asked about best practices in organizational dynamics and politics, CEOs had this to say:

- Bring in outside executives from big public companies to help establish operational efficiencies and company policies.
- Establish an audit and compensation committee composed of outside leaders.
- Create a board of directors to include both family and non-family and does not include CEO as board chair.
- Establish business and family governance.
- Build a culture of transparency through policies and practices which apply to the family the same as non-family.
- Invest in training and development programs and allow access to all employees.
- Develop the ability to collaborate and lead others effectively.
- If there is an issue or disagreement, address it quickly and succinctly. Allowing problems to fester causes them to create a toxic work environment.
- Listen to and research issues regardless of how trivial they might appear. All staff members (family and non-family) should be heard.
- Document everything.

4.14 Chapter Summary

Attempts at navigating the dynamics and politics of a family-owned business are not for the faint of heart. Regardless of the industry, issues they face may be of less concern to large companies or government agencies. Family members invested in the business outcomes must support the CEO and other leadership team members to develop sustainable business practices. They can start by ensuring ethics and values are aligned. Although competencies are essential, especially in family-member executive roles, the board and leadership's ability to assess candidate motivation in the selection process is vital, too. Both can have a long-term impact on the family and the business. And defining, establishing, and maintaining a desired organizational culture to inform how people should behave in the organization is essential.

R.J. noted that his company still experiences its fair share of challenges beyond a traditional non-family-owned business scope. They simply evolve with each generation. He added that a defined plan for executive leadership succession is a great place to address existing challenges while ensuring the organization's ability to lead through unforeseen family dynamics and politics.

Works Cited

APA Dictionary of Psychology. 2021. "Motivation." Accessed August 28, 2021, https://dictionary.apa.org/motivation

Aronoff, Craig, and John L. Ward. 2022. "Family Business from the Cousins' Perspective." *The Family Business Consulting Group®*. Accessed February 12, 2022, https://www.thefbcg.com/resource/family-business-from-the-cousins -perspective/

Cambridge English Dictionary. n.d. (1995) "values." Accessed October 16, 2021, https://dictionary.cambridge.org/us/dictionary/english/values

Family Business Institute. "Family Business in Transition: Data and Analysis." Accessed August 22, 2021. https://www.familybusinessinstitute.com/wp-con-tent/uploads/2019/01/Family-Business-Succession-Planning-White-Paper.pdf

Fry, Richard. 2018. "Millennials are the Largest Generation In the U.S. Labor Force." April 11, 2018. https://www.pewresearch.org/fact-tank/2018/04/11/millennials -largest-generation-us-labor-force/

Groysberg, Boris, Jeremiah Lee, and J. Yo-Jud Cheng. 2018. "The Leader's Guide to Corporate Culture," *Harvard Business Magazine*. Accessed February 18, 2018. https://hbr.org/2018/01/the-leaders-guide-to-corporate-culture

Hayes, Adam. 2021. "Generation Gap." *Investopedia*. Accessed August 30, 2021. https://www.investopedia.com/terms/g/generation-gap.asp

Indeed Editorial Team. 2021. "What Is a Tenured Employee? Top Benefits of Tenure and How to Stay Engaged as One." February 22, 2021.

Iqbal, Sonny, Jennifer Pendergrast, and German Herrera. 2020. "Managing the Trickiest Parts of a Family Business." *Harvard Business Review*. January 23, 2020. https://hbr.org/2020/01/managing-the-trickiest-parts-of-a-family -businesses

Jaffe, Dennis. 2018. "If You Want Your Family Business to Last Several Generations." *Harvard Business Review*. Accessed August 30, 2018. https:// www.forbes.com/sites/dennisjaffe/2018/08/30/if-you-want-your-family-business -to-last-several-generations/?sh=3e5af5ce7c16

Jaffe, Dennis. 2020. "Family Businesses Face Today's Crises: Constructive Tensions Emerge Across Generations." *Forbes*. Accessed October 9, 2020. https://www .forbes.com/sites/dennisjaffe/2020/10/09/family-businesses-face-todays-crises -constructive-tensions-emerge-across-generations/?sh=415195f43491

Kelly, Mary C., and Meridith E. Powell. 2020. "Sustaining Family-Owned and Closely-Held Businesses." In *Who Comes Next? Leadership Succession Planning Made Easy*, edited by Susan Priddy, 89. Dallas: Kaimana Publishing.

Levinson, Harry. 1971. "Conflicts That Plague Family Business." *Harvard Business Review*, March 1971. https://hbr.org/1971/03/conflicts-that-plague-family -businesses

Mazzella, Randi. 2021. "How to Make Working with Your In-Laws Work for You." *Next Avenue*, June 23, 2021. https://www.nextavenue.org/family-business -working-with-in-laws/

Merriam-Webster. n.d. "Ethic." Accessed October 16, 2021, https://www.merriam -webster.com/dictionary/ethic

Nacht, Joshua and Andrew Pitcairn. 2016. "Every Family Leader Should Pose Three Questions to Stakeholders." *Family Business Magazine*, September/October, 2016. https://www.familybusinessmagazine.com/every-family-leader-should -pose-three-questions-stakeholders

Pelligana, Dominic. 2017. "The Power of Governance in Family Business." *KPMB (blog): Family Business Governance*. February 21, 2017. https://home.kpmg/au/ en/home/insights/2017/01/power-of-governance-in-family-business.html

Pruitt, Sarah. 2020. "How John Adams Established the Peaceful Transfer of Power." Updated: January 14, 2021. https://www.history.com/news/peaceful-transfer -power-adams-jefferson

Rouse, Elizabeth. 2016. "Beginning's End: How Founders Psychologically Disengage from Their Organizations." *Academy of Management Journal* 59(5): 1605–1629.

Rüsen, Tom A., Torsten Groth, and Arist von Schlippe. 2021. "10 Golden Principles to Guide Your Succession Planning." *Entrepreneur & Innovation Exchange*. May 5, 2021. https://familybusiness.org/content/10-golden-principles-to-guide -your-succession-planning

Wong, Kellie. 2020. "Organizational Culture: Definition, Importance, and Development." *Achievers* (blog). May 7, 2020. https://www.achievers.com/blog/ organizational-culture-definition/

Yohn, Denise Lee. 2021. "Company Culture Is Everyone's Responsibility." *Harvard Business Review*, February 8, 2021. https://hbr.org/2021/02/company-culture-is -everyones-responsibility

Chapter 5

What Psychological Challenges Affect Small and Family Business Succession?

Shirley Adams

Contents

"Families are like fudge, mostly sweet with a few nuts."

—Unknown

Growing up, a very good friend lived on the next street over and her father owned his own small insurance business with offices near downtown. Coming from a long line of blue-collar, hard-working folk, it was fascinating that my friend's father was his own boss. He could take time off when he wanted, while my father was constrained to the week or two allotted to him at very specific times of the year. Her father went in later some days and came home early on others while my father left before daylight and was always home at the same time in the evening.

DOI: 10.4324/9781003281054-8

Over the years her older brother and sister both went to work for their father and I'm sure they were relieved to know they did not have to look for a job, one was already available to them. My family moved before my friend was of age to join the family business and since this was before the age of constant social media connection, it is not known if she joined them. The building they owned changed names and the family name disappeared from the front of the building. Did they assume the business when their father passed? Did he sell the business before he passed or did the children sell? That is the point of this book, what are you going to do with your business when it is time to move on.

As anyone who works in a small, family-owned business knows, many psychological challenges need to be considered when thinking about how to pass on the business, sell it to a third party or simply close its doors. In this chapter, we explore a few of the psychological challenges that need to be considered before you make the decision that will affect the future of your business and your family for years, decades, or possibly generations to come.

As we have explored in previous chapters, people look at entrepreneurs as being brave, heroic, and envied for their ability to make a dream a reality by starting their own business and even more so should that business succeed. However, what we rarely talk about are the sacrifices and long-lasting impacts on a family made along the way by those who are on the journey with the entrepreneur. A psychological toll is paid for making a dream a reality and we must be honest with ourselves about the effect this has on the family.

5.1 Family Dynamics

Family dynamics refers to the patterns of interaction among relatives, their roles and relationships, and the various factors that shape their interactions. Because family members rely on each other for emotional, physical, and economic support, they are one of the primary sources of relationship security or stress. Secure and supportive family relationships provide love, advice, and care, whereas stressful family relationships are burdened with arguments, constant critical feedback and onerous demands.

(Jabbari and Rouster 2021)

We could talk for days about family dynamics because we all know there are many layers to how a family communicates, interacts, and behaves with each other that can be hard to translate to others outside the family. Every family has characteristics which are strong and that see the family through times of trouble but also have unhelpful characteristics that cause tension which, when mixed with business, can contribute to what outsiders would consider unhealthy. In a blog for the Family Business Resource Center, Keith G. Baldwin (Baldwin, "The Four Biggest Challenges for Family-Owned Businesses" 2019) notes that "It's an unusual family-owned business where relationships are formed and thrive without emotional components like trust, love, and affection. But negative emotions like resentment, jealousy, and rivalry can create serious problems within the family business."

While preparing to write this chapter, the opportunity to interview several members of different family-owned businesses presented itself and one thing remained consistent with each family, the relationships within those families are very complex and this complexity makes it difficult to separate the family from the business and the business from the family.

In an interview conducted for this chapter, third- and fourth-generation members of a long-held family manufacturing company gave a candid interview as to the challenges this inter-mixing of family and business has had on their family.

The original patriarch of this family believed that the business was there to provide a living to the family but probably never dreamed that his business would survive nearly 100 years and the implications that bring to an ever-growing family and his descendants. Over the decades the business created several subsidiary companies to control order flow and provide an opportunity for extended family members to capitalize on the main business and provide them a means to make a living.

For sake of confidentiality and to condense the material, those interviewed will be called Frank (third generation) and Bob (fourth generation). Frank, like many children born into family companies, spent his entire life immersed in the family business in one way or another because his father, one son of the original founder, spent his entire life also immersed in the family business. Frank never explored another path and happily ran one of the subsidiary companies in another state along with other members of his immediate family. Like many of the extended members of the family, they were also stockholders which add another level of complexity to family dynamics.

It was assumed that Frank's son Bob would eventually take over the reins of the subsidiary company but as time went on, an opportunity for Bob to work at the main organization presented itself and he realized his path forward within the organization differed from his fathers'. Frank and Bob struggled with how to satisfy the needs of both individuals without leaving the other feeling guilty or remorseful.

Part of the solution was solved when the larger family entity as board members voted to sell the entire organization to an outside third party and Frank's company was dissolved as part of the overall restructuring of the company. Bob remained with the newly owned and managed company and has achieved his own level of success.

A solution to the problem of ensuring that the generation slated to assume the role of owner would be to encourage younger generation family members to work and explore other opportunities outside of the family business to ensure that they get needed skills and experience and to see if the family business is truly where their passion lies. This allows for growth of the individual and potentially be a catalyst for new ideas, thoughts, and innovation.

Family dynamics need to be considered so your succession plan succeeds. Who will be affected by your decision and what unintended consequences could result from your decision? Based on this information, you can formulate the conversations that will need to occur within the family.

5.2 Family Roles

As we instinctively know, each person within the family has their own unique role. The typical roles include the Hero, Rescuer, Mediator, Scapegoat/Black sheep, Lost child, Nurturer, Clown, and the Thinker (Innerchange 2021). Understanding the characteristics of these roles is helpful to know and it is possible to have more than one characteristic listed above. Knowing what role(s) each person holds is important and contributes to the success or failure of the company. In a book by Josh Baron and Rob Lachenauer, they use an analogy of a four-room house where roles are clearly identified and guide members to successfully manage their role in the business while maintaining their role in the family (Lachenauer 2021).

During the interviews, these roles were apparent and were critical in how successful some transitions were. Owners who believe that their role is irreplaceable, struggle with relinquishing control which eventually leads to hurt feelings, resentment, and general chaos for the business, family, and stakeholders.

One way to prevent this from happening is to hire outside board members, consultants, and business professionals who can guide you on how to avoid common pitfalls that can occur and to be honest with yourself. Open communication is key to preventing misperceptions of how the transition will occur and what happens afterward.

Just as businesses need to reinvent themselves as time changes with different leadership, new technology, and evolving trends, so does the family. Family businesses need to be intentional about bringing in different employees with the talent, skills, education, and foresight to propel the family business forward. The best way to do this is through strategic planning and honest communication about where the family business is headed and the roles that need to be filled.

Often, we make assumptions of our family members without discussing the implications of how our intentions may affect the other individual. We want to ensure that our decision to transition our company to either another family member(s) or an outside party, does not break up our family because the family is important. Again, communication is key to understanding expectations desires and fulfilling the needs of the organization and the family.

5.3 Sequel Fallacy

A fallacy is a certain reasoning logically incorrect which can lead to presumptions that might be accurate. A sequel is any item next in line or the continuation of a previous theme.

Let us consider first that you intend to pass along your business to one of your children. How have you framed this role, is it an obligation fostered with the child(ren) since birth or when you started your business? Have your children worked for the business since they were small and sweeping floors during the summer, or was this their first job as interns right out of high school or college? The assumption is that the second generation will automatically assume the business and can lead to a theory called the Sequel Fallacy.

Taylor Law writes about the common dilemma:

> Many well-intentioned family businesses succession plan is built around the idea that leaders from the next generation can simply step into the large shoes of their predecessors and run the business (and the family) exactly as their father or mother would have

done. But that fails to consider that each new generation of leadership likely has different skills and interests, and that business contexts and needs inevitably shift over time. When a family business assumes that the next generation can simply take over without pausing to consider the CEO job description, governance, or the evolving business context, they may be setting themselves up to fail.

(https://taylorlawjamaica.com/2022)

In my first interview listed above with Frank and Bob, the sequel fallacy played a pivotal role in how the family and business operated at both the subsidiary and main organization. This fallacy permeated how the organization decided at both the macro and micro levels of daily business since no one outside the family could achieve success beyond a certain level. Luckily for both of these individuals, their relationship had deep-rooted foundations of mutual respect and trust that carried them through the turbulent period of transition from one family owning the business to its sale to another individual outside of the family.

A suggestion to address the sequel fallacy is to allow every interested family member to have equal opportunity to rise within your family business. Instead of assuming that the oldest male will automatically assume control, it could be the youngest daughter who has a passion and capacity to lead the future organization. If you don't provide those opportunities for growth, you will be missing out on an opportunity for successful transition.

Another option would be to insist that succeeding generations spend time working with or for other companies not associated with yours. This allows them to grow in their formal and informal education and experience conditions and life outside the family business. If they then come back and work for the family business, they bring with them experiences, perspectives, and fresh ideas that can carry the organization forward for many years.

Again, open honest communication with the family about expectations, needs, and desires will go a long way to preventing misconceptions and misinterpretations.

5.4 Identity

For this section, I will be referring to identity as it relates to the family business and the owning family. How does one affect the other, and are they separate?

Who am I? Who are we? Many entrepreneurs spend years, up to decades building their company from the ground up, much the way you would raise a child and therefore, many entrepreneurs feel the same pride, emotional connections, sacrificial suffering, and beaming pride toward their company as they would toward a child. With this comes many psychological challenges that must be dealt with just as you would with your flesh and blood offspring.

Much like our feelings toward successful parenting, we can see our identity wrapped up in our companies which can erode our own self-identity. Once the child is ready to leave the nest, there is an adjustment period that must be dealt with. Many parents need to find their own identity again outside of parenting while others are happy to help their children pack the car up and wish them well as they pull out of the driveway. Or worse yet, what if your child does not identify with you as the parent. A disconnect emerges which can affect the relationship.

These same feelings are felt when handing over the keys to the family business. Once you have turned over ownership of your "baby," you need to know what you are going to do next. Are you going to travel, start another business, or go fishing? You deserve the newfound freedom now at your disposal but be honest with yourself there may be a period of adjustment you can expect.

One of the more successful transitions I have encountered involved a second-generation family business owner I recently encountered. Her name is Robin, and her father started a profitable boat-building operation in Arkansas. Her brother was also involved in the organization, running a branch of the business that sold boats for commercial purposes rather than recreational as the main company does. Due to some advantageous tax law, ownership of the organization technically belonged to Robin, but it was understood that the responsibility of selling the organization was between her father, brother, and her.

When it came time to consider selling, Robin asked her brother if he wanted to keep the business if his child, who is a teenager, might want to assume control at an appropriate time. She has no children of her own but was considerate of the only member of the successive generation. It was decided though this was not a valid consideration because of the number of years of schooling, experience, and training it would take to prepare for that assumption and the possibility existed that his interests would lie elsewhere.

What struck me was the apparent ease with which Robin walked away from the organization she played such a large role in creating and successfully running. What she explained is that the job was something that she did, it was not who she was. She had a clearly articulated identity outside of the company and was eager to invest more time in herself and her other interests. The other comforting factor she explained was that she had done her research on the acquiring business and that company was in complete alignment with her company's shared values, culture, and identity. While she still felt some guilt for the employees she had hired and trained, she felt comfortable enough that the new company would hold onto its founding values. And true to her feelings of trust, many of her former employees are working successfully within the current owned organization and one of her most trusted, loyal employees now runs that organization as president.

Her brother, however, struggled more than she or her father did as he saw his identity in the business he helped shape and struggled for a period to find a new identity. He is managing another business that their father had founded and is happily creating a new path for himself.

She shared with me that her father had a true entrepreneurial spirit and had founded numerous businesses over his lifetime and liked the thrill of starting a business but lost interest once it was up and was eager to start his next venture. This mindset allows him to not get his identity too wrapped up in one success or failure.

An interesting perspective I encountered was with another small, family-owned construction business that shifted my perspective as it relates to passing the business onto the next generation.

Tracy and her husband founded a construction business that erects metal buildings for commercial use. Like most small construction businesses, they have periods of success where business is booming requiring them to have many employees to complete projects and periods of shrinkage where jobs can be scarce, and employees are laid off.

During our conversation, I asked her about her thoughts on succession planning as it relates to their business. She was clear in her and her husband's thought that they would not consider passing along their business to their sons because they do not want them to work as hard as they have had to work to keep their business afloat. Their desire is to encourage a mindset of entrepreneurship but following a less stressful, more successful path of becoming project managers.

This thought process is not unique, because naturally parents have an instinctual nature to make the lives of their children easier than what they have experienced and that by working hard ourselves, our children will reap the benefits. This thought process however does have its flaws because each generation faces its own unique challenges, and it is through these challenges and difficult times that we grow as people, leaders, and business owners.

To wrap up this chapter, it is critical when considering your succession plan to consider the long-lasting implications for the family and its stakeholders. Look outside the company and the family for expert advice from consultants, accountants, lawyers, or other family-owned businesses that have either made a successful transition and unsuccessful so you can avoid the pitfalls that have happened to others.

How do you separate your identity from your business? This can seem impossible, especially if you spend your life giving the business everything that is within you to succeed. The most powerful thing to remember is that you control your identity and can change your identity to fit the situation of who and what you want to be when you complete your succession plan.

When the family business is sold or passed on, will we still be able to be a functional family that respects and loves each other?

Below we have listed some of the common psychological issues that are potentials for conflict within a small and family business with some coaching tips (Table 5.1).

5.5 Resource Tool

This worksheet is a questionnaire that should be done over a period, after deep reflection, and after having had many open and candid conversations with your family and or interested stakeholders.

You need to honestly ask yourself these questions as it relates to if your child(ren) want and are ready to assume the reins of the family business (Table 5.2).

You need to honestly ask yourself these questions as it relates to selling or handing off your company to a third party (Table 5.3).

5.6 Chapter Summary

Psychological issues affect succession planning in small and family businesses.

This chapter defined family dynamics as the patterns of interaction among relatives, their roles and relationships, and the factors that shape

Table 5.1 Coaching Tips to Address Common Psychological Issues in Succession for Small and Family Business

Common Psychological Issues in Succession for Small and Family Business	Coaching Tips
Transitions from one generation to the next.	A business consultant who engages a psychologist or psychological strategies to assist in the transition can increase communication issues so defined roles can be clarified and agreed to.
Younger generations do not care, care less, or care about the business in different ways than the founder.	A business psychologist can assist by teaching the family psychological characteristics, such as emotional control, problem-solving skills, and communication skills (Miller 2014).
Poor communication within the family that leads to misperceptions and expectations.	Have serious, honest discussions no matter how difficult it may be. Set up the discussion meeting from the beginning with the expectation that tough topics will be discussed. Business issues will be discussed, and the thrust of the conversations should not be taken personally (Baldwin, "The Missing Piece to Your Succession Plan," 2018).
Entitlement—Dealing with family members who may be employed by the business and others who are passive owners but desire a return on their equity.	Communication of roles, responsibilities, compensation, and profits is a critical part of the conversation. Work to diminish the culture of entitlement by having clearly defined roles. Address expectations and concerns before they become a crisis. Find ways to address challenges, to build and maintain relationships with other family businesses so that you can learn from, and support each other.

their interactions. Because family members rely on each other for emotional, physical, and economic support, they are one of the primary sources of relationship security or stress. Family dynamics is important in small family business succession planning and can influence how successors are chosen, who is chosen, and what impact that decision has on the business.

The assumption is that the second generation in a family will automatically assume the business can lead to a theory called the *Sequel Fallacy*.

Table 5.2 Questions to Ask Yourself about What Your Children Want Regarding Succession Planning

Questions to Ask Yourself	Notes
Have I created a strategic plan that includes all steps that need to happen before and after the transition?	
Have I created a job description for the position I am vacating?	
What is a comfortable timeline for the succession to happen and what parameters should I consider?	
What role do I see myself playing in the new company?	
Have I prepared my child(ren) for years to take over my company?	
Do they have the right education and experience to transition from worker, to leader, to owner?	
What role will my offspring's spouse play in the business if any and what influence do they have over my business?	
What are the different ways you see yourself interacting with the company after the succession?	

Identity, as this chapter has shown, relates to the family business and the owning family. How does one affect the other, and are they separate? Consider: Who am I? Who are we? Many entrepreneurs spend years, up to decades building their company from the ground up, much the way you would raise a child and therefore, many entrepreneurs feel the same pride, emotional connections, sacrificial suffering, and beaming pride toward their company as they would toward a child. With this comes many psychological challenges that must be dealt with just as you would with your flesh and blood offspring.

Table 5.3 Questions to Ask Yourself about Succession Planning

Questions to Ask Yourself	Notes
Have I created a strategic plan that includes all steps that need to happen before and post transition?	
Why am I selling/handing my company off to someone outside the family?	
What is a comfortable timeline for the succession to happen and what parameters should I consider?	
Have I been clear with my family about my intentions?	
Does the company/entity I am considering selling to have the same culture, business philosophy, and values as I do?	
What role do I see myself playing in the new company?	

Works Cited

Baldwin, Keith G. n.d. "The Four Biggest Challenges for Family-Owned Businesses | Davis Wright Tremaine." Accessed March 16, 2022. https://www.dwt.com/blogs/family-business-resource-center/2019/10/four-family-business-challenges.

Baron, Josh and Rob, Lachenauer. 2021. *The Harvard Business Review Family Business Handbook: How to Build and Sustain a Successful, Enduring Enterprise*. Harvard Business Review Press.

"Family Roles." *Innerchange*. Accessed August 19, 2021. https://www.innerchange.com/parents-resources/family-roles/.

Jabbari, Bahareh, and Sudra S. Rouster. 2021. *National Center for Biotechnology Information*. Accessed January 12, 2022. https://www.ncbi.nlm.nih.gov/books/NBK560487/.

Miller, Anna. 2014. "The Perils of the Family Business." Accessed January 12, 2022. https://www.apa.org/monitor/2014/11/perils-business.

"The Missing Piece to Your Succession Plan.". *Davis Wright Tremaine LLP*. Accessed January 12, 2022. https://www.dwt.com/blogs/family-business-resource-center/2018/11/the-missing-piece-to-your-succession-plan--the-psy.

"Taylor Law Williams Salmon: We Take the Time, Because You Matter." *Taylor Law Williams Salmon Attorneys*. Accessed March 16, 2022. https://lawfirmjamaica.com/.

Chapter 6

Questions and Answers about Legal Issues in Small and Family Business Succession

Ashley Ridgeway-Washington

Contents

DOI: 10.4324/9781003281054-9

6.1 Introduction

On June 5, 2021, publishing titan M. Richard Robinson Jr. died suddenly while walking with his son and ex-wife on Martha's Vineyard. At 84 years old, Mr. Robinson was the chairman and CEO of Scholastic Books and had been so for over 45 years. His father founded Scholastic in 1920 in the living room of their Pennsylvania home. Both of Robinson's sons were in the publishing business (Ramachandran 2021).

Although succession was often discussed at Scholastic, the turn of events following Robinson's death is a story made for reality TV, not Wall Street.

The fate of the largest publisher in the world lay in a plain manila envelope in Robinson's safe, unknown even to those it would affect the most.

Robinson left 30-year Scholastic veteran (and rumored paramour) Iole Lucchese 53.8% of Scholastic's Class A stock (Harris 2021). Robinson's bequest made Lucchese the most powerful woman in publishing and the Scholastic empire's controlling shareholder. In his will, Robinson also named Peter Warwick, the company's new Chief Executive, effectively bypassing his sons Ben and Maurice Robinson for immediate opportunities to step into day-to-day leadership or financial control of the Robinson family business. Robinson's bequest to Ms. Lucchese not only tipped the balance of power but shifted ownership of Scholastic to a person outside of the Robinson family. Robinson left Scholastic in an unusual position for a publicly traded company: adapting to a surprise succession plan, many key players, including those tapped to lead, did not know was coming (Harris 2021).

Not even Scholastic's general counsel knew Robinson's decision. Despite their long tenure with Scholastic, Lucchese and Warwick were not the logical choices for succession. Industry experts and investors have expressed public skepticism about the leadership and their ability to lead the publishing behemoth forward (Ramachandran 2021).

To further complicate matters, Robinson named Lucchese co-executor of his estate and gave Lucchese all his personal assets with the request (but not direction) to distribute his assets to his children as "she believed to be in accordance with Robinson's wishes" (Harris 2021). Ms. Lucchese's proximity to the personal family matters only intensified skepticism about the merits of her appointment. Nevertheless, Scholastic branded the changes in leadership as smooth and positive.

However, credible information suggests that Robinson's "wait and see" succession strategy left a huge mess and resulted in serious business disruption and family drama likely to spill into the halls of Scholastic's New York corporate headquarters (Ramachandran 2021). Scholastic already faced business volatility due to the COVID-19 pandemic, and while the fate of this company remains to be seen, the learnings from this succession blunder should not be missed.

6.2 Key Terms

■ **Business continuity**—Planning that anticipates a range of grossly disruptive scenarios and proactively establishes the processes, procedures, decisions, and activities that support the organization's ability to continue functioning through the disruption.

- **Business ownership model**—The legal plan which outlines the roles and responsibilities that each person or entity with a legal or equitable interest has in that business.
- **Business structure**—Refers to how a business is legally organized and how it is taxed and regulated as an extension of the organization structure.
- **Business valuation**—The process of determining the objective and subjective worth of all aspects of the business.
- **Conflict of interest**—Refers to scenarios or factors that compromise or may appear to compromise a fiduciary's ability to act in the best interests of one or more clients.
- **Fiduciary**—A person or organization that acts in the best interest of another ahead of their interests.
- **Governance**—Refers to the strategies companies employ to create checks and balances and ensure accountability.
- **Heirs**—One who inherits or is entitled to inherit from an ancestor by right or agreement.
- **Owner-centric**—Refers to a business environment where the "owners" are essential to all facets of the business, including but not limited to day-to-day decision-making, client/product development, governance, and oversight.
- **Power of attorney**—The authority for a person or entity to act on another's behalf, usually as specified in a legal agreement.
- **Successors**—A person or entity that follows another.
- **Representation agreement**—A legal agreement that outlines the terms and conditions of the attorney–client relationship.
- **Will**—A legal declaration of a person's wishes upon death or incapacitation.

6.3 Common Questions and Answers about Legal Issues in Small and Family Business Succession

The Scholastic succession debacle of 2021 is a real and tangible example of the importance of a trusted relationship with your legal partner. But, more important, this story offers a textbook case study in the perils of poor succession planning. If nothing, Scholastic's current plight is an instructive guide and a perfect backdrop to the most common legal questions and answers in family-owned and small business succession planning.

The Most Common Questions and Answers about Legal Issues in Small and Family Business Succession are intuitive and simplistic. Similarly, the answers are often straightforward.

Conversely, navigating the journey to executing these solutions can be very tricky. Fortunately, savvy small and family business owners use legal strategies to galvanize action and establish guardrails that equip these companies to withstand the only thing for sure in business—change.

Small and family businesses are the unsung heroes of the economy, making up 99% of all American companies with paid employees and adding 10.5 million net new jobs to the economy over the last decade (Small Business and Entreprenuership Council 2018).

These companies are foundational to entrepreneurship, and despite anecdotal beliefs, family businesses have staying power. Compared to typical companies, data suggests that family business outlive their counterparts (Lachenauer 2021). And while they may outlast other types of companies, they often do so without a founding family member at the helm of leadership.

In 2010, PricewaterhouseCoopers conducted a family business survey of over 1,600 family-run businesses and found that less than 30% of the companies surveyed survived passage into the second generation (2010/2011 PWC survey). And things only got worse from there, since only 13% of businesses survived into the third generation (Samuel Curtis Johnson Graduate School of Management-Cornell University 2022).

Anecdotally, owners of small and family-owned companies consistently prefer keeping the business in the family after retiring or passing. Despite technology and globalization leveling the playing field, these companies continue to see marginal progress in developing plans to ensure that the next generation of the family is ready, willing, and able to lead.

So why is the dichotomy between the founders' vision for the future and the eventual fate so different? If founders want to keep it in the family, why are more small and family-owned businesses not successful at sustaining multigenerational paths to family leadership? As we consider the innovation, ingenuity, and business savvy that fuels these companies, it becomes evident that small and family businesses need support to create roadmaps to generational success.

Perhaps, it is because, for founders, their company is far more than the "thing" they do or the "way" they earn. Instead, their companies are often "their" life's work." These innovative, courageous, resilient, fortuitous, and resourceful souls claw their way through the competition, business disruption, labor instability, consumer trends, and family disruptions to achieve success by relentlessly pursuing their service or product. And perhaps, they cannot let go when their time has expired.

According to Edelman's 2020 Trust Barometer Survey, small or family businesses are the most trusted enterprises. Of those surveyed, 67% said they trusted family businesses—against 58% for large public companies (Daniel J. Edelman Holdings, Inc. 2020). The commitment to manifesting their idea is why customers trust small businesses more than corporate titans. Unfortunately, it's also why it is tough for founders to plan for their departure.

Short-term business continuity planning and long-term succession plans ensure companies have staying power. If countless public cautionary tales were not warning enough, a global pandemic has only intensified the call to action in succession planning. Losing over five million people in less than 24 months has forced companies to traverse unprecedented business disruption fueled by a volatile economic environment, a bottlenecked supply chain, and unprecedented labor disruption. In addition, COVID-19 cast a remarkable spotlight on the importance of succession planning as unexpected death, and enduring illness caused circumstances to change instantly in ways that defy the most comprehensive plans and organizational controls.

This chapter will discuss four fundamental legal questions in small and family business succession and offer a road map for establishing legal strategies that empower you to undertake the actions that will help ensure your company's legacy is preserved well beyond your time in leadership.

1. What does my company's legal strategy have to do with succession planning?
2. How do I get started?
3. What will a legal expert partner work with me to do?
4. How will I know I have a sound succession plan?

6.4 What Does My Company's Legal Strategy Have to Do with Succession Planning?

"People are getting smarter nowadays; they are letting lawyers, instead of their conscience, be their guide."

—**Will Rogers**

Will Rogers, the American comedian, and vaudeville legend, was known for his wit and pragmatism but giving sound succession advice was not his claim to fame (Will Rogers Memorial Museum 2016). While his words were most certainly meant to be humorous and even sarcastic, in the context of this chapter, Will likely offered insights that ring true in the journey of legal partnership in succession planning.

As we will explore, succession planning can be messy and emotional, but the journey is essential to balance conscience and objectivity, both of which are needed in establishing a clear succession plan in small and family-owned businesses.

From a legal standpoint, the only strategy that is more important than how a small or family business will pass once the founders exit is the legal strategy used to form it. So what happens when a pivotal figure in the company passes unexpectedly or settles on departure? The answer is either chaos or business as (semi) usual, depending on whether that company had a succession plan that is objective and legally sound.

You may not realize just how important your legal advisor is to your succession plan. The building blocks of a seamless transition roadmap include objective and transparent guardrails and organized business affairs. From estate planning to business valuation to governance, a good succession plan relies on legal expertise to breathe life into your vision for your company's legacy. Most important, a consultation with the right legal partner may be just the nudge you need to activate the planning process.

One of the most common legal issues in succession planning is the absence of planning. The number of small business owners without a business succession plan is shocking. In a study conducted by Wilmington Trust, researchers determined that 58% of the small business owners surveyed had no business succession plan. Of those businesses without a business succession plan, 47% of the owners believed no succession plan was necessary (Thienel 2020).

These statistics defy logic, especially considering the success and complexity of many of these privately held organizations. Reason rarely explains humanity. It is easier for many small and family-owned business owners to push off succession planning than to acknowledge the inevitability of their diminished utility and mortality. To plan for the next generation of leadership is to acknowledge that their time will pass.

James Roberts, a succession planning and wealth management executive with Community Wealth Advisors in Rockville, Maryland, commented that

Many small business owners in their 50's and 60's seem to suffer from Ponce de Leon syndrome. They refuse to accept the possibility of their demise or assume that advances in medicine will keep them healthy indefinitely. … But deep inside, many are mentally ready to retire but do not know how to approach planning challenges or what they will do next.

(Thienel 2020)

Other barriers to action include making tough choices or acknowledging facts about people you love. To accept that an heir apparent for the business is not equipped to lead the company into the future or that your child wants to pursue other passions rather than work in the business can be tough to acknowledge.

Even worse, consider if co-founding siblings or spouses are not on the same page about the strategic direction of the business. Developing a succession plan involves confronting deeply personal, highly adversarial, or even painful truths that transcend the business. It is easier for founders to push the proverbial ball down the road.

With all the personal and psychological entanglements that commonly accompany succession planning, you may feel anxious or even guilty about critical decisions that drive your succession strategy. But, believe it or not, your legal partner is an indispensable asset in assisting you in wading through emotions to come to sound and objective decisions. Often, your legal partner is even comfortable being the proverbial "bad person." So, as you make the right choices, it may be natural to lean on sound legal strategy as the basis for executing the tough decisions you will need to make.

6.5 How Do I Get Started?

"The journey of a thousand miles begins with a single step."

–Lao Tzu

Congratulations! You have taken the first step by picking up this book. Since you are here, it's clear that you recognize that you need to ensure that the legacy you've worked so hard to build continues to thrive for generations to come. However, succession planning is not one size fits all, and it's also not a "one and done" process.

A sound succession plan is a living and breathing body of roadmaps, guardrails, and frameworks designed to change and grow with your company.

Succession planning begins with internal reflection on the goals of your company and envisioning the future of your organization. There is value in spending time thinking about and writing down what you want your company to be 100 years from now. But thinking about how you envision the company and writing down those goals is not enough.

Your company's future is your legacy, and you get to plan for its future the way you want to. So, the first step is to collect critical data points that will assist your legal partner in helping you to realize your succession goals.

Consider the questions below as you determine what you want your company and your life to look like. This exercise not only allows you to check your thoughts but will also help your attorney to guide you toward legal solutions that fit your needs and help you accomplish your vision, no matter how idiosyncratic they may be.

Table 6.1a and 6.1b offer a framework for clarifying your succession goals. Consider the questions below as you determine what you want your company and life to look like. I encourage you to answer honestly. This exercise not only allows you to check your thoughts but will also help your attorney to guide you toward legal solutions that fit your needs and help you accomplish your vision, no matter how idiosyncratic they may be.

Once you have organized your thoughts using the organizational vision framework, you are ready to vet professionals that can help you effectuate your vision. And before you ask, YES, you must work with licensed professionals to ensure your wishes are captured so it establishes legal guardrails for senior leaders now and in the future.

No matter how tempting (and cheap) it may be, legal templates and Google searches are no substitute for sound legal expertise! In addition, you will likely also need financial and human resources expertise to assist you in effectuating a comprehensive succession strategy, but we will address that in subsequent chapters.

6.6 The Role of Legal Partners in Succession Planning

Succession planning ranges from relatively simple to highly complex. Similarly, the investment you will make to ensure that you have a comprehensive succession strategy will vary based on the complexity, size of your business, and level of expertise of the legal professional you hire.

Table 6.1a   Succession Planning Legal Strategy Tips and Tools

Additional resources you'll find in this chapter…
This chapter includes several checklists, templates, and guides ("tools") to offer you general guidance as you begin your succession planning journey. Specifically, these documents provide insights into important documents, and business activities generally considered best practice when implementing legal strategy in succession planning.
How to use these tools…
The tools described above should be used as guidance but are not designed to be used in place of legal expertise. Please review each tool to determine which might be helpful to you as you begin assessing your needs.
Where you'll find the tools…
The tools (referred to as "tables" in the text) are embedded within the chapter…so read, read, read and take a few moments to review each table as it is introduced throughout the chapter.
Legal disclaimer…
PLEASE NOTE: The tools included in this chapter are a framework for your consideration based on general best practices. These documents are <u>not a substitute</u> for legal or professional advice. Should you decide to rely solely upon information provided in these tools, you do so <u>at your own risk</u>.   While the information presented in these documents has been verified to the best of our abilities, we cannot guarantee that the tools are comprehensive or a legally compliant solution for your organization. We reserve the right to change these documents at any time, with or without notice to you.
What if I have questions or can't figure something out?
Visit our website at www.ajaihumancapital.com or email us at info@ajaienterprises.com.

An attorney will look at the current state of your business with objectivity and assess foreseen and unforeseen risk factors that will empower you to ensure that your succession plan stands against legal challenges. In addition, an attorney will work with you to structure your business so authority is delegated to the appropriate decision-makers should you become incapacitated or exit the company abruptly.

In addition, your legal partner will call on you to make tough decisions now that will ensure the company's future later. Steps to mitigate risk may include establishing a board of directors, establishing criteria for your successor, and determining which legal strategy will empower you to transfer your company according to your wishes when the time comes. A business attorney can assist founders with identifying potential successors, developing a communication plan, and ensuring that all stakeholders' interests are protected as the next generation of leaders is prepared to step in.

Last, as a critical leader of your small or family-owned business, your personal estate may be an important element of your company's succession

Table 6.1b Thirty Questions to Ask Yourself about Preserving Your Legacy through Succession Planning

Directions: Consider the questions below as you determine what you want your company and your life to look like in the future. I encourage you to answer as honestly as possible. This exercise not only allows you to check your thoughts but will also help your attorney to guide you toward legal solutions that fit your needs and help you accomplish your vision, no matter how idiosyncratic they may be.

Questions to Consider	Your Initial Thoughts	Follow-Up?
1. What are my short-term and long-term goals for the company?		
2. What are my short-term and long-term goals for personal finances?		
3. What are my short-term and long-term goals for my personal life?		
4. Based on what I want and where the company is going, do my personal goals align with the company succession goals?		
5. When this is all said and done, what do I want to make sure happens with this business? (i.e., my company is passed to my children, I can pay for my grandchildren's college, the company stays in the local community ...)		
6. What is the magic of your company? (i.e., that intangible thing that sets you apart from your competitors)		
7. What are the behaviors of this magic?		
8. What does my company believe in and stand for? (mission, vision, values, cultural attributes)		
9. What's the company's one thing? (The one thing that can never change about who we are, how we do business, how we serve our customers/clients, where we do business ...)		

(*Continued*)

Table 6.1b (Continued)   Thirty Questions to Ask Yourself about Preserving Your Legacy through Succession Planning

Questions to Consider	Your Initial Thoughts	Follow-Up?
10. What character traits and skillsets (tangible/intangible) must future business leaders have?		
11. Based on the talent in the business today, who should take over my responsibilities when my time in leadership has come to an end? (Spend some time listing potential successors and mapping them to a function or role.)		
12. Do these people know that I am considering them to take over for me?		
13. Are they on board with my plan?		
14. What is being done now to prepare them to step in on my behalf?		
15. Do other key members of the business know this?		
16. Do key members agree with this approach? If not, what's the issue from your perspective?		
17. What are my potential successors' superpowers and opportunities for development?		
18. What is in my brain (or in the brains of other leaders) that needs to be put down on paper?		
19. How are we going to get all this knowledge recorded?		
20. What have we already done to document Standard Operating Procedure?		
21. How will I exit the business when it's time?		
22. Will the current ownership model work if there is more than one owner?		

(Continued)

Table 6.1b (Continued)   Thirty Questions to Ask Yourself about Preserving Your Legacy through Succession Planning

Questions to Consider	Your Initial Thoughts	Follow-Up?
23. How will I be paid for the value of my business?		
24. How do I know what the business is worth? (i.e., what has been done to assess business valuation?)		
25. How will leaders exit the business in the future?		
26. Who else needs to know my plan or weigh in?		
27. How will we communicate this to others?		
28. What are the triggering events and timetables that will guide my exit from the company?		
29. Who are the most critical internal and external stakeholders in the company? (description of critical employees, officers, vendors, customers, and managers and their roles, duties, or significance to the business)		
30. How will my vision for my exit and my company's legacy positively or negatively impact the people I care about most? (i.e., list decisions that may be popular/unpopular. Weigh the pros and cons and describe how you will communicate the information and mitigate risk.)		

Please note: The tools included in this chapter are a framework for your consideration based on general best practice. These documents are *not a substitute* for legal or professional advice. Should you decide to rely solely upon information provided in these templates, you do so *at your own risk*.

While the information contained in this document has been verified to the best of our abilities, we cannot guarantee that this document or any of the other tools in this chapter is a comprehensive or legally compliant solution for your business. We reserve the right to change these documents at any time, with or without notice to you. What if I have questions or can't figure something out? Email us at info@ajaienterprises.com strategy. An attorney can ensure that you have safeguarded your personal assets and reduced personal risk so your estate does not negatively affect the future of your business.

6.7 Selecting a Legal Partner

Selecting the right legal partner for your business is essential to successful succession planning. Your legal representative will be a trusted partner to you and your business. From my experience, there are several factors to consider when selecting the right lawyer for you and your business.

Succession planning may seem overwhelming. Your attorney will guide you in prioritizing tasks by dividing the work into smaller projects. As you complete each phase, you can realize meaningful progress. Each milestone offers space to reflect on legal strategies and make appropriate adjustments to achieve succession goals.

Once you have found a list of potential legal partners, you are ready to vet and interview legal counsel based on your business needs and interpersonal preferences.

Table 6.2 will help you clarify what is most important in selecting a legal partner and provide you with key insights on your preferences as you narrow your search. Referrals and the local bar association are great places to develop a shortlist, but only you can determine what is most important in selecting legal counsel based on your business needs and interpersonal preferences.

Table 6.3 offers questions that will aid you in ensuring that a potential legal partner's services, expertise, and business model align with the needs you have established using Table 6.2.

Once you've reflected on your goals and selected a legal partner, the real work begins. If you have not already done so, the firm you have selected should ask you to complete a client intake form. This document contains the baseline information the firm will need to perform a conflict-of-interest check and draft the representation agreement.

A typical client intake form will include:

■ Key Company Facts (name, address, state of incorporation, business organization structure, owners …).
■ Designated Points of Contact and Contact Information.
■ Summary of Legal Needs (high-level goals and desired outcomes).

Table 6.2 Selecting the Right Legal Partner Checklist

	Notes
Directions: Use this checklist to guide your thinking. For each question appearing below, record your thoughts under the right column below. There are no "right" or "wrong" answers in any absolute sense, but there may be some answers that are better than others.	
What do I need help with?	
☐ I'm not sure.	
☐ Succession planning?	
☐ Business valuation?	
☐ Negotiating contracts?	
☐ Establishing a board of directors?	
☐ Personal estate planning?	
☐ Zoning, licensing, and real estate matters?	
☐ HR compliance?	
☐ Trademark/copyright?	
How much money/time do I have to invest?	
☐ Overall budget? _____	
☐ Fee structure (retainer, a flat one-time fee, hourly rates, contingency)	
☐ I am willing to do some leg work on my own (smaller budget)	
☐ I want my attorney to handle everything (generous budget)	
How soon do I want to get started, and when do I need a plan in place?	
☐ Very Urgent	
☐ Somewhat Urgent	
☐ I've got some time	
Pro Tip: Some more sought-after attorneys/ law firms may take longer to schedule consultations and begin the succession engagement. If you have an urgent need, you may consider other alternatives. In some cases, larger firms can activate quickly as they generally have more resources (attorneys, case managers, etc.). To move quickly, ensure you have gathered all existing business and estate planning documents before your consultation.	

(*Continued*)

Table 6.2 (Continued)   Selecting the Right Legal Partner Checklist

	Notes
What level of expertise will you need?	
☐ How complex is my business model?	
☐ Is your business industry highly regulated?	
☐ Is there considerable family or business drama that needs to be sorted out?	
☐ How many decision-makers must be consulted?	
☐ How soon am I planning to exit the business?	
How much experience is enough?	
☐ Years in practice? _____	
☐ I would prefer a "partner level" attorney	
☐ I am comfortable working with an "associate level" attorney	
☐ I would like my legal partner to be Board-certified	
Pro Tip: The level of expertise you will need is directly correlated to the level of complexity within your organization. Complexity spans beyond your industry, business model, and organizational structure and could also include the number of decision-makers and anticipated interpersonal drama that may result. Less complex matters may be handled relatively quickly with the help of a legal partner with junior-level expertise. However, complex or highly-sensitive business needs may be best managed by more experienced legal partners.	
Geographical proximity to me or my business?	
☐ Do I need local representation?	
☐ Will I need an attorney with established relationships where I live or do business?	
How important is my legal partners' reputation?	
☐ I want a legal partner who is established as a trusted succession planning partner in my industry or circle of influence.	
☐ It's important that my legal partner is well respected in the community.	
☐ What examples can this attorney/firm share of success stories?	

(Continued)

Table 6.2 (Continued)   Selecting the Right Legal Partner Checklist

	Notes
How important is it to me that my legal partner has industry-specific experience?	
☐ Is this attorney/firm familiar with my industry or willing to learn it quickly?	
What size is the right size?	
☐ I like working with smaller firms	
☐ I am comfortable working with large firms	
Pro Tip: Smaller v. Larger Pros: smaller firms are often less expensive, offer a single point of contact, personalized service, and may foster a closer attorney–client relationship. Cons: Smaller firms may not be able to move as quickly to resolve your issues and may not be equipped to handle related legal needs that fall into other practice areas. Pros: Larger firms may have a longer consultation process but can often mobilize succession efforts quickly because they have more resources (people, tools, and partners). Many can handle your legal needs across practice areas internally. Cons: Larger firms may be more expensive and can feel less personalized. Often clients will have less interaction with their attorney and may work with various legal professionals to accomplish succession goals which could feel like a less connected attorney-client experience.	

6.8 Conflicts of Interest—A Common Succession Challenge

A responsible legal partner will always perform a conflict-of-interest check to ensure that taking you or your company on as a client does not create a conflict of interest for you or existing clients. While a conflict of interest may not necessarily bar a firm from working with you, it does require that the firm notify existing and new clients about the conflict and allow each party to make an informed decision (Monday 2020).

Pro Tip: When selecting a legal partner to represent the company, it may mean that your legal partner may not represent you as an individual owner of the company. Sometimes, business interests may not align with owners' or other key leaders' interests in the company. When this issue arises, a good legal partner will sit down with you to explain the issue and advise interested parties to secure independent representation with another firm (Monday 2020).

Once the conflict-of-interest check has been completed, expect to sign an engagement letter or representation agreement with your attorney. The

Table 6.3 Nine Insightful Questions Clients Should Ask When Selecting an Attorney—A Decision Matrix

Directions: Use this table to guide your thinking. Fill out the form below by offering a rating of how well prepared you are for each question below.

Total Rating: _____   Overall Rank: _____

Date: _____
Company: _____
Firm: _____
Attorney: _____
Practice Areas: _____
Board Certifications: _____

Suggested Rating:	1	2	3	4	5
	Won't Work	Not an ideal fit	A suitable solution	A great option	The ideal choice

1. Can you share a high-level overview of your areas of expertise and experience?
A thorough response will include: years of practice, industries serviced, practice areas, board certifications, geographic proximity, industry relationships, interdisciplinary relationships, or other relevant experience.

Rating: _____
Notes:

(Continued)

Table 6.3 (Continued) Nine Insightful Questions Clients Should Ask When Selecting an Attorney—A Decision Matrix

2. How will you use your experience and expertise to guide my company and me toward achieving my goals?
2a. Is there anything I should consider adding to my succession planning goals?
  This question gives you the space to briefly share your succession goals and gauge if your potential legal partner is an active listener.

Rating: ——
Notes:

3. Please describe your rates and fee structure? Are there additional costs above and beyond your standard fees? Are you willing to negotiable?
  This question is a great way to determine if this firm is within your budget and to determine (after you've consulted with several firms) if your budget is appropriate based on your goals.

Rating: ——
Notes:

(Continued)

Table 6.3 (Continued) Nine Insightful Questions Clients Should Ask When Selecting an Attorney—A Decision Matrix

4. Can you share examples of recent successes you've had with resolving or developing legal strategies to address business needs that are like mine?

This question gives a potential legal partner the space to share their record of successful outcomes.

Rating: _____
Notes:

5. Are you willing to provide client references? I prefer to speak with clients who are similarly situated. (i.e., similar in size, industry, age, level of complexity)

This question serves as a check and balance. Of course, potential legal partners can share their successes with you. However, successful outcomes are always more credible when a former client is willing to share a balanced perspective on the engagement relationship and outcome.

Rating: _____
Notes:

6. How soon can you begin working with me, and the estimated turnaround time?

This question allows you to provide insight into the level of urgency you have and may help you determine if your timeline expectations are reasonable based on the goals you've set.

(Continued)

Table 6.3 (Continued)   Nine Insightful Questions Clients Should Ask When Selecting an Attorney—A Decision Matrix

Rating: _____
Notes:

7. Will I be working directly with you or other members of the firm? If so, who and what is your level of oversight?
This question is an important data point as you determine what level of engagement you will need to feel comfortable with the nature of the attorney–client relationship.

Rating: _____
Notes:

8. Beyond legal guidance and document preparation, what else do you or your firm offer your clients?
This question helps you determine if you will get additional value for your investment (i.e., webinars, training, policies, processes, established relationships with key external stakeholders, inroads to opportunities, or other resources/professionals).

Rating: _____
Notes:

(Continued)

Table 6.3 (Continued)   Nine Insightful Questions Clients Should Ask When Selecting an Attorney—A Decision Matrix

9. **What is the most innovative approach your firm has taken to address a succession challenge? How do you ensure that your guidance includes solutions that incorporate diverse perspectives?**

   At first glance, this question may seem misplaced, but it is a great way to determine how experienced the firm is in handling complex, highly sensitive, or unique business needs. Experienced firms will have experienced all kinds of business issues and have developed out-of-the-box approaches that may not be found in the "textbook" approaches to succession planning.

   Rating: _____
   Notes:

*Feel free to add additional questions that are important to your unique goals and business needs.

engagement letter and representation agreement are similar documents. However, engagement agreements are generally less formal. A representation agreement has the typical look and feel of a contract. Regardless of the stylistic approach, both are legally binding contracts. These agreements cover important terms and conditions associated with legal representation and will override any informal discussions you may have had with your attorney during the consultation phase.

A representation or engagement agreement provides a clear path forward for the attorney and client. Some states provide attorneys with ethical guidelines that require key provisions in engagement letters or representations agreements. At a minimum, a good agreement should include the information described below but may also include additional information.

Table 6.4 offers a checklist of standard terms in a representation or engagement agreement. At a minimum, a good agreement should include the information described below but may also include additional information.

To work, the attorney–client relationship must be rooted in trust and confidentiality. You must be honest with your attorney about your goals to have a shot at achieving them.

Your legal partner is your fiduciary. Their goal is not to judge you but guide you toward realistic and attainable solutions. Your legal partner's job will be to push you, challenge you, and even disagree with you as you work as a team to ensure your business affairs have been legally protected, valued appropriately, and governed.

A wise client heeds the advice of their attorney and allows them to offer objective and balanced advice. An honest client will speak up when they know they cannot align with or agree to their attorney's recommendations. Ultimately, your attorney's job is to effectuate your vision, and the absence of ethical or legal concerns should align with your wishes.

6.9 What Will a Legal Expert Partner Work with Me to Do?

"You cannot live without the lawyers, and certainly you cannot die without them."

–Joseph H. Choate

Table 6.4   Common Terms in a Representation or Engagement Agreement

	Notes
Directions: Use this table to consider some issues to be addressed in a representation or an engagement agreement. If you have already identified each issue appearing below, check the box (X). If you have not identified or addressed each issue appearing below, leave the item blank and take notes on what you must do.	
☐ Identify the parties to the agreement (clients, attorneys)	
☐ Describe the scope of work to be performed and call out exclusions (especially if the service being excluded would typically be within scope)	
☐ Describe the duration of the engagement	
☐ Clearly describe the fee and cost structure, method of payment, billing, and payment dates, and consequences on non-payment	
☐ Outline the duties and responsibilities of each party	
☐ Describe the process for amending, revising, or terminating the agreement	
☐ Describe the process for resolving conflicts or disputes	
☐ Describe when the attorney may withdraw from the case or the consequences of breach of contract	
☐ Describe notice and permissions each party must get from the other before taking specific actions	
☐ Describe the effective date of the agreement	
☐ Explicitly state that the attorney makes no promises or guarantees about specific outcomes (as in the case of court proceedings)	

Legal counsel can be most helpful in your succession planning journey by helping you to answer four fundamental questions:

A. How do I know what I am passing on to my successors?
B. How do I create the right succession strategy?
C. When time to exit, how should I transfer business assets and control?
D. How do I know when I have a sound succession plan in place?

6.10 Market Business Valuation

Before owners can determine which exit strategy is best for them, they must understand what they are passing on to potential successors. Business valuation is a process and a set of procedures used to estimate the economic value of an owner's interest in a business (Monday, A Blueprint for Family Business Succession Planning 2018). Business valuation is a joint project between financial experts, legal experts, and business owners to determine the estimated value of the business. Business valuation, like succession planning, will change based on the state of the company and should be undertaken every two to four years to accurately capture the value of the business and the business assets (Monday, A Blueprint for Family Business Succession Planning 2018).

Business valuation is an integral component of succession planning and encompasses more than the objective and independent determination of the value of the business's assets.

Coming to an objective or "market valuation" of the business is the easy part. Establishing market valuation every three to five years is a best practice approach to understanding the company's value. In addition, a professional business evaluation helps you and your legal partner invite transparency into the business's economic health. Further, valuation sets realistic expectations about all stakeholders' economic benefits as they join or exit ownership. Most important, valuation guides risk mitigation planning, that is, adequate insurance and tax planning strategy (Monday 2020).

6.11 Subjective Business Valuation

Subjective business evaluation means determining the interests of the successive owners and clearly understanding their motivations for participating in the family business (Monday 2020). Subjective valuation should drive the "guts" of your business continuation and exit planning strategies, which we will discuss in greater detail later in this chapter.

Table 6.5 describes subjective valuation using a realistic family business scenario. In the table appearing below, Jason is the co-founder and Chief Business Development Officer of Sunshine Heating and Air. Jason's spouse, Amalia, is the CEO and co-founder. Together, Jason and Amalia have two adult children, A'Niyah and Gabriela. Jason also has an adult son from a previous marriage, Robert. Jason's protégé,' Devin, has been with

Table 6.5 A Diagram of the Subjective Interests of Sunshine Succession Stakeholders

Jason	Amalia
Chief Business Development Officer	**CEO**
Co-founder, Sunshine Heating and Air Interests: Ensuring the legacy of the business, succession to one or more children, gradual change of control, profit sharing for a defined period and then lump sum payout, quasi-independent governance. He wants to retire in 5–7 years.	Co-founder, Sunshine Heating and Air Interests: Ensuring the legacy of the business, governance that establishes succession requirements, succession plan that minimizes family drama. She wants to retire in 7–10 years.

A'Niyah	Robert	Gabriela
CEO, Beautique	**Sr. Director Bus. Dev.**	**VP, Finance**
Heir	Heir	Heir
Interests: Wealth accumulation and family legacy. A'Niyah is a successful business owner and has no interest in working in the family business. Instead, she would like to earn profits and pass her interests to her children.	**Interests:** Leadership in the family business, cash flow, family legacy. Robert has also worked in the family business since graduating college. With less than 10 years in the industry, he is still learning but hopes to become the CEO upon his parents' retirement.	**Interests:** Employment in the family business, cash flow, and wealth accumulation. Gabriela spent 15 years in big accounting before coming to work at Sunshine. She oversees finances in Sunshine and hopes to remain the CFO upon her parents' retirement. However, she does not want to assume the CEO's responsibilities.

Devin
VP, Operations
Trusted Employee
Interests: Leadership in the family business, an opportunity to purchase an interest in the company, and a new family legacy. Devin has been with Sunshine since she was 18 years old. She is the most experienced employee at Sunshine. She is loyal to Jason and Amalia, and wants the chance to buy into minority ownership upon their retirement. Devin is the Director of Operations and hopes to be the CEO one day. In addition, she wants to begin building a family legacy for her children.

Sunshine Heating and Air for over 20 years and oversees business operations and expansion. As Jason and Amalia think of the future of Sunshine, they envision Gabriela stepping into the CEO role when Amalia is ready to retire. Sunshine proudly promotes its majority women-owned designation. Gabriela not only has the financial acumen and level-headed demeanor, but she is also the perfect "face" of the future of the business. Jason and Amalia assume that Gabriela is on board with this plan. She left big accounting to work in the family business.

As Jason and Amalia work with their legal partner to discuss the future of Sunshine, they quickly realize that everyone is not on the same page.

By developing a clear understanding of the subjective value of the business, your legal partner can assist you with developing a right-size succession plan that addresses the individual motivations of each successor to the company. Seldom does a one-size-fits-all approach to succession planning yield the desired outcomes for succession stakeholders. Specifically, even-split approaches to succession can be detrimental to the legacy of the business, especially when successors opt out of working in the family business (Monday 2020).

As we explore the example of Sunshine Heating and Air, we see that each potential successor has different interests and motivations for the role that the future of the family business will play in their lives. This example also explores how key leaders, like Devin, may not be apparent successors but may affect the founding owners' succession goals.

Initially, Jason and Amalia assumed that Gabriela would step into her mother's footsteps. But upon further inquiry, they now understand this may not be a viable plan. By doing the work to understand what each stakeholder wants and needs from the family business, Jason and Amalia can work with Sunshine's succession team to create a succession plan that considers all these factors and communicates a clear plan in advance. This approach will undoubtedly make Amalia happy! It is clear that more than anything, she wants Sunshine to stay in the family and to avert family drama as critical succession decisions are being made.

6.12 Competing Motivations—A Common Succession Challenge

Pro Tip: where there are competing motivations (that is, multiple stakeholders vying for the CEO position), determining the subjective valuation is even more critical because it may be necessary to tailor the legacy strategy to ensure there are clear plans, defined roles and interests, and independent checks and balances.

Sometimes, the company's interests compete with the interests of your successors. There may be some friction, but total drama need not ensue. Instead, work with your attorney to take an objective assessment of your succession goals as it relates to your successors' subjective interests in the business. Establish clarity and set conditions that successors will need to meet to be considered for critical executive management roles. This is also an excellent opportunity to establish competency and experience requirements for key executive management roles so potential successors understand what they need to do to be considered for their desired position. Similarly, set clear expectations for successors who are not interested in working in the business about what they can expect to be different if they are not contributing to the business's day-to-day management. This way, successors are not blindsided by unexpected outcomes.

6.13 Developing an Effective Succession Strategy

One of the most common dilemmas in small and family business succession planning is how to arrive at the "right" succession strategy that accomplishes your goals and visions for the company's future and considers the motivations and interests of successors and critical internal and external stakeholders.

You may be asking yourself how your succession strategy and your succession plan differ. Your succession strategy includes the goals you have set for succession and the informed decisions you work with your legal partner to make, to achieve the succession goals you have set. Conversely, the documents and processes you put into place come together to create your succession plan.

Your attorney's job is to help you build the legal documents you need to effectuate your succession plan, but that is not an overnight process. The best succession strategy incorporates a short and long-term strategy.

While developing a final succession plan, a business continuation plan is a valuable tool for ensuring that the business can continue operating if it suffers the unexpected loss of a key leader without serious disruption or economic loss.

Perhaps you started this journey because you had some grand epiphany that succession planning was an important investment of your time and resources. However, if you are like most small and family business owners, your nudge toward succession planning came from a near-miss event or age milestone that caused you to take a sobering look at your own mortality and how your life's work will continue after you are gone. For many small business owners, the global pandemic was the wake-up call they needed and a master class in the chaos unexpected change can wield.

If COVID-19 has not taught us anything, it has made us understand that it is prudent to plan for the unexpected. Premature death or incapacitation is a real business risk that may necessitate an abrupt passage to successors who might be positioned to take on immediate leadership responsibilities.

Business continuation plans are not designed to substitute for a succession plan. Still, they can be an essential lifeline that offers the team immediate support, interim leadership assignments, and most of all, time to sort out how to move forward from the loss (Monday 2020).

6.14 Owner Centric Organizations—A Common Succession Challenge

Pro Tip: If the most critical information, relationships, decision points, and expertise in your company lie with you, you are your company's greatest risk. Though this statement may sound harsh, it is true. An owner-centric approach is a critical business vulnerability that founders must take head-on to develop a strong business continuation strategy. So, besides documenting the knowledge in your head, start transferring responsibilities and relationships now, no matter when you envision exiting the business. Not only does this practical strategy mitigate risk, but it also gives leadership the opportunity they need to develop the skills and organizational savvy they need to transition into leadership.

Your lawyer can assist you in executing a business continuation plan that is right for your business. Not only should the succession plan be socialized within the inner circle, but you should also work with your legal advisor to create a depth chart of leaders equipped to lead all or parts of the business while the ultimate successor gets up to speed.

The same is true of leveraging the limited durable power of attorney to delegate authority to named representatives for specified events, decisions, or periods. Business continuation plans often include standard provisions and legal documents, which are generally needed to enforce the emergency plan until a final approach is solidified (Meglathery 2001).

6.15 Business Continuation

Table 6.6 is a working checklist to assist you in gathering the essential elements of a business continuation plan.

The business continuity plan not only protects your company from unforeseen business disruption it is also an excellent springboard to developing your comprehensive succession plan. Through business continuity planning, your legal partner can assist you in exposing gaps in your legal succession strategy.

Once your legal partner has helped you finalize your business continuity plan as a short-term succession strategy, the in-depth process of formalizing a succession plan should begin. By this point, you should have a better grasp of the status of documentation, succession goals, and gaps so you are well positioned to start activating your formal succession plan.

6.16 Business Structure

As your company grows, so may your business structure needs. Business structure refers to how your company is legally organized and taxed. The most common business structures used by small and family-owned businesses are sole proprietorship, partnership, corporation, limited liability company, and an S corporation. Although these business structures are most common, they are not exhaustive. Several other legal business structures may better address your legal, risk, revenue, and taxation needs (Internal Revenue Service 2022). Your attorney might even recommend combining business structures to achieve specific succession goals.

Table 6.7 describes business structures most commonly used by small and family-owned businesses.

6.17 Business Ownership Model

If you are concerned that your successors may not be suited or mature enough to handle all elements of ownership responsibility, it is imperative

Table 6.6   Essential Elements of a Business Continuation Plan

	Notes
Directions: Use this table to consider whether you, as a business owner, have addressed the essential elements of a business continuation plan. Check (X) the box appearing in the left column below if you have addressed the issue. If you have not addressed the issue, take some notes in the right column about steps you should take to do so.	
☐ A description of the business and ownership structure	
☐ A schedule of ownership voting rights and designated proxies	
☐ A schedule of key leader's core authority and designated delegation of authority	
☐ Schedule on critical stakeholders and communication framework	
☐ Interim cashflow plan	
☐ Temporary management procedures	
☐ Communication and continuation strategy for key business relationships, external partners (i.e., lenders), and employees	
☐ Interim appointments	
☐ Voting instructions and emergency appointments to governing boards	
☐ Key terms and definitions	
☐ A description of the business and ownership structure	
☐ A schedule of ownership voting rights and designated proxies	
☐ A schedule of key leader's core authority and designated delegation of authority	
☐ Supporting legal documents and contracts	

Table 6.7 Common Small and Family-Owned Business Structures

Business Structure	Ownership Model	Liability	Taxation Pathways
Sole Proprietorship • A single-owner exercising complete control over a business. • The business has not been registered as a legal entity.	One person	Full personal liability	Personal tax Self-employment tax
Partnership • Occurs when two or more people own a business together. The business has not been registered as a legal entity.	2+	Full personal liability	Personal tax Self-employment tax
LP—Limited Partnership (state-specific requirements) • A legal entity, offering a general partner more ownership rights and control but full personal liability. Conversely, limited partners have fewer ownership rights and control and limited personal liability.	2+	General partner— Full personal liability Limited partner— Limited personal liability	General partner— Personal tax Self-employment tax Limited partner— Personal tax
LLP—Limited Liability Partnership (state-specific requirements) • A legal entity, offering partners certain protections from personal liability and allowing passthrough taxation.	2+	Partners likely not personally liable	Personal or Corporate Tax Self-employment Tax
C-Corporation • A legal entity; distinctly separate from owners in profits, taxation, and liability. • Offers the strongest protection from personal liability.	1+	Owners likely not personally liable	Corporate tax

(Continued)

Table 6.7 (Continued) Common Small and Family-Owned Business Structures

	Ownership Model	Liability	Taxation Pathways
S-Corporation • A legal entity, designed to avoid double taxation drawback of regular C-corporation (i.e., passthrough).	1+ but <100 US citizens	Owners likely not personally liable	Personal tax
LLC—Limited Liability Company (state-specific requirements) • A legal entity, offering certain protections from personal liability and allowing passthrough taxation.	1+	Owners likely not personally liable	Personal or corporate tax Self-employment tax
Nonprofit Corporation • A legal entity distinctly separate from owners in profit and liability. • Must be organized to do charity, education, religious, literary, or scientific work. • Tax-exempt, but profit distribution may be restricted. Business structure is separate from 501(c)(3) tax designation.	1+	Owners likely not personally liable	Tax-exempt Profit distributions restricted
Benefit Corporation ("B-Corp") (state-specific requirements) • Legal entity recognized by many US states. B-corps are mission and purpose forward but also profit-driven. • Verified social and sustainability standards.	1+	Owners likely not personally liable	Corporate tax

(Continued)

Table 6.7 (Continued)   Common Small and Family-Owned Business Structures

	Ownership Model	Liability	Taxation Pathways
Close Corporation (state-specific requirements) • Like B-corps but may require fewer business formalities and are often closely held and with a smaller group of shareholders.	1+ Max varies by state	Owners likely not personally liable	Corporate tax
Cooperative • Business or organization owned and operated for the benefit of its members or user-owners.	2+	Owners likely not personally liable	Corporate tax *Co-op deductions

Source: US Small Business Administration 2022.

that you create a succession plan that incorporates successors' strengths and protects the business from their vulnerabilities.

Your company's business ownership model refers to the strategies you use to establish ownership, voting, and decision-making rights, as well as the oversight or governance structures you employ to ensure that the company runs as planned (Monday 2020).

Just as companies grow out of physical space and scale business operations for growth, determining the right business structure and ownership model for the company's future is a wise succession strategy.

Founding owners are almost always owner-operators in the beginning. Even partnerships tend to start with an owner-operator model, where the founders both own and manage the business day to day. In most cases, this is a logical start to managing and building a new business. However, as founding owners envision their company's legacy, they may not always consider that the more people a company has with ownership interest, the more difficult it can become to appoint a single decision-maker that can lead the company (KPMG International 2020).

Recall the earlier example of Jason and Amalia of Sunshine Heating and Air. Their successors, Gabriela, A'Niyah, Robert, and Devin, had varied interests and motivations in the future of the family business. In fact, Jason and Amalia, who are founding members of the company, shared different interests and motivations for the future of the business. Recall, Amalia's primary goals were to keep the business in the family and keep the peace by minimizing family drama. On the other hand, Jason wants to ensure that the company's legacy is preserved for the benefit of the children and that when he exits, there is a gradual succession strategy that makes sure that future leaders are prepared to lead. There is value in Jason and Amalia's perspective, and their legal team will consider all these factors as they determine how to achieve varied succession goals.

As you recall, A'Niyah is the owner of Beautique, Inc., a successful wellness and self-care empire. She has no interest in working in the family business and instead is focused on preserving economic interest for her children. Notably, in family-owned businesses, family drama can ensue as second and third generations inherit ownership in the family business, but not all commit to the day-to-day work of the family business (Baron and Lachenauer 2016).

Based on the evolving needs of successors and the changing complexity of the business, it becomes clear why the business structure and business model may need to evolve over the years. Your legal partner can assist you in finding a business structure that is right for the next generation of business leaders.

Table 6.8 describes the common small and family-owned ownership models incorporated in common legal succession strategies to ensure the business reflects the interests and skill sets of successors and key stakeholders.

6.18 Owner-Operator Model

Where the number of heirs is small, and all parties will work equally in the business, partnership as owner-operators is a suitable ownership model. This approach ensures equitable distribution of the responsibilities and rewards associated with the company (Lachenauer 2021).

6.19 Distributed Ownership Model

As successors increase and some take up the family business while others pursue alternative fields of endeavor, the partnership approach can become tricky, if not risky. Using the distributed family ownership model, all heirs are vested with equitable ownership in the business and some level of decision-making authority. Those who work within the business are compensated separately for their roles as business employees.

6.20 Public Ownership Model

Profitable companies might also consider the public model. A family business behaves like a public company vesting shares to be traded publicly or distributed to employees. The controlling percentage is distributed among the family. This model decentralizes power and often vests day-to-day management to a CEO or other operational leader. As in the distributed ownership model, family members who work in the business are compensated for their professional role within the company, separate from their ownership interests (Lachenauer 2021).

Regardless of the model you choose, your attorney will guide you to the right decision and help you execute the legal documents and business filings required to achieve the desired outcomes. Once the structure is established, your legal partner may even work with you to determine what additional

Table 6.8   Common Small and Family-Owned Business Ownership Models

Business Model	Most Effective When …	Pros	Cons
Owner-Operator Ownership Model	• Small number of successors. • All successors work equally in the business.	Equal distribution of ownership and responsibility.	One or more successors may not be equal contributors. This can create resentment in successors who carry the heavier load of responsibility.
Distributed Family Ownership Model	• Larger number of successors. • Varied levels of engagement in the day-to-day management of the business	• Successors working in the business earn compensation for their work. • Ownership and decision rights are distributed equitably.	• Without additional governance, certain successors may question compensation decisions. • Can create family drama as successors compete for the most attractive internal roles.
Public Ownership Model	• Larger, more profitable business. • Large numbers/multigenerational successors. • Varied levels of engagement in the day-to-day management of the business.	• Successors collectively has a controlling interest in the business. • Decentralized decision-making. • May incorporate executive leaders who are external to the founding lineage. • Successors working in the business earn compensation for their work.	• Successors must be in alignment to effectively leverage their controlling interests. • Leadership is more likely not to be a generational successor.

expertise you will need to ensure that you revise your accounting, risk/compliance, communications, and human resources strategies to align with the new business structure.

6.21 Oversight—Ownership Rights and Responsibilities

Though we often use the term "ownership" broadly to refer to the persons who possess or control a business, this definition is misleading in succession planning. Upon closer inspection, the term "ownership" includes possession but may not necessarily indicate other controlling rights and responsibilities.

- Voting Rights, that is, having a vote in significant business decisions.
- Board Authority, that is, holding a seat on the governing board.
- Executive Management Authority, that is, established as a day-to-day decision-maker.
- Economic Interests, that is, being entitled to a share of the worth and profits of the business.

Founding owners of small or family-owned businesses rarely create clear guardrails or define ownership roles in the way we have explained above. In first-generation companies, the responsibilities are often so interdependent that they can be virtually indistinguishable. Key stakeholders work together and do whatever needs to be done to keep the business, often without regard to their economic interests or area of expertise (Monday 2020).

But just as organizations grow and build out departments to focus on specific strategic goals, successors' roles within the business should be tailored to their interests and strategic skillsets. As each generation of successors is added to the organizational footprint, it becomes necessary to establish guardrails and create a structure that clarifies the key players and their role in the business (Ballini 2020).

6.22 Voting Rights

Formal voting rights are most often established in the second generation and beyond and generally are used to give successors a voice in decisions that make core changes to the business. Voting rights are rarely utilized to vest day-to-day decision rights in successors. They may be best established when successors do not wish to have daily involvement in the business but rightfully have a say in decisions that may affect their economic interests.

6.23 Governing Boards

Governing boards come in many forms but are most established as compliance, insider, inner circle, or quasi-independent boards in small and family-owned businesses. The focus of governing boards is not to engage in day-to-day management activities. Instead, governing boards offer oversight (that is, compliance and fiscal accountability) and advise the business as owners retain decision-making authority (Cloyd 2014).

Table 6.9 describes common governing board structures used in small and family businesses. Governing boards ensure greater transparency and establish accountability as companies grow in scope and complexity.

6.24 Executive Management

In first-generation businesses, the founders almost always hold executive management authority. However, as the business grows in scope and complexity, it may become necessary to vest day-to-day decision-making authority in others based on their function, interests, and expertise. Officers and executives develop the overall vision and strategy for managing the daily needs of the business and may include a mix of successors, closely trusted leaders, and other experts. The governing board often assists owners in selecting officers and executives and may work to hold them accountable.

6.25 Reaffirming the Importance of Each Role—A Common Succession Challenge

Pro Tip: Successors who are not selected for the future role they envision may become disappointed or angry by your succession decisions. Still, disappointment need not lead to disillusionment or disengagement. Founders must be transparent and realistic with successors about the executive management role they see them filling. Successors' interests and skillsets are not created equally, so founders must work with their attorney and human

Table 6.9 Common Governing Boards in Small and Family-Owned Businesses

Type	Function	Focus
Compliance Board	• Often a first-generation approach to governance. • Required as a condition of formation in most states. • Often start with a single member (the founder). • Board might comprise other family members or industry experts as business grows.	• To ensure that governance is prioritized. • Board does not make day-to-day business decisions. • Owners retain decision-making authority.
Insider Board	• Often a later first-generation approach and beyond. • Commonly found in family-owned businesses. • Usually include family members and members of senior management.	• To offer guidance on governance and day-to-day management. • Board provides mentorship and acts as a sounding board for owners. • Owners retain decision-making authority.
Inner Circle Board	• Often a second-generation approach and beyond. • Generally comprised of the close confidants and experts of founding members. • Commonly include legal, financial, and human resources partners.	• Board is advisory in nature. • May take a more formal approach and closer oversight of the company's practices. • May include CEO that is not an owner. • Owners retain decision-making authority.
Quasi-independent Board	• Often second-generation and beyond. • Found in more profitable or well-established companies. • Include external board members who have no interest in business outside of the board seat.	• To approach governance from an objective and structured approach. • Focus on fiscal and compliance accountability. • May include governance sub-committees. • Recommendations of the board not taken lightly. • May include CEO that is not an owner. • Owners retain decision-making authority.

Invalid source specified.

resources experts to establish expectations for successors who hope to step into key executive management roles. Just as a large company would not hire a computer scientist expecting them to be a marketing and communications guru, founders should not expect that their successors are naturally prepared or inclined to step into senior leadership. Through conversations, formal training, and apprenticeship, founders should work with their trusted advisors to determine if their successors are the right leaders for the company. It may feel challenging to converse with your successors, but the sooner you breach this subject, the better. It gives everyone involved time to process the plan, ask questions, and respond by either moving forward or moving on.

6.26 Economic Interests

Economic interest is simply the equity or percentage of ownership each person has in a small or family-owned business. Financial interest does not translate to control, but it generally vests owners with voting rights to weigh in on significant business decisions. Where there is passive ownership or a successor that wants nothing to do with business matters, voting rights can be delegated to another party. This is called a proxy and gives another person the ability to step into an owner's shoes for voting.

Founding members may want to ensure that a single family member has a controlling interest in the business to reduce the risk of evenly dividing the company among family members who may not be ready, willing, or able to step into leadership. A best-in-class approach to succession planning includes working with your legal advisor to establish a nucleus of control with additional oversight and checks and balances.

Checks and balances could consist of creating a pathway for heirs who opt out of management to sell their interest to a family member vested in the day to day of business. This can be effectuated through a shareholder or owning interest agreement which establishes the process for selling an ownership interest in the company, including guidance that covers the first right of refusal and the triggers for forced sale.

Oversight might also include exploring boards' role in advising leadership, establishing governance, and offering objective insight on critical business decisions. Whatever the path forward may be, prudent founders work with legal partners to ensure those leadership roles are defined, and heirs are clear on their role in managing the affairs of the business.

6.27 Confronting Reality—A Common Succession Challenge

Pro Tip: Founders should not assume that their successors wish to stay in the family business. While these conversations might be difficult and even emotional, they are worth having early and often if the succession plan will be a practical roadmap into the future. Similarly, founders should be clear about how disinterested successors will earn from the business and build these guardrails into the formal succession plan.

6.28 Transfer of Assets and Control

There are four ways to transfer your business to a successor. Like all facets of succession planning, transferring assets and control is not a "one size fits all" approach, but the size and complexity of your organization often guides the final decision. We will explore each transfer strategy and discuss where each strategy is most commonly applied. As we explore the pros and cons of each approach, you will be introduced to some essential legal documents that will likely be incorporated into your succession plan.

6.29 Passing Ownership Interest to Heirs—A Singular Event

The most common and straightforward way to transfer a small or family-owned business is passing the interest in the company to family members or a single heir upon retirement or death. A survey conducted in 2020 by Family Enterprise USA suggests that as much as 84% of small or family businesses are passed to successors as a gift, with 65% of these gifts manifesting as a partial ownership arrangement (Family Enterprise USA).

At first, glance, passing a business to family members seems like a reasonably simple methodology for ensuring that the company stays in the family. Many owners are attracted to the approach because it is often the least expensive and noisy way to transfer ownership interest to heirs. Unfortunately, owners who take this approach can limit their ability to steer their company's legacy beyond their time at the helm of leadership (KPMG International 2020).

But if done properly, the process is not as simple to effectuate as it appears. The passing down of your company requires proper planning and timely communication to avoid the risk of family drama. Like any major family decision, establishing who will steer your company after your exit can cause an array of positive and negative emotions.

If you intend to pass your ownership interest and management authority upon your death, this can be accomplished through your personal will or trust. Depending on the complexity of your business, your legal advisor may draft additional legal documents to ensure that your final wishes are effectuated. Vesting ownership can be effectuated as a gift or sale and is not synonymous with preparing for the disruption that your passing will leave if your successors are not prepared to lead the business (Monday, A Blueprint for Family Business Succession Planning 2018).

In addition, you may leave the assets of your family business to your heir while trusting the leadership responsibilities to one or more additional stakeholders. Your leadership team and legal advisors should objectively assess who should inherit business assets and who will lead the day-to-day operations of the business. You will also need to decide if and how your heirs will compensate you once ownership has passed to them. Determining how you will be paid once you pass the company on is especially important if you plan to pass the business on before your death.

Once critical decisions are made, there needs to be a clear and concise direction as to who will take over the business, who will retain ownership but not leadership, and how business leaders will be compensated for their work. Most important, key leaders must communicate the plan to all stakeholders and work to prepare named successors for leadership positions sooner than later. The transition of leadership should not come as a surprise to anyone involved.

6.30 Taking an Incremental Approach—A Common Succession Challenge

Pro Tip: Passing the business to family members without a transition period can be catastrophic. This is particularly true when a business does not have well-documented standards of practice, policies, and procedures. In addition, the complete and immediate transition of power to family members is especially risky if they have not spent considerable time working in the business.

Established leadership can mitigate the risks, but only if the successor keeps leaders in place.

This is where it is prudent to work with your attorney and human resources expert to establish a talent succession plan. This plan should provide business leaders with clear requirements and growth and development milestones they will need to meet or exceed to step into executive leadership. The sooner this plan is drafted and communicated, the better. It not only gives successors a clear path forward but also paves the way for one or more successors to step up and demonstrate that they have what it takes to take the helm of leadership. Similarly, a structured talent succession plan should create opportunities for successors to lead various business areas, develop client relationships, and assess if working inside the business is sustainable and, if so, at what level.

6.31 Passing Ownership Interest to Heirs—A Phased Approach

A similar but more thoughtful approach to business succession is the gradual transfer of operational control from founders to heirs of the business and the gradual divestment of the ownership interest. This approach leverages gradual change of power by establishing a transition timeline that offers the owners the space and time to mentor the next generation of leaders. This approach also gives the potential successor a chance to learn critical aspects of the business, develop strategic business relationships, and become immersed in the organizational culture before taking the helm of leadership.

6.32 Transferring Assets

The mechanics of a gradual transfer can be effectuated through a sale or gift or a combination of the two. Where successors' financial resources are limited, or liquidity is an issue, phased change of control coupled with profit-sharing can be a great way to transition ownership and decision authority. Your legal and financial experts will assist you in structuring a profit-sharing arrangement that aligns with the cash flow of your business and fairly compensates you along the way (Monday, A Blueprint for Family Business Succession Planning 2018).

6.33 Change of Control

The gradual change of control is perhaps the most challenging component of the phased transition succession strategy. By ramping down over time, founders face the most vicious variables of all time. Over a defined transition period, the business can change a lot. Profit and loss may fluctuate wildly, key stakeholders may exit the business, or unlikely talent may emerge. Commonly, your vision for your company's future and your exit strategy or timeline may change (Lachenauer 2021).

A solid legal partner can work with you to anticipate business volatility and structure your succession plan to withstand it. They can also assist you with drafting a succession plan that provides precise requirements for named successors, contingency plans for unexpected exits or departures, and a framework for making substantive changes to the succession plan. By anticipating that change will occur and including checks and balances that invite other perspectives to the table for consideration, founders can ensure that their exit strategy and vision remain relevant and timely as they gradually step away from the business.

An incremental buyout over a predetermined period is among the most common ways founders realize the value of the business. Often founders continue to earn income from the company well beyond retirement (Monday, A Blueprint for Family Business Succession Planning 2018).

The succession plan should articulate delegation of authority and transition of power. In addition, limited durable power of attorney can establish clear triggers for vesting power with successors and clarify decision-making authority these future leaders will have and when.

6.34 Timing the Exit Strategy—A Common Succession Challenge

Pro Tip: It is worth noting that founders who leverage the phased transition strategy will need to practice self-awareness and check their ego as they gradually step away from the business. It can often be difficult for owners to relinquish control, but drawing the transition out for an unreasonable time period can be as detrimental to the business as having no succession plan.

A KPMG study of over 1,800 small and family-owned businesses indicated that despite having a succession plan in place, over 50% of family business leaders did not have a formal retirement plan in place, making the path uncertain for their potential successors and the future of the family business (KPMG International 2020).

The succession dilemma of Walsh Bros. Office Equipment in Phoenix is a textbook example of how failure to yield to the next generation of business can cause unintended consequences (Dahl 2011).

Pete Walsh was made for the family business and grew up in it, rising steadily through the ranks of leadership and earning a VP title by the age of 36. In his time at Walsh Office Equipment, Pete had spearheaded key innovation and been given the autonomy to run one of the most important divisions. Pete was a named successor to the top position, and after spending what felt like his entire life in the business, he was ready to take the helm of leadership as he approached his forties (Dahl 2011).

The problem was that Pete's uncle, then 55, had been the CEO for over 30 years and was not ready to step down. His uncle projected an additional decade or two in leadership before he would be prepared to retire (Dahl 2011).

After spending several more years in what Pete aptly described as the waiting room from hell, Pete left Walsh and started his own consulting business (Walsh 2012).

His decision surprised family and those inside the business, leaving a wake of business disruption and mixed family emotions. Ultimately, Walsh Office Equipment lost its heir apparent, and in 2009 Pete's uncle sold the business to an external stakeholder. Pete's Peak Performance Coaching has seen more than a decade of success, but in hindsight, you can't help but wonder whether Pete's uncle held on too long or Pete gave up too quickly. Either way, the family business did not pass on to the next generation (Walsh 2012).

6.35 Selling To External Buyers—Inner Circle—Management or Employees

As small and family-owned businesses mature, founding employees and leaders can become like family. Similarly, these members of the inner circle are often well suited to step into leadership or assume ownership interest in a company when owners exit.

Selling to members of the inner circle involves many of the same legal preparation selling within the family. Still, other legal strategies are employed when effectuating a full or partial sale to members of the inner circle.

A common practice that is more profitable for small and family businesses is issuing employee stock option plans. Employees earn shares as part of the compensation plan through employee stock programs. Thus, employees are invested in the company's success as minority owners. Over time, the owner's controlling interest is reduced, vesting ownership in those responsible for the day-to-day execution of business goals (Monday 2020).

Owners may also effectuate a sale using a shareholder or purchase and sale agreement if they plan to sell interest in the business during a single event. The purchase agreement should contain all the terms and conditions of the sale.

Owners may also ensure that successors in the inner circle have support and a transition period by requiring that they agree to a service agreement, where the buyer contracts the consultancy services of the seller for a defined time after the sale. In addition, prudent sellers who stay on in an advisory capacity should ensure to work with legal partners to document indemnity protections. These clauses ensure that former owners and key leaders are defended against and held harmless from the consequences of legitimate actions they took during their time in the business. These clauses also ensure former owners are not held liable for decisions made after they exited the company (Monday 2020).

Prospective buyers should work with independent legal partners to perform due diligence when deciding whether to invest in ownership in any business, and businesses they have worked in are no exception. Nothing disrupts the family environment or inner circle more than a new owner feeling as if their trusted partner or beloved employer misled them in the valuation or overall health of the business they have purchased.

6.36 Selling To External Parties—Independent Buyers

Small and family-owned businesses may face the decision of looking outside of their family or community of trust to source a buyer for their interest in the company. The sale of a company to an independent and unaffiliated buyer can be far more complex than the succession strategies we have discussed.

Table 6.10 describes common legal documents that external parties will want to review to consider whether your business is the right investment.

Unlike passing ownership interest to family or members of your inner circle, selling to an independent buyer is a more objective transaction.

Table 6.10 Common Legal Documents—Selling to External Parties

	Notes
Directions: Use this table to consider whether you, as a business owner, have the common legal documents needed to sell to external parties. Check the box at left (X) if you have the documents. Leave the box blank if you do not have the document and make notes in the right column about the steps you will need to take with competent legal counsel to secure those documents.	
☐ Articles of Incorporation	
☐ Service Contracts	
☐ P & L Statements/Tax statements	
☐ Employment Contracts	
☐ General Ledgers	
☐ Trademarks, Copyrights, Patents	
☐ Mortgages, Leases, Deeds	
☐ Active litigation	
☐ Investor relations	
☐ Inventory	
☐ Standards of Practice (policies and procedures)	
☐ Safety Logs/Emergency management	
☐ Insurance documents	
☐ Licensure and permits	
☐ Succession Plans	

Similarly, the level of control or influence a former owner may have once the sale is complete is likely to be limited to the purchase agreement.

Besides effectuating the sale documents, prospective buyers will likely require due diligence, which means reviewing every facet of the business to access the status of corporate governance, financials, people operations, and business strategies. Prospective buyers will get in the weeds on the inner workings of your business when determining if your business is a good investment. A great starting point would be to ensure that corporate documents are intact and up to date (Monday 2020).

6.37 Preserving Company Culture—A Common Succession Challenge

Pro Tip: Even when selling to an independent buyer, owners have the power to preserve key elements of the company culture they have created. By leveraging legal strategies such as legal covenants, and other controls, founders can ensure that core cultural attributes remain hardwired in the organizational footprint post-sale (Cancialosi 2017).

Zappos is a perfect example of the power of company culture and the lengths leaders go to maintain the traits that distinguish a business from its competitors (Cancialosi 2017). Former CEO Tony Hsieh felt so strongly about the organizational culture as a tenet of success that he disrupted the status quo in skillfully negotiating to be an independent operator as a condition of Zappos acquisition by retail behemoth Amazon (Askin 2016).

Zappos saw tremendous success and made Amazon even more profitable by engraining the Zappos culture in every facet of the business (preacquisition and post-sale) (Askin 2016). Though Tony stepped down as CEO in 2020 and passed that same year, his bold commitment to preserving the cultural heritage of Zappos is likely to endure (Cancialosi 2017).

6.38 Lacking Documentation—A Common Succession Challenge

Pro Tip: Just get started. Utilize the checklists in this chapter to determine what you have compiled to this point. As you list each document, categorize it as complete or incomplete. Also, note what is current and what may need revision. Each phase of succession planning allows you to formalize your plan by developing or revising documents. By the time your formal succession plan is in place, you will have a much better handle on documentation.

A strong succession plan contemplates who will be best served in each function and establishes criteria for who should do what. In the graphical depiction of Sunshine's future state, we see how each successors' responsibility within the company varies. This hypothetical succession matrix resembles a typical small or family-owned business second-generation scenario. Notice that not every successor has the same rights and responsibilities.

Table 6.11 depicts a typical succession strategy based on the Sunshine Heating and Air–Scenario.

Table 6.11 Sunshine Heating and Air—Succession Strategy

Name	Role	Current Economic Interests	Future Economic Interests	Current Voting Rights	Future Voting Rights	Current Board Insider	Future Board Inner Circle	Current Day-to-Day Mgmt.	Future Day-to-Day Mgmt.	Current Earns Salary	Future Earns Salary
Jason	Founder	49%		X			X	X COO		X	X 5 yrs. post transition
Amalia	Founder	51%		X		X	X	X CEO/Bus. Dev.	X Fractional CEO/Bus. Dev.	X	X Fractional and 3 yrs. post transition
Evans Family Trust	Founders' Trustee		26%		Proxy to Trustee		X				
Gabriela	Successor		21%		X			X Finance	X CFO	X	X
A'Niyah	Successor		20%		Proxy to Trustee						
Robert	Successor		20%		X			X Bus. Dev/ Operations	X Fractional COO In-waiting	X	X
Devin	Trusted Employee		10%			X		X Bus. Dev/ Operations	X Fractional CEO In-waiting	X	X
Vacant	External HR Leadership								X VP Human Resources		
Sylvester	Family Attorney					X	X				
Gail	Accountant					X	X				
David	Trustee				X						

As we look at the succession strategy for Sunshine as depicted in the diagram above, we see that many of the critical stakeholders' subjective interests were incorporated into the final succession plan. Jason and Amalia have a target retirement date and can begin operationalizing their succession strategy. They have chosen a phased approach to transition ownership and executive management responsibilities. The succession plan will include a hybrid ownership structure. The family will continue to be the majority owner of the business. Devin, a loyal and long-tenured employee, will be offered the opportunity to purchase a minority interest.

To ensure their vision for the legacy of Sunshine Heating and Air they have created a family trust that will own a controlling share of the business. The trust not only works to ensure that the collective voice of the family is represented when voting on significant business matters, but it also allows Jason and Amalia to step out of business at a defined time and empower successors to step up into leadership.

By yielding their individual voting rights to a family trust, they pave the way for the next generation of Sunshine leadership to shape many elements of the future of the business. In addition, Jason and Amalia will retain seats on the inner circle board of directors, which will enable them to influence critical areas of oversight such as business strategy, risk management, crisis management, capital expenditures, and executive accountability.

Gabriela will undertake specific development efforts to step up as the chief financial officer over the next three to five years. As the succession plan states, the board can vet external talent to fill the position should she fail to meet development milestones.

Jason and Amalia must do the difficult work of explaining to Robert why he is not slated to step into the CEO position upon Amalia's retirement. Despite Robert's value to Sunshine, Jason and Amalia have determined that Robert is not ready for the position. Another consideration is the impact of having a man at the helm of leadership at Sunshine. The company has been designated as a Women-Owned Small Business and must continue to be majority-owned (51%) and run to maintain the designation. The change could affect the overall business strategy.

While this decision likely will not be popular with Robert, he will be invited to undertake specific development efforts to step into the chief operations officer role. Based on his current experience, he is well-positioned to grow into the position within the next three to five years. However, as the succession plan states, the board may vet external talent to fill the position should he fail to meet development milestones.

Devin is best positioned to serve as CEO upon Amalia's retirement, considering Gabriela's disinterest in the role. Devin has extensive experience in business development and operations. She has demonstrated loyalty to the company and will be rewarded with an offer to purchase a minority ownership stake in the business. Devin is the right choice and aligns with Sunshine's diversity strategy. In addition, she will be slated to begin development efforts to be ready to become Sunshine's next CEO. As the succession plan states, the board can vet external talent to fill the position should she fail to meet development milestones.

A'Niyah will remain free from the day-to-day responsibility of managing Sunshine Heating and Air. Still, her economic interest in the company is key to maintaining the women-owned business designation. A'Niyah has her hands full with Beautique, Inc. She has proxied her voting interests to Gabriela, whom A'Niyah trusts to make sound decisions for the business. Unlike her siblings, who are working in the business, A'Niyah, is ineligible to receive a salary from the business. Her economic interests will be limited to equity and any shareholder earnings she is eligible to receive.

Under the guidance of their attorney, Jason and Amalia have developed a triad executive leadership model that vests the chief executive officer, chief financial officer, and chief business development officer with equitable weight in making executive management decisions. They will also build out a people and culture position to provide internal human resources expertise to the leadership team. This framework balances executive management power and responsibility. While this legal guardrail may not appease Robert, it is a thoughtful response to his career aspirations and subjective interests of Sunshine.

Jason and Amalia will continue to rely on their team of trusted advisors to serve as board members.

They feel good about the succession plan based on the state of the business today. The founders have charged the board of directors with committing to reviewing the succession strategy and updating the plan every two years to ensure it remains relevant. They have also committed to working with their attorney to develop comprehensive communication and talent development plan leveraging industry experts recommended by their attorney. Jason and Amalia began the journey to succession planning feeling overwhelmed but understand the importance of legal counsel in answering some of the biggest questions they had about the process. They will partner with their attorney to execute the legal documents and develop controls necessary to bring the succession plan to life.

6.39 How Will I Know When I Have a Sound Succession Plan?

"However beautiful the strategy, you should occasionally look at the results."

—Sir Winston Churchill

Business owners do not fully ever know if their succession plan covers every possible risk scenario. For example, before March 2020, the business community had little insight on a succession strategy that included a global pandemic. With that in mind, working with an attorney to anticipate common issues in business is a great start. In addition, committing to flexibility and cyclical review of your plan is the best strategy to ensure that your plan remains relevant and responsive to ever-changing business needs.

A sound succession plan requires a multidisciplinary partnership with business owners, legal, human resources, and financial expertise. A successful legal succession strategy assists the owners with:

■ Assessing the reality of the business and establishing the legal infrastructure that positions the company to grow.
■ Documenting owners' vision for the company's future and establishing a legal plan for how owners divest their ownership and authority upon their exit or death.
■ Establishing checks and balances that ensure that owners, the company, and potential successors have the benefit of business expertise and governance to support the decisions they make.
■ Engaging in personal estate planning that mirrors the company succession plan, as appropriate.
■ Reviewing business and personal risk and creating mitigation plans that empower the company to withstand business disruption without facing destabilization.

6.40 Interplay between Personal Estate Planning and Business Succession— A Common Succession Dilemma

Pro Tip: If you have done the work to solidify your vision for the business, but have not stopped to consider how your personal goals and finances will affect the business succession plan, you have got more work to do.

While we will not spend time exploring this in Chapter 6, you'll need to work with your legal team to engage in personal estate planning. As the Scholastic succession dilemma teaches us, poor private estate planning can destabilize key stakeholders in a small or family-owned business, causing the family drama to spill into business matters. When loved ones are not adequately cared for or communicated with when key leaders pass, it almost always affects how they approach established succession plans within the business. Poor private estate planning sets the stage for in-fighting and legal challenges that diminish the business brand and jeopardize the future of the business.

As you consider our example of Jason and Amalia, you will notice they worked with their attorney to create a family trust with their economic interest in the business upon retirement. While this approach is demonstrative, it is a great example of the interplay between business succession planning and personal estate planning. The two go hand in hand, and one is rarely effective without the existence of the other.

Table 6.12 offers key considerations for creating a personal estate plan that compliments your business succession plan.

6.41 Chapter Summary

This chapter addresses common legal questions about small and family business succession planning and offers practical solutions that assist decision makers in finding answers for their organization. This chapter was not written to supply you with answers. Instead, it arms you with a practical framework for deciding the path forward to reach your succession goals.

This chapter is not intended to be a comprehensive legal guide. The topics discussed in this chapter fill a book alone. Instead, Chapter 6 offers a roadmap for common legal strategies and considerations that will guide you toward the appropriate legal partnerships, planning, and documents you will need to create to establish the business legacy you have envisioned.

While your legal partner and strategy are essential, these tools are not enough to yield a strong succession plan. The process is not expedient. Despite a roadmap, there will be detours, road closures, and potholes along the journey. Success in succession will require owners to modify, revise, re-route and improve their initial plans. The conversations you must initiate will

Table 6.12 Personal Estate Planning Checklist

Directions: Use this Table to consider whether you, as a business owner, have addressed the essential elements of a personal estate plan. Check (X) the box appearing in the left column below if you have addressed the issue. If you have not addressed the issue, leave the box at left unchecked and take some notes in the right column about steps you should take to address that issue.

	Notes
☐ Schedule of Heirs	
☐ Balance Sheet with schedule of itemized debts	
☐ Schedule of Assets with vendor, account representative contact, and named beneficiary	
☐ Retirement Accounts/IRA	
☐ Health Savings Accounts	
☐ Checking/Savings Accounts	
☐ Schedule of Life and Accidental Insurance	
☐ Schedule of Disease/Disability Insurance	
☐ Properly Executed Will	
☐ Codicil which includes your beneficiary designations (i.e., jewelry, family heirlooms, etc.)	
☐ Limited Durable Power of Attorney (financial and other)	
☐ Living Will	
☐ Advanced Health Care Directives with Resuscitation Directives	
☐ Trust Accounts	
☐ Lifetime Gifts and Charitable Contributions	
☐ Specific End-of-Life Instructions	
☐ Burial Instructions/Funeral Arrangements	
☐ Designated Resting Place (burial place/ headstone)	
☐ Misc. End of Life Wishes/Instructions	
☐ Specific Instructions for Minor Children	

be difficult and emotionally charged, but as Jack Welch once stated, "Good business leaders create a vision, articulate the vision, passionately own the vision, and relentlessly drive it; to completion." Your relentless pursuit of legacy and your commitment to establishing a transition to secure your life's work will make this journey worth the ride.

Works Cited

Askin, N., G. Petriglieri, & J. Lockard. 2016. *Tony Hsieh at Zappos: Structure, Culture and Radical Change. INSEAD Case Study.* Cambridge, MA: Harvard Business Review Publishing.

Ballini, Beatrice. 2020. "Every Family Business Needs an Independent Director." *Harvard Business Review*, January 27.

Baron, Josh and Rob, Lachenauer. 2016. *The 5 Models of Family Business Ownership.* Cambridge, MA, September 20.

Baron, Josh and Rob, Lachenauer. 2021. "Do Most Family Businesses Really Fail by the Third Generation?" *Harvard Business Review*, July 19.

Cancialosi, Chris. 2017. "Preserving A Culture People Love As Your Company Grows: Lessons from Zappos." *Forbes*, May 30.

Cloyd, Mary Ann. 2014. *What Is a Board's Role in a Family Business?* July 30 https://corpgov.law.harvard.edu/2014/07/30/what-is-a-boards-role-in-a-family -business/.

Dahl, Darren. 2011. "Succession Stories: The Good, the Bad, and the Ugly." *Inc.*, March 29. https://www.inc.com/articles/201103/succession-stories-keeping-the -business-in-the-family.html

Daniel J. and Edelman Holdings, Inc. 2020. "2020 Trust Barometer Survey." January 19.

Harris, Katherine Rosman and Harris, Elizabeth A. 2021. "The Real-Life Succession Drama At Scholastic." *The New York Times*, October 25: 1.

Internal Revenue Service. 2022. *Business Structures.* January 19. Accessed February 3, 2022. https://www.irs.gov/businesses/small-businesses-self-employed/busi- ness-structures

KPMG International. 2020. *The Courage to Choose Wisely: Why the Succession Decision May be a Defining Moment in Your Family Business.* Survey, KPMG.

Meglathery, Sally. 2001. "Overview of Business Continuity Planning." In Business Continuity Planning: Protecting Your Organization's Life, by Ken Doughty, 79–96. Boca Raton: CRC Press LLC.

Monday, Gregory F. 2018. "A Blueprint for Family Business Succession Planning." *American Bar Association.* American Bar Association - Business Law Section.

Monday, Gregory. 2020. The Lawyer's Guide to Family Business Succession Planning. Chicago: American Bar Association Book Publishing.

Ramachandran, Shalini and Jeffrey A. Trachtenberg. 2021. "Succession Drama Rattles Scholastic." *The Wall Street Journal*, August 2.

"Samuel Curtis Johnson Graduate School of Management - Cornell University." 2022. *Family Business Facts*. Accessed January 3, 2022. https://www.forbes .com/colleges/cornell-university/samuel-curtis-johnson-graduate-school-of-man-agement/?sh=46742ff28352 johnson.cornell.edu/smith-family-business-initiative -at-cornell/resources/family-business-facts/

Small Business and Entreprenuership Council. 2018. "Facts & Data on Small Business and Entrepreneurship." Accessed September 17, 2021. https://sbecoun-cil.org/about-us/facts-and-data/.

Thienel, Steve. 2020. *Death & Business in 2020: Succession Planning Tips for Small Business Owners*. June 19. Accessed October 29, 2021. https://www.thienel-law .com/blog/2020/6/19/death-business-in-2020-succession-planning-tips-for-small -business-owner

US Small Business Administration. 2022. *Choose a Business Structure*. Accessed February 1, 2022. https://www.sba.gov/business-guide/launch-your-business/ choose-business-structure

Walsh, Pete. 2012. *Peak Workout Business Coaching: Waiting Room Hell: Family Business Succession*. Accessed April 19, 2021. https://peakcoach.com/2012/04/ waiting-room-hell-family-business-succession/

Will Rogers Memorial Museum. 2016. "Learn About Will." *Will Rogers Memorial Museum and Birthplace Ranch*. Accessed January 17, 2022. https://www.will-rogers.com/learn-about-will

Chapter 7

Valuing the Small and Family Business for Succession Planning

Kyle S. Meyer

Contents

DOI: 10.4324/9781003281054-10

7.1 Introduction

Many years ago, the author was involved in the buyout of certain members of a family business. The transaction was between cousins in the third generation of the family and the negotiations were contentious. Both sides hired experts to help them value the business as a starting point for the negotiations. At the outset, the parties were far apart in their values for the business. The selling family members valued the business at approximately US$100 million, while the buying family members valued the business at approximately US$10 million. Helped by a skilled mediator, the parties finally agreed upon a value and the transaction closed (the agreed-upon value was closer to US$10 million).

The transaction described above represents one of the many scenarios encountered with succession planning. The concepts used to value the business in this negotiation are the same as those used for succession planning purposes in other scenarios. Whether transferring ownership interests is from parents to children or between siblings (and/or cousins), or the sale of all or a part of the business to third-party investors or employees, the valuation methods described in this chapter are applicable.

As you can see from the preceding example, two parties valuing the same business arrived at different valuations. The selling family members used aggressive cash flow projections and ignored some basic (and substantial) discounts typically applied to the valuation of small and family businesses. But the buying parties were much more conservative in their projections of future cash flows and aggressively applied discounts. The moral of the story is that business valuation is as much art as it is science. It is wise to engage a credentialed valuation professional when involved in valuing a small or family business in any context, but especially when involved in succession planning. Valuation professionals will assist in establishing a value for the business and will do battle with the IRS if they or some other party challenges the valuation.

This chapter aims to cover concepts used to value small and family businesses for succession planning purposes. In this chapter, we will discuss issues related to the valuation of small and family businesses in succession planning. We will cover the reasons valuations are needed, the most used approaches to valuations, and provide an example to illustrate the methods. It is imperative that the reader understand this chapter is not intended to provide tax or estate planning advice. Readers should seek tax professionals who specialize in this area of tax law to be sure that their questions are properly addressed.

7.2 Defining Terms

Here are terms we will be using throughout this chapter:

- **IRS**—The Internal Revenue Service, an agency of the federal government.
- **EBITDA**—Earnings Before Interest, Taxes, Depreciation, and Amortization. The computation of this is illustrated later in this chapter. EBITDA is used in certain valuation methods.
- **Revenue Ruling 59-60**—This is a document issued by the IRS in 1959. Despite its age, it is still considered the road map for valuing businesses.
- **Attest function**—Services provided by independent accountants to provide reliability for financial statements.
- **AICPA**—American Institute of Certified Public Accountants. This body, comprised of practitioners of all accounting services, guides the accounting profession in providing attest functions to small and family businesses.
- **Principle of alternatives**—Based on the assumption that buyers have alternate investments that provide comparable risks and returns.
- **Principle of substitution**—Based on the assumption that a potential buyer's other, similar investments provide a reasonable substitute for the asset (that is, the small or family business) that is being valued.
- **Principle of future benefits**—Based on the assumption that buyers are purchasing expected future benefits (that is, cash flows) of a business.
- **Fair market value**—estimated value of an asset (for example, a small or family business) that is based on the price that a willing buyer would pay to a willing seller if neither were under any pressure to consummate the transaction and both parties have sufficient knowledge and understanding of potential risks and rewards associated with the asset. This is the basis for most asset valuations.
- **Normalization adjustments**—Adjustments made to net income to compute what the business would generate in net income and EBITDA if certain family-related expenses were not incurred. Typically, these adjustments increase net income and EBITDA.

7.3 Why Business Valuations Are Important in Succession Planning

First, let's discuss why the valuation of small and family businesses relates to succession planning. When small and family enterprises face succession planning, they have several alternatives. Owners of small and family enterprises can transfer all or part of the ownership to subsequent generations either by gifting ownership interests or by selling their ownership interests to the next generation. Owners could also sell all or part of the business to a third party or to their employees. Regardless of how the transition is structured, the business must be valued properly. This chapter discusses some of the most common approaches to valuing small and family businesses.

The author once worked with a multigenerational family business. As the owners approached retirement, they assessed the ability and the desire of their children to take over the business. After much soul searching, they decided that it would be in the best interests of the family to sell the business outright to a third party. While their children had the desire to take over the business, they understood and supported the decision, and the owners enjoyed their retirement with no connections or worries related to their former business. When they marketed the business, they needed an asking price. The asking price was developed using the valuation methods discussed in this chapter.

Ideally, the transition of a small or family business to new ownership is handled in an orderly fashion via estate and gift planning. This planning is best handled assisted by professionals trained in gift and estate planning; it is not advisable for most owners to attempt this on their own. Attorneys and accountants who specialize in these transactions should be consulted early. But what about situations when the owner dies suddenly? What if the spouse of the deceased owner has little to no experience in running the business or has little to no desire to run the business? In these cases, the disposition of the business would be handled by the heirs; however, the same methods discussed in this chapter would be used to value the business.

Even with the best estate planning, there may be issues related to transferring ownership to the next generation of family members. For example, a larger ownership share may be bequeathed to one child to the dismay of the other heirs. The chosen child has spent more time working in the business or he or she may just be the favorite of the owner. Regardless, the same methods discussed in this chapter would be used to value the business. Dealing with the issues arising among the heirs in these scenarios are addressed in other chapters of this book.

While each alternative has unique challenges regarding valuations, they share common issues. The valuation methods discussed in this chapter can be applied in each scenario. Several valuation professionals were interviewed and their practical insights for valuing small and family businesses are included in this chapter.

7.4 The Impact of How the Transfer Is Structured on Business Valuation

If the small or family business is to be transferred to the next generation, the owners have competing priorities. If the ownership is transferred via gifts while the owners are still alive or bequeathed after death, there is a desire to minimize the value of the business to minimize estate and gift taxes. If the interests are to be sold to a third party or to the company's employees, then there is a desire to maximize the value of the business to maximize the retirement nest egg. A sale to a third-party buyer will be arm's length, so the value established in that transaction will be a fair estimate of firm value. The values set for an arm's length transaction will be derived using the methods described in this chapter.

Business valuations for the options discussed are straightforward. Minimize business value for transfers to the next generation and maximize business value for sales to third-party buyers. However, if the business is to be sold to the next generation, now the owners (current generation) and the buyers (the next generation) having competing interests. The selling party (the current generation) has the incentive to maximize value to provide a retirement nest egg. But the buying party (the next generation) has the incentive to minimize the purchase price to keep their initial investment at a more affordable level. This purchase and sale transaction will not be an arm's length transaction. In cases such as this, the methods used to value the family business should follow the methods described in this chapter. If the business is valued using these accepted methods, it will be more easily defended should the IRS or any other interested parties challenge the valuation.

7.5 Revenue Ruling 59-60

The guiding practices of valuing small and family businesses are based on Revenue Ruling 59-60, which was published by the Internal Revenue Service in January 1959. All these years later, this document still serves as the primary guide for valuing businesses for estate and gift tax purposes. Business valuation professionals look to this Rev Ruling, along with Tax Court rulings, for guidance when valuing small and family businesses.

A valuation is a supportable opinion as to the value of something--such as the value of a small or family business. According to Revenue Ruling 59-60, a business valuation is a prophesy of the future (Internal Revenue Service 1959). This prophecy of the future is our best guess of what will happen based on what we think we know today. While we can make educated and well-studied forecasts of the future, we do not have complete knowledge. As forecasts go farther into the future, our crystal balls grow cloudier. Once we recognize that, valuing a business, whether for succession planning or for the sale or purchase of a business, is as much art as it is science.

7.6 Why You Need to Value Your Small or Family Business

Anyone planning to pass their business on to the next generation will need to value the business for estate and gift tax purposes. Planning for estate and gift taxes is beyond the scope of this chapter. A quick Google search of estate and gift tax planning will show there is a plethora of law firms and accounting firms that specialize in this area of tax law. Volumes have been written on the topic of estate and gift taxes, outlining tax planning strategies for the alternatives described above. Therefore, in this chapter, we will only address methods used to value small and family businesses for tax. It is therefore recommended that qualified tax professionals be engaged to assist with estate and gift tax planning.

If the succession plan is to sell the business, there are several valuation approaches available. But the price paid by a willing buyer to a willing seller, with neither one under any duress to complete the transaction and both knowing the facts and circumstances surrounding the business (that is, an arm's length transaction), is the value of your business (Internal Revenue Service 1959). While some approaches are specifically for valuing a business regarding the sale of the business, the valuation approaches discussed in this chapter can value a business whether it is being sold or transferred to the subsequent generations.

7.7 Sophistication of the Small or Family Business

Family businesses vary in size and sophistication. Many are first-generation organizations with only rudimentary accounting and reporting systems. The more sophisticated the accounting system in place, the more accurate the valuation is likely to be. Mid-sized family businesses usually have better accounting and reporting systems, making it easier to get accurate numbers to be used in the valuation.

Larger, more established family businesses (for example, ALDI Group and Cumberland Farms) have very sophisticated accounting and reporting systems. These entities are typically audited by independent accounting firms. Valuations of these business entities are supported by more reliable numbers.

The size and sophistication of the business are important because the more reliable the financial statements are, the more likely that the resulting valuation will be a valid, defensible estimate of value. The reliability of financial statements is enhanced if they are subjected to attest services by an independent Certified Public Accountant (CPA).

Attest services vary in scope and content. There are three types of attest services that small and family businesses are likely to utilize. These are compilations, reviews, and audits (American Institue of Certified Public Accountants 2016). Each level of attest services provides a different level of assurance as to the fairness of the financial statements.

Compilations provide the lowest level of assurance. When a CPA prepares compiled financial statements, their work is limited to using the books and records of the client to prepare financial statements. There is little in the way of analytical procedures performed and the notes to the financial statements are limited.

When a CPA performs a review, it starts with financial statements prepared by the client. The CPA then performs certain limited analytical procedures, such as variance analyses, which are applied to the data to help the accountant identify any unusual activities or trends. Typically, in a review performed under standards promulgated by the American Institute of Certified Public Accounts (AICPA), the CPA provides financial statement users with negative assurance as the fairness and completeness of the financial statements. The review report states that the CPA did not learn of any material misstatements in the financial statements.

Compiled or reviewed financial statements are considered less reliable than audited financial statements. An audit provides the highest level of assurance as to the fairness, reliability, and completeness of the information in financial statements. A typical audit report has a scope paragraph that outlines the measures used by the CPA to obtain reasonable assurance as to the fairness and completeness of the financial statements. Language recommended by the AICPA to describe procedures performed during an audit is as follows.

> An audit involves performing procedures to obtain audit evidence about the amounts and disclosures in the financial statements. The procedures selected depend on the auditor's judgment, including the assessment of the risks of material misstatement of the financial statements, whether due to fraud or error. In making those risk assessments, the auditor considers internal control relevant to the entity's preparation and fair presentation of the financial statements to design audit procedures appropriate in the circumstances, but not for the purpose of an opinion on the effectiveness of the entity's internal control.

(American Institute of Certifed Public Accountants 2013)

Audits are considered a minimum level of assurance for most transactions involving the purchase or sale of a business. Any transactions involving capital markets require audited financial statements. However, many small and family businesses cannot afford audits, nor do they feel the need for audits. Many years ago, the author worked for a small family business that did business through several legal entities. The family had a good reputation within the local business community and obtained financing for the projects and business units using internally prepared tax basis financial statements. The family had a Big 4 accounting firm review our tax returns, but the firm provided no type of attest services.

The foregoing discussion is to make the reader aware of the importance of having reliable financial information available when valuing small and family business. The more reliable the financial information, the more reliable and defensible the resulting valuation is. Ideally, the firm will have audited financial statements, but reviews or compilations will suffice.

Valuation professionals who were interviewed for this chapter indicated that five years of financial statements were needed to prepare a quality valuation. Any firm involved in succession planning will have at least that many years' worth of operating results available. The only questions relate to the quality and reliability of the financial information. This is where audits can remove much uncertainty by the person doing the valuation. Note that the responsibility for the reliability and accuracy of financial statements and other information rests with the management of the business being valued—that is, the owner. Auditors provide opinions as to the fairness of the financial statements, but they rely on management to provide complete information.

7.8 Valuation Principles

Three principles provide the conceptual framework for business valuations— the principle of alternatives, the principle of substitution, and the principle of future benefits (Understanding Business Valuation 2017). The principle of alternatives is based on the buyer having the option of either investing or not investing in a particular asset, in this case, the asset is the business being valued. The seller has the option deciding whether to sell the asset, to whom the asset would be sold, and at what price the asset would be sold for. The buyer can invest in other companies or other income-producing assets. The value of the business is based on the desirability of it as an investment compared to all other similar investments for that investor.

The principle of substitutes states that the buyer of a business will pay only what they would pay for an equally desirable business. The buyer can invest in other companies or other income-producing assets of similar quality. The value of the business is based on the desirability of it as an investment compared to all other similar investments for that investor. A buyer would not agree to pay more for an asset than he or she would for a similar asset (an equally desirable substitute). The principle of future benefits is discussed later in this chapter.

7.9 Going Concern

A business valuation typically assumes that the business is a going concern. It is assumed that the business will continue to operate as it has up to the valuation for the near future (the accounting profession defines going concern as the expectation that the organization will still be in business 12 months from the audit report). If the business is in poor financial condition and is not likely to survive, then forecasting future cash flows is a meaningless exercise (The Small Business Valuation Book 2008). In cases such as these, the business is valued at liquidation value.

Liquidation value is an estimate of what the assets could be sold for as of the valuation date less any costs of disposal and net of the amount that the business's liabilities could be settled for as of the valuation date. Liquidation values assume an orderly sale of the underlying assets (not a fire sale). Liquidation values will produce the lowest value for the business. While this may sound attractive for minimizing estate and gift taxes using liquidation values is neither appropriate nor would it be acceptable to the IRS if the business is a going concern.

7.10 Valuation Methods

The most used business valuation method is based on the fair market value of the business (that is, the principle of future benefits). Revenue Ruling 59-60 defines a valuation as

> the amount at which the property would change hands between a willing buyer and a willing seller, when the former is not under any compulsion to buy, and the latter is not under any compulsion to sell, both parties having reasonable knowledge of relevant facts.

A key takeaway here is that for business valuations value is based on an arm's length transaction between two willing and able parties. Neither party is under duress to either buy or sell, both parties understand the facts and circumstances related to the business, and both parties can consummate the transaction. This also assumes that the property is marketed for a reasonable period to find the buyer willing to pay the highest price. According to valuation professionals interviewed for this chapter, for estate and gift tax purposes, the fair market value approach is the standard used by business valuation professionals.

Fair value is a relative concept. It is not a fixed, exact number. Instead, it is within a range of values, much like the appraiser of a home provides a range of values with an estimate somewhere between the maximum and minimum values. Judgment is used when applying valuation standards. It is possible, and even likely, that two independent business valuation professionals could come up with two very different values for the same business (see the example from the beginning of this chapter). Differences result from individual judgment applied to the facts and circumstances surrounding the valuation.

The most common valuation method used to estimate fair value is based on estimated future cash flows for the business. The next section will discuss how business valuation professionals estimate future cash flows for businesses.

7.11 Earnings Before Interest, Taxes, Depreciation, and Amortization (EBITDA)

Most business valuations are based on estimated future benefits generated by the business. Future benefits are defined as future cash flows. Reported net income is not a good proxy for future cash flows. Reported net income includes deductions for noncash expenses, such as depreciation and amortization. It may also include deductions for nonrecurring expenses such as asset impairments and reorganization costs.

Earnings before interest, taxes, depreciation, and amortization (EBITDA) is a proxy for cash flows used in estimating business values. The goal is to get back to pretax cash flows generated by the business's operations. Income taxes are added back because we want to estimate how much cash the business generates without regard to the payment of taxes. Interest is added back to remove the impact of capital structure on operating cash flows. We are looking at the cash flows the business would have generated from its operations if the business had no debt outstanding and was financed completely by owners' capital investments. Another way of looking at this is that businesses will have different capital structures, so the impact of debt service (payment of principal and interest on debt) will have varying impacts on cash flows generated by businesses. That is why interest expense is added back to net income—it levels the playing field in terms of capital structure.

Depreciation and amortization are noncash expenses deducted in determining pretax income. These noncash expenses are simply the allocation of initial (historical) costs to the periods that benefit from those assets (for example, productive capacity). Since we are trying to determine cash generated by business operations, these expenses are added back to net income to arrive at EBITDA.

Table 7.1 provides net income for Acme Family Business. A valuation date will not coincide with the end of the business's fiscal year. Therefore, we use data from the last 12 months of operations (trailing 12 months, or TTM) to compute the income statement will the starting point for our valuation exercise.

Table 7.1 Acme Family Business Reported Net Income

Revenues	$10,000,000
Cost of goods sold	4,800,000
Gross profit	5,200,000
Sales and marketing expenses	1,750,000
General and administrative expenses	1,500,000
Interest expense	125,000
Depreciation and amortization	150,000
Pretax income	1,675,000
Income taxes (40%)	670,000
Net income	$1,005,000

7.12 Normalization Adjustments

Often, expenses recognized by family businesses differ from the amounts normally incurred by a business of the same size and scope as the business being valued. Certain adjustments are made to reported net income to make it comparable to other, non-family, businesses in the same industry. These adjustments are called *normalization adjustments*. Common normalization adjustments include, but are not limited to, those related to

- Officer compensation (over or under market rates).
- Compensation paid to family members (sinecure-type positions).
- Above-market or below-market rent paid to the owner or to a family limited partnership controlled by the owner.
- Costs associated with perquisites consumed by the owner and the owner's family that are unrelated to the business, such as the ski lodge in Utah or the beachfront condominium in Florida.

The idea behind normalization adjustments is to conform the business's reported net income to what a non-family-member owner would expect to derive from the business under normal operating circumstances. Often, net income is understated due to certain expenses being overstated or unnecessary for the business. We are looking for operating income that a comparable business would report, absent these excessive expenses.

Compensation paid to the owner may be reasonable and customary for the services provided to the business. If it is, then no normalization adjustments are needed. If executive compensation is above market, then the excess of actual compensation over comparable market compensation should be added back to pretax income when computing normalized income. If the owner is paid less than the market value of his or her services (many owners take little or no salary from their businesses), then the difference between actual compensation and market compensation should be deducted from pretax income when computing normalized income. Compensation paid to the owner should follow compensation paid to executives in comparable businesses within the same industry and geographic area. A good place to find comparable businesses is industry trade association websites, publications by placement firms, and compensation paid to executives of publicly held companies.

The author recalls working with a manufacturing client many years ago. The owner/founder was president and chairman of the business. The owner/founder was getting up in his years by that time and every morning, the owner/founder's nurse wheeled him into the office in his wheelchair. He then spent the better part of the day napping in his office. For this, he was paid a handsome salary. He was no longer involved in the day-to-day decisions affecting the business and his compensation was not based on the value of the service he provided to the business. Instead, the firm (and the IRS) considered this to be a distribution of earnings rather than reasonable compensation. His salary was added back to determine pretax income for the business and to compute normalized income.

Often family businesses employ members of the owner's immediate family in various positions within the firm. We are not worried about family member employees who contribute directly or indirectly to the success of the firm. We are concerned about those family members who have jobs in name only. These are more likely to be considered sinecures than they are actual line positions within the business. In these cases, wages paid to family members with sinecure-type jobs should be added back to compute normalized income.

Sometimes a family business occupies space in a building owned by the owner/manager or by a member of the owner/manager's immediate family. If the lease requires the business to pay market-rate rent, then there are no issues. However, if the lease calls for above-market rents, then rent expense should be reduced to what the business would pay in an arm's length leasing transaction to arrive at normalized income. Similarly, if the lease is at below-market rates, rent expense must be adjusted to reflect rent paid to a third-party lessor to arrive at normalized income.

Often, the owners of a business will use the business to purchase assets solely to benefit the owners and their families. Examples would be a ski lodge in Utah, an oceanfront condominium in Florida, or an expensive boat used for family excursions. When assets such as these are included with the business's operating assets, net income should be adjusted to eliminate the carrying costs of those assets to compute normalized income. And all operating and maintenance costs associated with those assets run through the business's books must be added back to compute normalized income.

For our Acme example, assume that the owner/manager receives total compensation of US$200,000, while the market rate for the president/CEO of a business of the size and scope of Acme is US$100,000. The owner's compensation expense is included in administrative expenses. The difference of US$100,000 represents excess executive compensation paid by the business. This means that if the business were managed by a professional manager rather than the owner, executive compensation would be US$100,000 lower than the amount reported by the business. Therefore, Acme's general and administrative expenses must be reduced by this amount to normalize business expenses, increasing normalized income.

Also assume that the owner's children are provided sinecure-type jobs with the business. The children's compensation included as operating expenses of the company amounts to US$50,000. These costs must be added back to net income, thereby increasing net income, to compute normalized income.

A similar adjustment is often made for rent paid by the business. In our Acme example, assume that market rent for the space occupied by the business in the building owned by the owner/manager is US$125,000 per year. However, the lease requires the business to pay rent of US$200,000. Had this been an arm's length leasing transaction, rent expense would have been US$75,000 less than what the business reported as part of general and administrative expenses. General and administrative expenses are therefore reduced by the amount to compute normalized net income, increasing normalized income.

Table 7.2 shows how normalization adjustments are applied to Acme Family Business to compute normalized income. We start with the data

Table 7.2 Acme Family Business Computation of Normalized Income

	As Reported (US$)	Normalization Adjustments			
		Excess Executive Compensation (US$)	*Children's Salaries (US$)*	*Over Market Rent Paid to Owner (US$)*	*Normalized Net Income (US$)*
Revenues	10,000,000				10,000,000
Cost of goods sold	4,800,000				4,800,000
Gross profit	5,200,000				5,200,000
Sales and marketing expenses	1,750,000				1,750,000
General and administrative expenses	1,500,000	(100,000)	(50,000)	(75,000)	1,275,000
Interest expense	125,000				125,000
Depreciation and amortization	150,000				150,000
Pretax income	1,675,000	100,000	50,000	75,000	1,900,000
Income taxes at 40%	670,000				760,000
Net income	1,005,000				1,140,000

reported in Table 7.1 and then apply the normalization adjustments. Because of the normalization adjustments made to reported net, pretax income increases from the US$1,675,000 reported by the business to US$1,900,000. Also note that taxes are computed based on normalized pretax income. The rationale for this is that, had the business not overpaid for executive compensation and building rent, it would have recognized more income and paid more in income taxes than what it reported for the period.

Now that we have computed normalized income for Acme, we can compute normalized EBITDA for Acme. EBITDA is computed by adding back certain expenses to reported net income. Normalized EBITDA starts with normalized income and adds back interest, taxes, depreciation, and amortization. Normalized EBITDA, while not perfect, is a good proxy for cash flow generated by the operations of the business without distortions caused by including family-related expenses in the operating income of the business. To compute normalized EBITDA, we add back interest expense, income tax

Table 7.3 Acme Family Business Computation of Normalized EBITDA

Normalized net income	$1,140,000
Add back:	
Interest expense	125,000
Income taxes	760,000
Depreciation and amortization	150,000
Normalized earnings before interest, taxes, depreciation, and amortization (EBITDA)	$2,175,000

expense, depreciation, and amortization to normalized income. Normalized EBITDA for Acme is US$2,175,000, as shown in Table 7.3.

7.13 Common Valuation Methods

Now that we have computed normalized EBITDA, we can use this to estimate the value of Acme using approaches commonly used by valuation professionals. These methods include the guideline business method, the discounted cash flow method, and the asset-based approach. Each method has its pros and cons, and each will be discussed here along with an example of how these methods are used to value Acme.

7.14 Guideline Company Method

The guideline company method uses data of companies that are as closely comparable to the business being valued to compute an estimated value of the business. This approach is like what we see with real estate appraisals. With real estate appraisals, comparable sales of similar properties are the starting point for valuations. Adjustments are made to account for differences between the property and the comparable properties. When using the guideline company method, the comparable company is publicly traded, so financial data for the guideline company should be readily available.

Once a guideline company is identified, EBITDA is computed for that company using publicly available data. The market capitalization for the guideline company is used to determine the EBITDA multiple for that company. Market capitalization is the number of shares outstanding multiplied by the market price of the company's stock. The market capitalization is divided by EBITDA to compute the EBITDA multiple for the guideline company. This multiple is then used to estimate the market value of the small or family business being valued based on normalized EBITDA.

With Acme, assume that a suitable publicly traded company was identified. If the guideline company has 25 million shares of common stock outstanding and, as of the valuation date, the market price is US$12.50 per share, then total market capitalization would be

$$25,000,000 \times \$12.50 = \$312,375,000$$

If the company's EBITDA is US$60,750,000, then the EBITDA multiple would be 5.14:

$$\$312,375,000 \div \$60,750,000 = 5.14$$

Applying this multiple to Acme's normalized EBITDA results in an estimated value for Acme of US$11,183,796, as shown in Table 7.4.

If an appropriate publicly traded company cannot be found, industry benchmarks can be used in place of the guideline company's multiple. A source for industry benchmarks is the Stern School of Business at New York University website (Damodaran 2021). This link provides access to an Excel file prepared and maintained by Aswath Damodaran, PhD, a finance professor at the Stern School of Business. Dr. Damodaran provides EBITDA multiples for 92 industries. Multiples range from a high of 47.57 (real estate development) to a low of 5.75 (retail grocery and food). The average multiple is 16.43.

Duff & Phelps also provides EBITDA multiples for North American industries (Duff & Phelps 2020). The list of industries is less extensive than the list provided by Dr. Damodaran, but it does provide a good reference use when valuing a small or family business.

Table 7.4 Acme Family Business Estimated Value Using EBITDA Multiplier

Acme's Normalized EBITDA	$2,175,000
Guideline company multiple	5.14
Estimated value	$11,183,796

7.15 Discounted Cash Flows Method

Since a valuation is a prophesy of the future, the most used method to esti-mate business values is the discounted cash flow method. While the guide-line company method uses multiples as of a specific date, the discounted cash flow method considers estimated future cash flows expected to be generated by the business. Since we are forecasting future cash flows of the business, we need to dust off our crystal ball. Forecasts of the future are highly speculative, but if they are based on an understanding of the busi-ness's recent operating history and trends, they provide reliable estimates as the basis for computing the value of small or family businesses.

It is best to have several years of income statements available to identify trends that may affect the business. At least five years of income statements and cash flows are considered optimal. We use past income statements and cash flows, along with our understanding of current and prospective condi-tions affecting the overall economy and the local economy where the busi-ness operates, to project future cash flows for the business. We must also look at what the company's competition is doing and how that may affect market share, volumes, and selling prices.

Forecasts of future cash flows will include estimates of increases in prices and volumes to forecast product sales and estimates of inflation likely to impact inputs (materials, labor, etc.). To prepare our forecast for Acme, we start with normalized income and assume a 5% growth in revenues (a com-bination of selling price increases and volume increases) and a 3% increase in input prices. The discounted cash flow method also requires an estimated terminal value, which is the estimated value of the business at the end of the forecast period. Including a terminal value in the computations recog-nizes that the business will have value at the end of the forecast period. That value will accrue to the owners of the business, whether the business is sold or is retained within the family.

One of the biggest challenges with the discounted cash flow method is determining the rate to use for discounting the future cash flows. As the IRS puts it so eloquently in Rev Ruling 59-60, "the determination of capitaliza-tion rates presents one of the most difficult problems in valuation" (Internal Revenue Service 1959). Discount rates applied to future cash flows impound risk inherent in the business. This includes systemic risks, which includes risks associated with the general economy, risks associated with the specific industry, and risks associated with the specific geographic area in which the business operates. Also impounded in the discount rate are non-systemic risks, those risks specific to the business. Non-systemic risks would include such things as customer concentration (one or few large customers vs. a large number of smaller customers), reliance on foreign operations or customers, and key person risk (business success relying on one specific individual rather than a strong and competent management team).

Discount rates for small or family businesses are in the 20–30% range; these could be higher if the perceived risk associated with the company is higher than other companies in a particular industry. Discount rates would also be higher for start-up businesses as they typically are perceived to have risk much higher than established businesses. The Graziadio School of Business at Pepperdine University (Everett 2020) publishes an annual survey that includes required rates of return for private capital investors. These rates provide guidance as to the discount rates that investors must have to justify investments in privately held firms. Required rates of return for investors range from a low of 21% for private equity investments in larger firms (greater than US$50 million EBITDA) to a high of 38% for seed funding by venture capital firms.

The rationale behind using discounted forecasted future cash flows is that a dollar today is worth more than a dollar expected to be received. The farther into the future that a cash flow is expected to be received, the higher the risk it will not be received or that the amount received will be materially different (that is, lower) from the amount forecasted. By discounting forecasted future cash flows, we are bringing them all back to today's dollars. There is an inverse relationship between the discount rate and the present value of the future cash flow. As the discount rate increases, the present value decreases, and vice versa. The higher discount rates quoted above for private capital investors would cause much lower valuations.

We now need to forecast annual net cash flows for Acme for the next five years. We will start with normalized income (Table 7.2) and grow revenues and expenses from this base year. Table 7.5 shows the forecasted growth of revenues, expenses, and net cash over a five-year forecast period. Revenues are expected to grow at an annual rate of five percent and expenses are expected to grow at an annual rate of three percent. Depreciation and amortization are expected to increase by US$10,000 per year. Five years is a typical time frame since the farther into the future that forecasts go the cloudier the crystal ball becomes.

The numbers in Table 7.5 result from computations that grow revenues and expenses based on anticipated percentage annual increases. The numbers convey precision (for example, cost of goods sold in Year 5 of

Table 7.5 Acme Family Business Forecast of Cash Flows

	Normalized Income (US$)	Year 1 (US$)	Year 2 (US$)	Year 3 (US$)	Year 4 (US$)	Year 5 (US$)
Revenues	10,000,000	10,500,000	11,025,000	11,576,250	12,155,063	2,762,816
Cost of goods sold	4,800,000	4,944,000	5,092,320	5,245,090	5,402,442	5,564,516
Gross profit	5,200,000	5,556,000	5,932,680	6,331,160	6,752,620	7,198,300
Sales and marketing expenses	1,750,000	1,802,500	1,856,575	1,912,272	1,969,640	2,028,730
General and administrative expenses	1,275,000	1,313,250	1,352,648	1,393,227	1,435,024	1,478,074
Interest expense	125,000	125,000	125,000	125,000	125,000	125,000
Depreciation and amortization	150,000	160,000	170,000	180,000	190,000	200,000
Pretax income	1,900,000	2,160,750	2,4639,323	2,736,752	3,054,130	3,392,605
Income taxes at 40%	760,000	862,100	971,383	1,088,264	1,213,182	1,346,598
Net income	1,140,000	1,2963,150	1,457,075	1,632,397	1,819,774	2,019,898
Add back depreciation and amortization	150,000	160,000	170,000	180,000	190,000	200,000
Estimate net cash flows	1,290,000	1,453,150	1,627,075	1,812,397	2,009,774	2,219,898

US$5,564,516) than exists. Remember that when we put together a forecast, we are making our best guess about what will happen based on what we think we know today. You notice that business valuations, especially those using discounted cash flows, are as much art as they are science.

Now that we have our forecast of future cash flows, we need to compute the terminal value of the business at the end of the five-year forecast period. The descriptor "terminal value" is the nomenclature used in the valuation profession. It is not intended to imply that the business will be sold or will terminate operations at some specific point. Terminal value is an estimate of the value of the business at a specific point (with Acme, five years into the future). Terminal value recognizes that the business has value, and that value will inure to the owners of the business. Often the terminal value will have a significant impact on the value of the business. With small or family businesses that provide services as opposed to goods to their customers, the value of the business may be linked to the owner. Without the owner, the business has little to no value. In our Acme example, we are assuming that Acme provides goods to its customers and that its value will continue beyond the retirement or death of the owner.

The author recalls doing a valuation for a retail shopping center and finding that the cash flows for the forecast period (10 years) did not support the value of the shopping center. The author pondered how that could be because the anchor tenant and the local tenants lined up were all financially strong and forecasted cash flows were substantial. Until the author realized that he had forgotten to include the terminal value in the valuation computations. Once the terminal value was included, the value of the business was supported.

The estimated annual cash flow numbers from Table 7.5 will now be discounted at the appropriate discount rate. With Acme, we determined that 20% was the appropriate discount rate. Discount rates combine the cost of capital, the cost of debt, and a risk premium added for non-systemic risk. Systemic risk is impounded in the cost of capital; non-systemic risk, since it relates to the specific firm, must be added to the firm's cost of capital to compute an appropriate discount rate. Computation of the cost of capital, the cost of debt, and risk premium for non-systemic risk is beyond the scope of this book.

A capitalization rate is used to forecast the value of a business at a particular point. Forecasted cash flows for the last year of the forecast period are divided by the capitalization rate to forecast the terminal value. Capitalization rates are defined as the discount rate (20% for Acme) minus

Table 7.6 Acme Family Business Computation of Present Value

	Year 1 (US$)	Year 2 (US$)	Year 3 (US$)	Year 4 (US$)	Year 5 (US$)
Estimate net cash flows	1,453,150	1,627,075	1,812,397	2,009,774	2,219,898
Terminal value					14,799,317
	1,453,150	1,627,075	1,812,397	2,009,774	17,019,215
Present value at 20%	1,210,958	1129,913	1,048,841	969,220	6,839,641

the revenue growth rate (5% for Acme) (Understanding Business Valuation 2017, p. 561). Acme's terminal value is

$$\$2,219,898 \div (20\% - 5\%) = \$14,799,317$$

This amount is added to operating cash flows in Year 5. This sum is then discounted at 20% to arrive at the present value of future cash flows (estimated business value today) of US$11,198,572. Computations are provided in Table 7.6.

Note that the value of Acme Family Business using the discounted cash flow method is approximately US$14,776 more than the value derived using the guideline company method. The value derived from each method is neither right nor wrong; valuations derived from both methods both are acceptable to the IRS, so the choice of which method to use is up to the person valuing the business, although long applied consistently.

7.16 Asset-Based Method

The asset-based valuation method focuses on the balance sheet of the company being valued. The assets and liabilities on the balance sheet of the company being valued are marked to market. Assets are adjusted to their fair market value as of the valuation date and liabilities are adjusted to the value they could be settled for as of the valuation date. This method is the preferred method for valuing holding companies and real estate companies. Each asset is appraised under this method. This method is acceptable for use with the IRS, but it is not always the best method for valuing companies that provide goods or services to their clients.

According to a survey by the Graziadio Business School, approximately 52% of business appraisers used discounted cash flow models or capitalization of earnings method to value companies, while another 26% used the guideline company method. Only 8% used the asset-based method to value companies (Everett 2020).

7.17 Discounts on Valuations

Now that we have computed estimated values for Acme Family Business, we need to adjust the values for certain discounts typical for the valuation of small and family businesses. The most common discounts are the discount for lack of marketability (DLOM) and the discount for lack of control (DLOC).

The DLOM is due to the business being a closely held business. Shares of publicly held businesses are traded every day on active exchanges involving a large number of arm's length transactions. Therefore, it is easy for the owner of shares stock in these companies to buy and sell shares. With closely held businesses, the ability to buy or sell shares is limited. Sometimes shareholder agreements exist that state the terms under which shares in the company can be bought or sold. The value of the company is discounted for this lack of ability to buy and sell shares. Typically, DLOM is in the 25–30% range.

The DLOC is applied to minority interests in the business. The founder of a small or family business will transfer ownership interests to their children or grandchildren. If there are over two recipients (heirs) of such shares, each shareholder will own less than 50% of the business. Each recipient cannot control the direction of the company. The value of the company is discounted to reflect this lack of control. Typical discounts for lack of control are in the 25–30% range.

The DLOM and DLOC are not additive. If the person valuing the company believes that a 25% DLOC and a 25% DLOM are appropriate, the total discount is not the sum of these two discounts (50%). The formula for computing the total discount is (Understanding Business Valuation 2017, pp. 597–599)

$$1-(1-\text{DLOC})\times(1-\text{DLOM})$$

If a 25% DLOC and a 25% DLOM are used, the resulting combined discount is

$$1-(1-25\%)\times(1-25\%)=43.75\%$$

Table 7.7 Acme Family Business Discounted Company Value

	Guideline Company (US$)	Discounted Cash Flows (US$)
Undiscounted company value	11,183,796	11,198,572
DLOC and DLOM (at 43.75%)	(4,892,911)	(4,899,375)
Discounted company value	6,290,885	6,299,197

If we assume these discounts are appropriate for Acme, the value of Acme would be adjusted downward by 43.75%. Table 7.7 provides these computations.

There is also a swing premium for minority interests. This could occur when a minority shareholder has the swing vote on major decisions. For example, assume there are three shareholders. Two shareholders own 49% of the stock of the company and the third shareholder owns 2% of the stock. In major decisions, the 2% shareholder can provide the swing vote if there is a disagreement between the other two shareholders, by voting with one or the other shareholder. In cases such as this, the swing vote premium effectively reverses the DLOC.

7.18 Chapter Summary

This chapter provided a 30,000-foot overview of valuations for small and family businesses. Volumes have been written on this topic. Many professionals have lucrative careers providing valuation services. It has been assumed that the business valuation is for estate and gift tax purposes and that the business being valued is a going concern. This chapter, due to scope limitations, cannot prepare the reader to do battle with the IRS. It is therefore recommended that anyone needing a valuation for estate and gift tax purposes engage a business appraiser qualified to engage with the IRS to assist you with the valuation. These professionals are credentialed by organizations such as the American Institute of CPAs and the American Society of Appraisers, among others.

Works Cited

American Institute of Certified Public Accountants. 2013. "Illustrative Auditor's Report on the Financial Statements." https://www.aicpa.org/content/dam/aicpa/interestareas/frc/industryinsights/downloadabledocuments/inv/ep-inv-clarified-audit-reports.pdf

American Institue of Certified Public Accountants. 2016. "Adopting the Comprehensive Definition of Attest: Protecting the Public." https://www.aicpa .org/advocacy/state/downloadabledocuments/what-are-attest-services.pdf

Damodaran, A. 2021. "Stern School of Business." Accessed March 17, 2022. http:// people.stern.nyu.edu/adamodar/New_Home_Page/datacurrent.html#multiples

Duff & Phelps. 2020. "Duff & Phelps." Accessed March 17, 2022. https://www.duf-fandphelps.com/insights/publications/valuation-insights/valuation-insights-first -quarter-2021/north-american-industry-market-multiples

Everett, C.R. 2020. *2020 Private Capital Markets Report.* Malibu, CA: Pepperdine University. https://bschool.pepperdine.edu/

Internal Revenue Service. 1959. *IRS Revenue Ruling*, 59–60. https://www.pvfllc.com /files/IRS_Revenue_Ruling_59-60.pdf

Trugman, G.R. 2017. *Understanding Business Valuation: A Practical Guide To Valuing Small To Medium Sized Businesses.* 5th edition. Newark: Wiley.

Tuller, L.W. 2008. *The Small Business Valuation Book.* Avon, MA: Adams Media.

Chapter 8

Questions and Answers about Financial Planning Issues in Small and Family Business Succession

Kelsey Lovett

Contents

My passion for succession planning comes from my own family history and experience. My grandfather was a successful pharmacist and business owner for most of his life. The pharmacy and his work were an integral part of our family structure. The notion this was a part of our family identity was only reinforced when my aunt followed in his footsteps and became a pharmacist and partial owner in the pharmacy. All went according to plan for years. Together they built a strong reputation, a thriving business, and trust in the community. However, the unexpected happened in 2011. In one calendar year, both my grandfather and my aunt passed away from cancer. Our family was left inextricably changed, and so was the business.

DOI: 10.4324/9781003281054-11

Had you asked anyone in our family, we would have clearly stated there was a backup plan. The backup plan was my aunt. It was assumed, as it should have been, that she would outlive my grandfather and she would take over as the sole owner of the business. No one expected what would transpire, and so during grieving the loss of our loved ones, we also had to come together to keep the business alive. Our family was lucky enough to have three strong women ready to do whatever was necessary to keep my grandfather and aunt's legacy intact. My grandmother, mom, and cousin all stepped up to the plate and poured their heart and souls into the business. They did what most people see as impossible, and they have now been running the business solely together for ten years.

My story is personal, but unfortunately not unique. In my role as a financial advisor, I have heard many stories like my own. The stories are hard to hear, especially knowing they could have been avoided. Now I strive to work with business owners to plan for the uncertain and unlikely. I understand intimately that it is the only way we can protect the business owner's assets, effort, legacies, and families.

Financial planning is only a singular part of the succession planning process. What we look to do as financial advisors is help the business owner client look at the bigger picture, examining both pre- and post-transition. Once we have created that mindset, we work with the business owner to create a personal financial plan that aligns with the business, with the transition plan, and with the family. When the financial plan is aligned with the transition strategy and the family, we see that a succession plan is much more likely to succeed.

In this chapter, we will discuss issues related to the financial planning options of small and family-owned enterprises in relation to exit planning or succession planning. We will cover why you need an exit or succession plan, the common themes to address regarding financial planning combined with succession planning, and a few of the most used options for transitioning the business.

8.1 Why You Need an Exit Plan

So, what is an exit plan? Richard Jackim, the co-author of *The $10 Trillion Opportunity* and co-founder of EPI, defines exit planning this way:

> An exit plan asks and answers all the business, personal, financial, legal and tax questions involved in transitioning a privately owned

business. Exit plans include contingencies for illness, burnout, divorce, and death. The purpose of an exit plan is to maximize the value of the business at the time of exit, minimize taxes and ensure the owner can accomplish all his or her personal and financial goals.

(Snider 2016, p44)

Most business owners do not have business transition as a top priority during their working years because they are too busy with the day-to-day tasks associated with a successful and ever-moving entity. It is a common mistake to not consider, create, or formalize a succession plan. Plan for and consider what will happen to your business after you are gone, whether by choice or by circumstance.

What is at risk if a business owner does not have an exit plan in place? The answer is everything.

Consider these scenarios:

1. The business owner passes away unexpectedly with no succession plan in place.

    If a business owner passes away unexpectedly, there is an extreme burden placed on the family to make important and time-sensitive decisions regarding the business. Many business owners have most of their assets tied up in their business, an asset illiquid without a well-thought-out and documented succession plan. Even if a business owner is confident in their loved ones, the pressure is often too much for ill-prepared or uninformed family members who might be left making all the decisions for the business. Most business owners want to avoid passing on these burdens to their loved ones.

2. The business owner becomes disabled and cannot run the business anymore and there is no succession plan in place.

    If a business owner becomes disabled and cannot run the business anymore, their livelihood may well depend upon the successful transition of their business. For many family-owned enterprises, their business is their retirement plan. Many business owners do not fund outside/separate retirement plans with cash because their cash is needed internally in the business for growth and expansion opportunities. This lack of liquidity can create a huge burden for a business owner who has experienced a major illness or disability.

Timing is critical. Far too often an ill-prepared family member will make decisions that affect the livelihood of the business and the family financials because of the pressures associated with time-sensitive issues. With the proper plan in place, business owners can rest easy knowing that even if the unimaginable happens, their families and their legacies will be intact.

A well-thought-out succession plan can create harmony, security, and freedom for business owners and their families.

8.2 Common Themes to Address

Owners of small businesses and/or family businesses have several unique challenges to face and consider for transitioning out of or away from their business. This chapter will discuss a few themes to address when beginning the process of succession planning. These are the common themes we see when working with business owners, and they are challenges that can and need to be addressed head-on.

1. **Procrastination**—There are many reasons we see procrastination plague the succession planning process and why it is the number one challenge to overcome. Succession planning takes time and time is a valuable commodity in the business world. Most business owners are not willing to take time away from their thriving businesses or distract themselves with issues that are not time sensitive.

   Business owners always underestimate the time it will take to complete a transition. Transitioning a business is a tedious process, and action should be taken immediately to think through options, plan for contingencies and engage professionals to help you along the way. It important to have experienced advisors on your team to help advise you on the legal, tax, personal and financial aspects of the deal.

   For many family business owners, there are not only financial issues to address but also emotional ones. For most business owners, their business is their largest asset, and the one they have put many years not only investing their money into but their life's work. Many business owners cannot determine where they start and their business begins. They are inextricably linked and intertwined.

   There are many factors at play, and we must plan for and create space and time for exploration, cultivation, and implementation. A strategic and thoughtful timeline is important to the succession planning process. Failing to carefully plan can create significant roadblocks for the actual completion of a successful transition.

Questions to consider:

a. What will happen if an exit plan is not in place and a crisis such as a death or disability occurs?

b. Is there an estate plan in place that addresses the business ownership?

c. What is at risk when a business owner procrastinates in planning?

d. What is the appropriate timeline for transitioning the business?

e. Can the business owner take time to detach from the day-to-day tasks to consider the long-run picture?

f. What emotional hurdles are there for a business owner to overcome so there are fewer distractions during the succession planning process?

2. **Legacy goals**—Once a small business owner has accepted the importance of succession planning, address legacy goals. The business owner often needs to be empowered to address their legacy goals and to consider what is pragmatic and realistic. They are the creators and protectors of their legacies, and goals often are not reached if they are not defined.

Questions to consider:

a. Has time been taken to flesh out and document what is wanted?

b. How does the business owner define succession goals?

c. Should the business owner sell the business to an outsider, or is there someone within the family or internally that the business could transition to?

d. Have the goals been communicated with others in the business and family?

e. Do others share the goals and/or are there competing interests?

f. Can the family goals be aligned with the business and financial goals?

g. Is there time to cultivate alignment for the owner's legacy goals if they are not already aligned?

h. Can "buy in" be cultivated for other generations?

3. **Family politics**—Giving up control of a business, whether to another family member or an outsider, can create emotional stress and disrupt family dynamics. Consider how to navigate the personal and familial politics as you embark on the succession planning process.

There are family dynamics to address regardless of how you plan to exit the business, but especially if the business will be passed down to the next generation. As an example, one major hurdle to consider is if multiple members of the succeeding generation will take on different roles in the business. For example, there may be one child who plans to succeed you and one child who does not plan to be associated with the business. How do those decisions affect you as the owner/parent and specifically how does that affect your estate and estate gifts?

Questions to consider:

a. Is there a common goal among the family regarding the business?
b. How does the owner work within and through the family politics?
c. What are the silent issues that will affect a succession plan?
d. Are there multiple members of the next generation to consider?
e. Is there an open line of communication between a potential successor and the business owner?

4. **Over-valuation**—Many business owners have pegged a value on their business that has no merit or has not been fleshed out in many years. Valuation is a critical part of the succession planning process, and business owners should work with and partner with CPAs and certified valuators to help value their business.

An owner should find a firm that specializes in the specific industry of the business for valuations. If an owner is not already working with a valuator, take the time to find a qualified partner. A business owner should ask their personal account/CPA, their financial advisor, their attorney, or peers if they have recommendations. A vital source to reference would be the website for The National Association of Certified Valuators and Analysts (www.nacva.com) to find a professional to partner with.

When a business owner works with valuators, they are looking for the strategic value of the business if it went to market and was sold to a third party. Many business owners overestimate the value of their business, so they must make sure that the business valuation is done with accuracy, precision, and care. It is essential to establish the value of the business before creating the business succession strategy. Taking the preparatory steps in completing a business valuation can add value to the business when it comes time to transition.

Questions to consider:

a. When was your business last valuated?
b. Have you worked with professionals to create and document the valuation needed for an exit plan?

c. What external market forces should we know that will affect your business valuation?

d. What internal factors can you control that would affect your valuation?

8.3 Financial Planning and Succession Planning

Financial planning is an integral part of the exit planning process. It starts with a personal financial plan. This personal financial plan focuses on the business owner itself. It looks at the owner's cash flow, taxes, savings, insurance coverages, real estate assets, investment assets, and dependency on the business.

The following topics are the foundation for personal financial plan. In reviewing the financial health of the business owner, we often find strengths and weaknesses that might impact the success of a transition for the business owner. In order to make the transition as smooth as possible, to understand the full picture and to make improvements it is important to analyze the following pieces of the business owner's financial life:

Cash flow—The financial plan should examine the business owner's cash flow, both inflows and outflows. Inflows would include income taken or received from the business, other family member salaries, income from other investment sources or businesses, income from real estate, and any other income source such as alimony or child support. The financial plan should then uncover and examine any outflows the business owner has. Outflows would include high-level commitments like liability payments, rents, insurance costs down to everyday spending like food, utilities, vacations, and hobbies. Examining the cash flow allows the financial advisor and the business owner to identify how money is managed. The examination also allows for the advisor to project what the owner might expect to need in retirement to cover their costs and keep their standard of living should they sell the business.

Taxes—The financial plan should examine the business owner's personal taxes. The personal taxes will likely include the business, depending on how the ownership of the business is set up. The examination of the tax return will also allow the financial advisor to see what tax strategies are being utilized and to see if any opportunities are being passed over. There are many things that can be gleaned from a tax return, and it is important to review them in the financial plan.

Savings/emergency fund—The financial plan should examine the business owner's current savings and ideal savings level. Each business owner will have different goals and needs when it comes to savings. The financial advisor should work to uncover what is needed and desired and help the business owner create that savings level. Once the savings level has been met, it is important to use the financial plan to help the business owner manage the dollars.

Insurance coverages—The financial plan should examine the business owner's current insurance coverages. All insurance policies should be reviewed in the financial plan including life, disability, property and casualty, long-term care, liability, etc. The financial advisor and business owner should review coverage levels, premiums, deductibles, and insurance carriers. A full review of all insurance coverages is important to make sure the business owner has the proper level of protection in place for himself/herself, his/her family, and his/her business.

Real estate assets—The financial plan should examine the business owner's real estate assets. Real estate assets can vary drastically including the business owner's home, vacation property, rental property, property the business is located on, undeveloped land, and family land. Each type of property will add its own layer to the complexity of the business owner's financial plan. It is important for the financial advisor to understand the liabilities associated with each property and the long-run plans for the properties.

Investment assets—The financial plan should examine the business owner's investment assets. Many business owners will consider their business their main asset/investment, but they will likely have other investments. It is important to work with the business owner in the financial plan to uncover and review any other assets including investment accounts, retirement accounts, former employer-sponsored accounts, and cash-like accounts. Each account will need to be reviewed to see if the account fits the business owner's risk tolerance and goals. The financial advisor should work closely with the business owner to understand the goals and objectives of each separate account. It is important for the investment accounts to be reviewed and managed quarterly.

Dependency on the business—The financial plan should examine the business owner's dependency on the business, mainly the cash flow from the business. The financial advisor needs to understand how the business owner uses the business cash flow and understand what cash flow will need to be replaced if the business owner sells the business. The more reliant a business owner is on the cash flow, the more that will be needed from the sale of the business.

The financial well-being of the business owner is the basis for a well-laid-out exit plan. As financial advisors, it is our job to examine and understand the financial wants vs. needs so we can help the business owner navigate options for transitioning the business. If all the owner's wealth is tied up in the business, the business owner will rely much more heavily on a successful transition or sale. If they do not receive what they are expecting or needing, then their livelihood and retirement will likely be affected.

During the transition process, the financial advisor should work closely with the business owner and the business owner's team to consider the financial impact of a sale or transition. The financial advisor should work with other professionals to help advise the business owner on areas outside of their expertise like deal structures, tax impacts, and estate considerations.

After the sale or transition of the business, it is a financial advisor's job to help guide the business owner client. There will be a new influx of liquidity that will need to be invested to replace the income from the business. There will be new challenges to address like investment risk tolerance, time frame, tax implications, and product selection.

As you can see, a financial advisor is a critical part of the exit planning team. The overall goal of the financial planning process in relation to succession planning is to find tools that will help business owners put their vision into reality. The end goal is to create a framework that will accomplish the wishes of the business owner in the most efficient way.

A Personal Financial Plan can help the business owner answer the following financial questions:

How much money is needed from the sale of the business to fund my income and retirement needs?

What type of tax exposure will I have with different transition options?

How do I maximize my wealth?

How do I manage my wealth once the sale of the business is complete?

How will potential changes in tax legislation affect my plans?

What financial gaps are missing in my plan?

What financial tools are available pre- and post-transition to help achieve my goals?

Table 8.1 Topics to Address in Financial Planning

Topic	Comments	Person Responsible
Personal Goals and Objectives		
Personal & Family Timelines		
Emergency Funds		
Assets		
Net Worth		
Life Insurance		
Long-Term Care Insurance		
Personal Taxes		
Professional Goals and Objectives		
Professional Timelines		
Cash Flow		
Liabilities		
Estate Planning		
Disability Insurance		
Property and Casualty Insurance		
Education Planning		

A Personal Financial Plan will also look to address the following topics with the business owner (Table 8.1).

8.4 Options for Transitioning the Business

The inevitable question most small and family-owned business owners ask is what are my options? This chapter is not meant to detail out all the options, because each situation is unique; however, when small and family-owned enterprises face succession planning, these are the most common options:

1. Intergenerational Transfer
2. Internal Sale
3. External Sale
4. Sale to no one/Close the business

Intergenerational transfer—An intergeneration transfer allows the business owner to keep the business within the family and pass it to the next generation. This transfer can be done through a gift or a financial transaction.

Internal sale—An internal sale allows the business owner to sell to an existing partner, manager, or even an employee group. This is considered internal because the buyer is an individual or a group already familiar and involved with the business.

External sale—An external sale allows the business owner to sell to an outside party. This can be facilitated directly by the seller and buyer or through a third party like an investment banker. The external market will allow the business owner a wider range of potential buyers.

Sale to no one/close the business—Some business owners decide that their succession plan will be to simply liquidate the assets left in the business and close their doors. This option is sometimes used because of a lack of marketability for the business. This could be because the business or industry itself is obsolete or is not profitable anymore.

This is by no means a complete list of options for a business owner considering a transition strategy, but it is a good basis for where to start your planning.

While a business owner may want to and plan for selling or gifting ownership to the next generation or to key employees already within the business that does not always happen. A sound succession plan should have both a Plan A and Plan B if the ideal scenario does not come to fruition.

Once you have decided whether you will transition the business through internal or external measures, you will face another set of decisions. There are numerous ways to structure each of the primary routes—including a lump sum sale, an installment sale, an earn-out sale based on a percentage of future profits, and others. Each option requires a different approach and different financial tools. In addition, each option brings its own set of tax and financial impacts to the business owner and acquiring owner. We want to structure the plan thoughtfully and consider all the repercussions, good and bad.

Selling a business can create many financial planning issues and opportunities related to cash flow, investment portfolios, retirement plans, and wealth preservation. Therefore, it is imperative that you find a financial advisor who can help you identify and address these issues. A financial advisor is only one of the important professionals you should consider consulting before, after, and during a business transition.

So, who else needs to be on your team?

Banker—The business owner needs to work with the banker who can assist with the everyday banking needs of a business owner. The banking relationship is important because business owners need assistance with a variety of things from basic cash flow accounts to access to financing for loans.

Investment banker—The business owner needs to work with an investment banker if considering an external sale. The investment banker will help take the business to market and introduce potential buyers and sellers.

Business broker—The business owner needs to work with a business broker when considering all their options for succession planning. The business broker can help the business owner understand that market for their industry and the likelihood of a successful sale.

CPA—The business owner needs to work with a tax professional like a CPA that can help with tax planning and tax management. The tax professional will also be instrumental when it comes time to consider succession planning options.

Business valuator—The business owner needs to work with a business valuator to conduct a proper business valuation. The business valuator should have experience in the owner's industry and should work to help the business owner understand how the business is valued.

Business attorney—The business owner needs to work with an attorney who can help properly structure the business and advise the business owner on any legal issues pertaining to the business.

Estate attorney—The business owner needs to work with an estate attorney who can recommend and implement necessary estate documents. These estate documents are a critical part of any financial plan and succession plan.

Insurance agent—The business owner needs to work with an insurance agent or advisor. This advisor should be in place to advise the business owner. There are a variety of types of insurance agents, so there may need to be more than one agent involved.

Business advisor—The business owner needs to work with a business advisor while working through the succession planning process. This

advisor could share valuable advice and insight into the process and
can also help the business owner avoid some commit pitfalls.

Mergers and acquisitions professional—The business owner needs to work
with a mergers and acquisitions professional if the owner is considering
an external sale.

Advisor of philanthropy—The business owner needs to work with a
philanthropy specialist if their business succession goals include philanthropy. There are many complicated tax tools and strategies that can
be used to fulfill philanthropic wishes, and someone who specializes in
this type of gifting can be contacted for help.

I recommend that you start building your team now. If you don't have these
roles filled, look to your peers and local professional organizations for referrals. Keep track of your team by creating an inventory of your team members and contacts (Table 8.2).

Table 8.2   Succession Planning Team Inventory

Directions: Use this inventory to identify your team members. Place their names under the second column below opposite each identified role. Then, indicate in the right column if a referral is needed.		
Role	**Team Member**	**Referral Needed: Yes/No**
Banker		
Investment Banker		
Business Broker		
CPA		
Business Valuator		
Business Attorney		
Estate Attorney		
Financial Advisor		
Insurance Agent		
Business Advisor		
Mergers and Acquisitions Professional		
Advisor of Philanthropy		

8.5 Chapter Summary

Succession planning is a process. It takes time, a willing business owner, and a dedicated team of professionals to put all the pieces together. The financial planning piece of the picture is foundational and must be addressed in the beginning stages because so many other parts of the plan rely on it. The financial plan should encourage the business owner to think about the current and future financial needs and wants in a way that will create a road map for the business owner. The financial plan will uncover weaknesses, identify opportunities, identify areas to improve, and ultimately force the business owner to think and plan for the short and long run.

If a business owner can embrace the succession planning concept early and often, the business owner will likely have more control of the sale, a more lucrative transaction, and a better long-run plan after the sale is complete.

If you're reading this book, I think you are already thinking about your plan. You are investing your time and energy into educating yourself around the idea of succession planning. Learning these concepts and ideas is important, but it will just be the first step. For you to experience the successful transition of your business, you must take immediate action! "Succession planning is not just a single event symbolized by signing thoughtfully designed estate planning documents. It is an evolving, lifelong process" (Collier 2012, p7).

Works Cited

Collier, Charles W. 2012. *Wealth in Families*. 3rd edition. Cambridge, MA: President and Fellows of Harvard College.

Snider, Christopher M. 2016. *Walking to Destiny: 11 Actions An Owner MUST Take to Rapidly Grow Value & Unlock Wealth*. 1st edition. New Delhi: ThinkTank Publishing House.

Chapter 9

Talent Management in Small and Family Businesses

Larry Baldwin, William J. Rothwell, and Robert K. Prescott

Contents

DOI: 10.4324/9781003281054-12

9.1 Opening Vignette

Kerry Nelson owns a small shop in a suburban shopping mall. Kerry has struggled to keep the business going in recent years due to the high cost of the rent, the diminishing foot traffic in the mall, and (most recently) the devastating effect of the COVID-19 virus on mall shopping. Nelson employs three people in the shop since it is impossible for her to be in the shop at all times. The mall is open from 9 am to 10 pm, seven days per week, and the rules of the mall require all stores to be open during the mall's business hours.

Kerry is now at retirement age. She just turned 66 years old and has qualified for Social Security. For years she sacrificed to put money aside for retirement, and she has a nice nest egg that will carry her into the golden years.

Now Kerry needs to make decisions about what to do next. She has thought about selling the shop, which is an appealing option. But few buyers would have interest if they looked over the sales records over the last few years. Those sales figures are disappointing because of the COVID-19 pandemic. Kerry has also considered having a fire sale, selling whatever inventory remains after the sale, and then just closing the shop permanently. That is also a possibility. Kerry has children, but neither of them is interested in taking over the shop. Her son is an electrical engineer, and her daughter is a Registered Nurse. They both earn more than they could make in the shop. When she discussed her options with her children, they suggested she close the shop, enjoy her remaining years without worrying about daily business, and use the proceeds from the shop's sale to fund her time in a retirement community.

Kerry would like to keep the shop open if she can. To her it has sentimental value. She lived most of her life in that shop. She met her husband when he dropped in as a shopper. She was working in the shop when she was rushed to the hospital twice to give birth to her children. As toddlers her children played in that shop, and years later her children brought their future spouses into the shop to introduce them to her. Kerry's parents visited the shop, and they told her that what she had done with it made them feel proud. Tears formed in her eyes when she thought about her life and that shop. She does not want to sell or close the shop.

But Kerry realizes that small and family businesses like her shop face major challenges in talent management. Recruiting good workers is difficult because a small business cannot pay what larger, more successful organizations can. It is impossible, and Kerry has found training new hires and keeping the best people to be quite an effort.

What can Kerry do now to recruit, train, and retain workers? How can she find a successor if she wishes to keep her shop open after she retires? She thinks about promoting one of her three workers or else hiring someone to groom to take over the shop as General Manager.

As she thinks about succession and all the employee issues she faces, she wonders whether she should approach the matter with dedication and careful planning. That she thinks of as a formal approach, which would encompass (among other topics) the management implications of workforce actions, legal considerations of what she does, tax and accounting issues, and family dynamics. She could keep doing what she has always done—and as many small and family business owners do. That means she would only focus on succession or employee issues as she was forced to do so by expediency to meet immediate business needs like filling vacancies or making new hires productive. Informal methods may rely on such methods as mentoring (Rothwell and Chee 2013) and daily actions intended to groom individuals or employee groups for more responsibility (Rothwell, Chee and Ooi 2015).

9.2 Introduction

As the opening vignette has shown, talent management poses special challenges for small businesses and for family businesses. These special challenges can complicate the succession planning process in those settings.

But what is meant by the term *talent management*? How does talent management relate to succession planning? What precisely are the unique challenges faced by small business owners and family businesses in planning for, acquiring, developing, deploying, engaging, rewarding, promoting, retaining, and (sometimes) releasing talented workers, and how can the effects of those unique challenges be mitigated or overcome? What recent challenges are small and family business owners experiencing? This chapter addresses these questions.

9.3 Defining the Term *Talent Management*

Talent management is a term in search of meaning. It can have more than one meaning. The meaning of the phrase *talent management* hinges largely on the meaning of the word *talent*.

Talent can refer to:

- How well people perform their jobs (their productivity).
- What potential people have for promotion.
- Both present job performance and future potential for promotion.
- Natural gifts with which people are born.
- Personal strengths—what people do best.
- What special knowledge people may have ("what you know" [Rothwell 2011]).
- What special social relationships people may have ("who you know").
- How much you can innovate ("how creative you are").
- Other, specialized definitions unique to an industry or organization.
- All of the above.

Talent management is about working to manage and develop talent. It usually refers to efforts to attract, develop, and retain individuals with talent. But it can go well beyond that simplistic definition, too. Some would define talent management as integrated efforts, focused on talented people, to:

- Plan for talent.
- Attract talent.
- Select talent.
- Onboard talent.
- Train talent.
- Develop talent.
- Reward talent.
- Engage talent.
- Deploy talent.
- Retain talent.
- Release talent.

All those talent management issues affect small and family business owners in their efforts to find successors—and to conduct their normal business operations.

A formal approach to each issue is planned and carried out deliberately. But few small business leaders do that in ways that comprehensively address the issues covered in previous chapters of this book—such as tax/accounting, legal, management, family psychology, and financial considerations. Most focus on informal methods centered in expediency. Many large organizations enjoy an advantage with employees because they carefully plan for workforce needs and implement those plans.

9.4 How Talent Management Relates to Succession Planning

Succession planning can be understood to mean developing people for more or different responsibilities. It does not mean guaranteeing people promotions. It does not mean rewarding loyalty for long service. It does mean preparing people to step up on the organization chart to different job duties.

Talent management includes development but goes beyond it to include integrated efforts to planning for talent, acquiring talent, engaging talent, deploying talent, assessing, or rating talent, retaining talent, and (sometimes) releasing talent. When succession planning and talent management are defined in that way, succession planning is included in—and part of—talent management.

9.5 Unique Talent Management Challenges and Mitigation Efforts of Small and Family Business Owners

Consider the full range of challenges that small and family business owners face when dealing with human resources (Carasco and Rothwell 2020). They include issues associated with planning for workers, acquiring workers, developing workers, deploying workers, engaging workers, rewarding workers, promoting workers, retaining talented workers, and releasing people who are not productive. All aspects of human resources can be different in a small or family business compared to a big business or a multinational corporation. It is worth considering what these challenges are and how to mitigate or address them.

9.5.1 Planning for Workers

Workforce planning has grown to be a popular topic for discussion in business circles in recent years. Organizational leaders realize the importance of planning the quantity and quality of people they will need to execute their strategic goals (Rothwell, Graber and McCormick 2012). And, given several factors (Hetrick et al. 2021), labor cannot be taken for granted as plentiful as it often has been in years past.

How do small and family business owners undertake that challenge of planning for future workers? It begins by thinking about it. How many workers are likely to be needed to keep the organization operating? How many people are likely to resign, be on disability or family leave, and how many are likely to be promoted or moved around? Those questions need to be considered. Family business owners may wish to consider how to handle new family members who enter through marriage or how to deal with in-laws who become divorcees.

9.5.2 Acquiring Workers

Large companies often have an advantage in talent acquisition in that they can support a full-time recruiting staff to source talent in all its meanings. But small companies struggle to attract anyone. There are reasons they struggle.

First, because they rarely have a full-time recruiting staff, small businesses must approach the labor market cold whenever a vacancy occurs. Recruiting is handled in fits-and-starts because the organization does not have the workers to focus on it full time. Without a continuing presence in the labor market, small businesses do not have the same established reputation in their industries or communities that large organizations do. Small businesses do not establish a large footprint in the labor market because few workers are employed there. People rarely hear about that employer—and do not think to seek employment with that employer.

Second, large companies can afford the time and effort to research their employment brand and their employee value proposition. *The employment brand* refers to the reputation of the organization as an employer. What do people say about working there? Why do they say it is good? The *employee value proposition* refers to the promise made to workers in return for their services or loyalty. What is the full list of benefits that workers receive from working in one organization?

The employment brand should not be confused with the organization's brand name; rather, the employment brand is best identified by asking workers why they stay in the organization rather than seek alternative employment.

The employee value proposition for a small business may be more limited than for a large organization. Workers often receive fewer benefits and must fight to get health insurance or other benefits routinely provided in large organizations.

To overcome these problems, small business owners must simply be more innovative in their recruiting methods and their human resource practices. One way to do that is to create and implement creative employment policies that larger organizations do not use. Some are familiar: signing bonuses; spot bonuses for good work; or special gifts for holidays. A second way to do that is to seek people in labor groups traditionally overlooked by larger employers. That may include protected class employees and retirees. A third way to do that is to find clever approaches to recruiting workers that other employers traditionally have not tried. Examples might include hosting open house career fairs in the business and invite in people from the community or industry or giving talks in community organizations about the business as a scouting approach.

9.5.3 *Developing Workers*

Small businesses rarely have large training budgets. And onboarding and on-the-job training in small businesses may be handled informally and without the well-planned structure sometimes present in larger organizations.

Without a well-organized onboarding and training program, small business owners may struggle to attract and retain workers who often regard employee development as critical when they search for jobs and compare employment choices. A Gallup report in 2016 revealed that 59% of millennials regard learning opportunities as critical to them to preserve their competitive advantage (Adkins and Rigoni 2016). But they are not alone, because the same study found that 44% of GenXers and 41% of Baby Boomers believe the same. It thus turns out that work is regarded as a career-enhancer, but few small businesses have a well-planned employee development program that will appeal to top talent. While some managers believe that investments in training will lead to higher turnover as workers take their new skills and leverage them into better-paying opportunities in other organizations training is an excellent way to attract, develop, and retain good people (Grensing-Pophal 2021).

9.5.4 *Deploying Workers*

Small business owners devote much time and effort to hiring. But once people are hired, they are not always carefully deployed. *Deployment* means making sure that people remain in the right place doing the right things.

Small businesses often need to deploy people across many jobs in a way that rarely happens in larger organizations. Workers need to perform many roles because there may be more work than there are workers available to do it. Stated another way, in a small business workers must "wear many hats." Cross-training workers is critically important (Why Cross-Training Employees Is Great for Small Business 2016). Employers must know how to establish a systematic approach to training workers on how to fill in for others when they are out sick or on vacation—or when the job vacancy extends for some time.

Deployment gives small businesses an advantage that large businesses rarely enjoy. Work experience is the best way for people to be developed for more responsibility. There are simply more opportunities for that in small businesses.

9.5.5 Engaging Workers

A study of 700 small businesses found that workers had higher levels of job satisfaction and commitment—what many people call *engagement* (Rothwell et al. 2014)—than in larger organizations (Perna 2020). But the biggest challenge that workers in small businesses reported facing was higher levels of isolation and feelings of loneliness. Employers can address those issues by hosting regular get-togethers and daily check-ins to see how people are doing. Still, small business enjoys an advantage in engagement over larger organizations.

9.5.6 Rewarding Workers

Small business owners often complain that they cannot afford to pay their workers as larger organizations can. They feel that their organizations experience a competitive disadvantage in pay practices. And employee surveys bear out the truth of that impression. A survey of small businesses cited by *Forbes* indicates that 44% of small business employees are dissatisfied with their pay, and 49% feel that their pay has not kept pace with inflation (Lesonsky 2020). The same study found that workers do not live close to their employers, so travel costs and commuting time are more than for employees of larger organizations.

Employee benefits in a small business are rarely as robust as they are in larger companies. Every employer in the United States must provide the mandatory benefits:

- Social security.
- Medicare.
- Unemployment insurance.
- Workers' compensation.
- Overtime pay.
- Time for jury duty.
- Leave for COVID-19.

Employers providing these required benefits cannot compete based on a better benefits package than other employers. Where they can compete is funding, voluntarily, benefits that may be especially appealing to some workers. These include:

- Paid leave (vacation, sick leave, funeral leave, personal leave).
- Unpaid leave.
- Health insurance.
- Life and disability insurance.
- Retirement benefits.
- Fringe benefits (such as daycare, tuition reimbursement, employee discounts, gym memberships).
- Free benefits (such as special uniforms, nice office furniture, company cars).

No benefit is free. They must be funded, and they are costly. And that will raise the employer's costs and reduce profits. Still, if the goal is to attract, develop, and retain the best, most talented people, funding more-than-competitive pay and benefits may be essential. That is especially true if the goal is to attract a pool of promotable people for a succession plan.

9.5.7 Promoting Workers

Small and family business owners also worry, just as they do about wages and benefits, that they cannot offer the opportunity for career advancement or promotions that larger employers can. The value of promoting from within is that it encourages employee loyalty and is thus a retention strategy. If word is advertised that workers can be promoted in a small business that can also be a way to attract talented people.

Often, employee development in a small business depends on the willingness of individual workers to take advantage of the opportunities presented to them to broaden and deepen their work experience (Lee no date). If employers provide opportunities for cross-training, that can also broaden the workers' potential. But employee development efforts must be managed if workers are to be prepared as successors, since success at one level on an organization chart is not necessarily a guarantee of success at higher levels (Rothwell 2015). Grooming people for more responsibility—essential to effective succession planning—cannot be left to manage itself!

There is more than one way to promote workers (Sessoms n.d.). Promotions can be competitive, which may involve succeeding on job performance tests. Promotions can be based on demonstrated acquisition of new knowledge and skills, a common approach for technical workers such as engineers or scientists. Promotions can be based on time-in-position, adding new duties, or merit. Merit-based promotions are based on comparing the worker's education, experience, and other qualifications against the job requirements in the same way an external hire would be evaluated for selection. All these methods can be considered by small business owners.

A word of caution: family business owners sometimes face a dilemma in which family members expect special consideration for jobs or promotions in the organization. While bowing to that expectation may lead to family harmony, it is not a wise approach for long-term business success. The reason is simple: picking people for jobs other than their ability to perform will rarely read to successful placements.

9.5.8 Retaining Talented Workers

Employee retention has emerged as one of the biggest employer challenges in the wake of the pandemic. Many reasons have been offered to explain it. Among them: (1) workers want more meaningful work; (2) many workers have learned that they can do work from home while saving money on commuting, childcare, and eldercare; (3) workers realize that, if they stay where they are, they usually get smaller pay raises than what they get if they jump to alternative employers; (4) workers are pursuing more meaning in their jobs; (5) workers want their employers to be more active in social issues that affect their lives—such as diversity, climate change, social justice; and (6) the sheer number of job openings available (Cook 2021).

The Great Resignation has had a big impact on small and family business owners—and particularly those who own restaurants, hotels, gas stations, and other labor-intensive but low-tech-based firms. It is hard for employers to keep people.

But what are the solutions? There are many. Some are costly; some are inexpensive. Addressing turnover starts with wanting to do it.

9.5.9 Releasing Workers

Not every employee works out. Some must be let go. Small and family business owners cannot afford to keep unproductive people around. But there is need to have a good policy and procedures in place to ensure that workers targeted for release are let go for the right reasons—that is, an inability to do the job or an inability to work productively with co-workers.

9.6 Recent Challenges Small and Family Business Owners Are Experiencing

The pandemic has had a profound effect on all people—and organizations. That is especially true of small businesses. Among those challenges that affect talent management, workers expect their employer to:

- Offer more flexibility in how they do their work.
- Make first-rate efforts to ensure health and safety in the workplace.
- Pay some attention to the psychological issues faced by employees.
- Take proactive steps to create a better world.
- Offer reasonable pay raises that keep pace with inflation.
- Demonstrate sensitivity to diversity, equity, and inclusion issues in the workplace.
- Ensure timely and effective communication about workplace issues.

9.6.1 Offering Workers More Flexibility

Flexibility is a word loaded with meaning. Workers who ask for more *flexibility* from their employers usually mean they want more autonomy in making decisions affecting them (Reisinger and Fetterer 2021). Among those, workers want a say in work schedules, productivity requirements, benefits, how they will work (onsite or online), and much more. The old days of imperial bosses who dictate from on-high with little or no regard for worker opinions will find themselves abandoned by their workforces.

An employer that can demonstrate flexibility will create an employment brand that will attract talented workers. How can that be done? Ask the workers for their input and then follow through in good faith, regularly checking with the workers they are seeing and "feeling" a more flexible work environment.

9.6.2 Making Efforts to Ensure Workplace Health and Safety

The pandemic has raised worker sensitivity to health and safety. Workers do not want to get sick at work, and they want reassurance that their employer is taking serious steps to ensure their well-being. That means following local mandates about masks and vaccinations. That means forming worker committees to track worker well-being—and then taking serious steps to follow through on what those committees recommend.

An employer that can show a willingness to ensure health and safety in the workplace will create an employment brand that will attract talented workers and can avoid the excessive turnover faced by many other employers. How can that be done? Ask the workers for their input on what it would take to feel that their work setting is safe. If that means cleaning toilets every 30 minutes—as some employers did during the peak of the pandemic—then that is the action that should be taken. Often, what employees feel ensures their health and safety will also please present or prospective customers.

9.6.3 Paying Attention to Psychological Issues

During and after the pandemic, many workers in small businesses experienced a profound sense of isolation and loneliness. That prompted skyrocketing conditions for suicide rates globally. While feeling isolated is most acute for remote workers, it can also be felt by workers who are in work settings with other people. Nobody enjoys a workplace that feels "psychologically cold" where people do not want to go to work because they do not like their supervisor, their co-workers, their customers, or find meaning in the work they do.

What can employers do to create a corporate culture that supports camaraderie and esprit-de-corps? The first step is to take it seriously. Ask people how they feel. Survey them. Feed back the survey results. Act on what the workers indicated would help improve worker cohesiveness. Consult the action strategies suggested in publications (see, for instance, Murphy n.d.).

9.6.4 Trying to Create a Better World

Workers—particularly millennials—expect their employers to do more than just make money. They expect businesses to take the lead in driving social change and improving the world (Patterson n.d.). That includes the expectation that businesses will try to deal with climate change, deal with social justice issues, and community development.

If small business owners want to establish an employment brand that attracts and retains workers, it would be wise to demonstrate action toward improving the world. Finding successors may hinge on just what the employer has done to improve global conditions. It is a serious issue.

9.6.5 Offering Pay That Keeps Pace with Inflation

Earlier in this chapter, pay was mentioned as a perennial problems for small businesses. They simply cannot compete with larger organizations. That is true at a time of inflation when prices rise faster than salaries everywhere.

But small businesses can have advantages in working conditions that larger organizations may lack. That may be the key to competing. If small business owners give workers the flexibility to deal with childcare issues or eldercare issues, they may establish an employment brand that other organizations cannot match—even if they pay more.

9.6.6 Demonstrating Sensitivity to Diversity Issues

Workers today—and particularly millennials—insist that their employers live up to the values that the workers support. That means diversity, equity, inclusion, and social justice are not just "nice to have" efforts; rather, they are essential for an employer to attract, develop, and retain the best people (Miller 2021). That is true in the United States, and it is true elsewhere (see Kershaw 2021).

In many job interviews today, that is a question that job applicants will ask an employer. It may take the form of a question like "what is your organization doing to demonstrate an appreciation for diversity?" Business owners wanting to attract, develop, and retain workers will try to be able to answer that question with confidence.

9.6.7 Ensuring Timely and Effective Communication about Workplace Issues

Communication does not mean telling workers what you want to do and expecting them to follow eagerly. Workers today expect to receive information as events are occurring. They do not like to be taken by surprise.

Table 9.1   A Worksheet for Brainstorming Effective Talent Management Strategies

Directions: Use this worksheet to structure your thinking on ways to make your small or family business stand out. The goal is to improve your organization's employment brand as an employer of choice so as to enjoy the benefits of a competitive advantage in attracting, developing, and retaining workers. For each issue listed in the left column below, make notes in the right column about creative ways that your organization could stand out from the pack of other small or family businesses. Involve others in your brainstorming. When you are finished, take steps to follow through and implement the actions you identify.

Employment Issue		What Creative Ideas Can You Identify to Give Your Organization an Advantage in Talent Management?
1	Attracting workers	
2	Selecting workers	
3	Onboarding workers	
4	Training workers	
5	Developing workers	
6	Rewarding workers	
7	Engaging workers	
8	Deploying workers	
9	Retaining workers	
10	Offering workers more flexibility in how they do their work	
11	Making first-rate efforts to ensure health and safety in the workplace	
12	Paying attention to employees' psychological issues	
13	Taking proactive steps to create a better world	
14	Offering reasonable pay raises that keep pace with inflation	
15	Demonstrating sensitivity to diversity, equity, and inclusion issues in the workplace	
16	Ensuring timely and effective communication about workplace issues	

Workers believe that good communication is essential for them to do their jobs (Workplace Communication Statistics 2021).

Much has been published on how to improve workplace communication. But the key to it is ensuring that workers get the information they need when they need it. If your organization has a reputation for fostering good communication, it can attract and retain workers in ways that other organizations cannot.

Use the Tool in Table 9.1 to help your organization brainstorm ways to improve key issues in talent management.

9.7 Chapter Summary

This chapter defined *talent management* as acquiring talent, engaging talent, deploying talent, assessing, or rating talent, and retaining talent. An important issue is how the word talent is understood. *Succession planning* was defined as developing people for more or different responsibilities. Small and family business owners face special challenges in dealing with talent management if it is understood to mean, in the simplest sense, efforts to attract, develop, and retain good workers. Some challenges have long existed for small and family businesses when it comes to all human resource issues; other, newer challenges have been prompted by the pandemic and its aftereffects. Among those newer challenges is that employees expect their employer to: (1) Offer more flexibility in how they do their work; (2) Make first-rate efforts to ensure health and safety in the workplace; (3) Pay some attention to the psychological issues faced by employees; (4) Take proactive steps to create a better world; (5) Offer reasonable pay raises that keep pace with inflation; (6) Demonstrate sensitivity to diversity, equity, and inclusion issues in the workplace; and (7) Ensure timely and effective communication about workplace issues.

Works Cited

Adkins, A., and Brandon Rigoni. 2016. "Millennials Want Jobs to be Development Opportunities." *Workplace.* June 30, 2016. https://www.gallup.com/workplace/236438/millennials-jobs-development-opportunities.aspx

Carasco, M., and William Rothwell. 2020. *The Essential HR Guide for Small Businesses and Startups: Best Practices, Tools, Examples, and Online Resources.* Alexandria, VA: Society for Human Resource Management.

Cook, I. 2021. "Who Is Driving the Great Resignation?" *Harvard Business Review*. September 15, 2021. https://hbr.org/2021/09/who-is-driving-the-great -resignation

Doyle, A. 2021. "What Is Workplace Flexibility?" *The Balance Careers*. July 6, 2021. https://www.thebalancecareers.com/workplace-flexibility-definition-with -examples-2059699

Gonzalez, E. 2020. "The Ultimate Guide to Employee Benefits for Small Businesses." *The Blueprint*. July 30, 2020. https://www.fool.com/the-blueprint/ employee-benefits/

Grensing-Pophal, L. 2021. The Critical Link Between Effective Training and Retention, *HR Daily Advisor*. October 29, 2021. https://hrdailyadvisor.blr.com /2019/11/18/the-critical-link-between-effective-training-and-retention/

Hetrick, R., Hannah Grieser, Rob Sentz, Clare Coffey, and Gwen Burrow. 2021. "The Demographic Drought." *Emsi*. https://www.economicmodeling.com/wp -content/uploads/2021/07/Demographic-Drought-V18.pdf

Kershaw, R. 2021. How to Meet Employees' Growing Expectations around Diversity. *People Management*. June 4, 2021. https://www.peoplemanagement.co.uk/ voices/comment/how-to-meet-employees-growing-expectations-diversity#gref

Lesonsky, R. 2020."Small Business Owners Ask: Am I Paying My Employees the Right Salary?" *Forbes*. https://www.forbes.com/sites/allbusiness/2020/02/12/ employee-salary-small-business-owners/?sh=b868a4764f93

Miller, J. 2021. "For Younger Job Seekers, Diversity and Inclusion in the Workplace Aren't a Preference. They're a Requirement." *The Washington Post*. February 18, 2021. https://www.washingtonpost.com/business/2021/02/18/millennial -genz-workplace-diversity-equity-inclusion/

Perna, M. 2020. "Small Businesses Go Big on Employee Engagement During Pandemic." *Forbes*. September 15, 2020. https://www.forbes.com/sites/mark- cperna/2020/09/15/small-businesses-go-big-on-employee-engagement-during -pandemic/?sh=4a0dfafb626f

Reisinger, H., and Dane Fetterer. 2021. Forget Flexibility. Your Employees Want Autonomy. *Harvard Business Review*. October 29, 2021. https://hbr.org/2021/10 /forget-flexibility-your-employees-want-autonomy

Rothwell, W. 2011. *Invaluable Knowledge: Securing Your Company's Technical Expertise-Recruiting and Retaining Top Talent, Transferring Technical Knowledge, Engaging High Performers*. New York: Amacom.

Rothwell, W. 2015. *Effective Succession Planning: Ensuring Leadership Continuity and Building Talent From Within*. 5th ed. New York: Amacom.

Rothwell, W., and Peter Chee. 2013 *Becoming an Effective Mentoring Leader: Proven Strategies for Building Excellence in Your Organization*. New York: McGraw-Hill.

Rothwell, W., James Graber, and Neil McCormick. 2012. *Lean But Agile: Rethink Workforce Planning and Gain a True Competitive Advantage*. New York: Amacom.

Rothwell, W., R. Alzhahmi, C. Baumgardner, O. Buchko, W. Kim, J. Myers and N. Sherwani. 2014. *Creating engaged employees: It's worth the investment.* Alexandria, VA: ASTD Press

Rothwell, William J., Peter Chee, and Jenny Ooi. 2015c. *The Leader's Daily Role in Talent Management.* New York: McGraw-Hill Education.

Sessoms, G. n.d. "Ways to Promote Employees." *Chron.* https://smallbusiness.chron .com/ways-promote-employees-17676.html

"Why Cross-Training Employees: Employees Is Great for Small Business." 2016. *Small Business Expo.* https://www.thesmallbusinessexpo.com/news/why-cross -training-employees-is-great-for-small-businesses/

"Workplace Communication Statistics." 2021. *Puble.* Accessed March 18, 2021. https://pumble.com/learn/communication/communication-statistics/#:~ :text=A%20Statista%20report%20on%20the,people%20had%20the%20same %20difficulties

Chapter 10

Transitioning the Business and Executing the Succession Plan

William J. Rothwell

Contents

DOI: 10.4324/9781003281054-13

Once you have made your choices about the future and chosen one or more possible successors, then it is time to plan for the transition and to execute the succession plan. But how do you do that? This chapter answers that simple, yet exceedingly difficult, question.

Please note at the outset of this chapter that much has been written about leadership entrances and exits to organizations (see Coffee 2021; Dowdy 2011; Franc 2019; Gust 2019; Keyes 2020; Muehlhausen 2020; Sleger 2021; Stern 2019; Tepper 2014; and Wolfred 2009). Much of it applies to transitions of small business owners and family business owners.

Vignettes

Consider the vignettes below as short examples of common situations that come up as small or family business owners transition out of their businesses and install someone else in their stead.

Vignette 1

Mary Roswell sold her restaurant to one of her waitresses, Joanna Prestonson. Mary inherited the business 20 years ago but, at age 72, decided it was time to sell it and enjoy what remained of her life. Joanna had been Mary's most loyal employee and was with her from the time Mary took over the business from her father

David Roswell. The restaurant employs four people: a cook, two waitresses, and the owner. While it never made a large profit, it made enough to eke out a living for those four people. As Mary finalized the paperwork for the sale, she realized that she owed it to Joanna to give her some coaching on aspects of the business with which she had no experience—such as the bookkeeping challenges, efforts to market the restaurant, and community action with the local Chamber of Commerce, United Way, and other groups that contributed to visibility (and subtle advertising) for the business. Mary began her "to do list" of steps about how to coach Mary on a napkin from the restaurant.

Vignette 2

Larry Michaelson owns a car wash. He has owned it for 33 years. But recently he decided that he would have to choose between upgrading the car wash with new equipment or else getting out of the business. After spending his life with the business, Larry was not eager to sell the business. So, he decided he would hire someone to fill his shoes as owner-operator. The business had succeeded, a fact that Larry attributed to the excellent location his business enjoyed. (Larry did not originally choose the business site for location, but local business conditions changed while his business continued to be where it always was. The result: the car wash enjoyed perhaps the best location of any business in the city for attracting traffic.) Larry began his search for a replacement by asking his friends, family members, and business acquaintances if they knew of anyone who would be a good choice. When that did not result in any names, Larry asked the small accounting firm that had always done his books keeping whether they knew of anyone. He also asked his attorney and financial advisor. But those efforts did not result in any names, either. Growing desperate, Larry put an advertisement in the local newspaper and posted a short notice on bulletin boards in grocery stores around the city in lower to middle-class neighborhoods. That effort paid off. He found three excellent candidates who wanted to learn about the car wash business and had graduated from local high schools.

Larry did not consider himself very knowledgeable about human resource issues. But, as luck would have it, his girlfriend Mae—Larry was divorced—had a friend who was the Vice President of HR at a local bank. Mae arranged for Larry to meet Meg Smithers, the VP of HR for Middletown Trust. That began a three-year-long coaching effort in which Meg guided Larry through the steps of coaching and developing one applicant, Danny Right, to be the new General Manager of the Logan Automatic Car Wash. The transition succeeded, and Larry retired while Danny continued to run the business with as much success as Larry ever had. But Larry attributed the successful preparation of Danny to Meg's guidance and the step-by-step, logical plan they developed for him.

10.1 Definitions

- **Individual Development Plan (IDP)**: An IDP describes, step by step, how to guide an employee or worker through a development process. When the term is used in succession planning, it usually refers to a plan negotiated between worker (who is being developed) and the manager (who is guiding or carrying out the development process) to prepare the worker for more responsibility (a vertical promotion on the organization chart) or to prepare the worker for applying greater technical expertise (a horizontal promotion on the organization chart from one level of technical expertise to a higher level of technical proficiency). While an IDP is usually planned annually, it can have a lifespan longer than that. IDPs can be simple or complex; IDPs can be based on a rigorous assessment of what the worker needs to know to do the job for which he or she is being groomed or a very informal assessment based on the manager's impressions.
- **Execution**: Implementing a plan.
- **Key job incumbents**: Individuals occupying important jobs on the organization chart. Typical examples include the CEO or General Manager and his or her direct reports.
- **Key people**: Individuals whose loss would be devastating to the business. Key people are not always at the top of the organization.
- **Transition management**: The term has many meanings. In the simplest sense, transition management refers to changing from one thing to another. When applied to succession issues or business transfers, it refers to transitioning from one owner or business leader to one or

more others. Transitions can be stressful for employees. They can occur because of the death, disability, or sudden departure of the business owner. They can also result when the business is sold or gifted to others. Often business owners focus on the business sale or the family drama involved with the business transition. Often they forget about the loyal employees and customers who have been a part of their businesses for so long.

10.2 How to Plan the Business Transition

The direction of a business transition depends on several factors. First, what has the business owner chosen as the means to transfer the business? For instance, will the business be sold to a third party, handed over to a family member, given to a partner, sold to a partner, and so forth? These choices were listed in Chapter 1. But the nature of the business transfer will shape the nature of the transition management challenge.

Second, who is chosen to lead the business? Will the new leader be promoted from within, hired from outside, or will a family member be tapped to run things? The new leader is important because he or she might be intimately familiar with the operations of the business. If the person is approaching the business cold—with limited information—then obviously more attention needs to be devoted to planning the transition.

Third, how supportive are others of the transition? Small business owners should consider the likely reactions of their workers, customers, suppliers, and dealers/distributors to a transition. When word gets out that the owner, perhaps the founder or owner of many years, is planning to sell or else pass on the business to another, different stakeholders—that is, people with a stake in the business operations—may have different reactions. Some reactions may not be good or favorable to the business, and steps should be taken to anticipate and try to head off any negative reactions. One example: if one worker expects to be appointed General Manager (GM) upon the departure of the former or present GM but that does not happen, what will that worker do? It may not be desirable to have that worker instantly leave the business out of anger. Likewise, a family business owner has to consider the family implications of a business transfer—before or after the death of the owner or founder. Were the family members consulted on the transfer? What are they expecting—money? A promotion? A nicer office? Do they have expectations based on a transition from one owner/manager to another? Do the family members agree on the choice of the replacement, and what happens if they do not?

Fourth, due consideration must be given to issues discussed in this book already. Have the tax implications of the transition been ironed out? Have the legal issues associated with the transition been addressed? Has the small business owner considered financial advice, if needed, for a windfall of cash? Has the family business owner considered family psychology—and family conflicts—that may have an influence on the transition?

Fifth, has the full impact of the transition been considered? For instance, if someone is promoted from within the business to assume the duties of the GM, what happens with the vacancy created from that promotion? In succession planning, it is common to encounter the so-called "domino effect"—some call it the "musical chairs problem"—whereby one promotion triggers vacancies at all lower levels that then must be addressed and can have serious consequences on business operations. If someone is hired from outside the organization, how knowledgeable are they about the people (the who), the business operations (the what), the facilities (the where), the special issues associated with time demands like peak and valley business cycles (the when), the unique philosophy that sets the organization apart from its competitors (the why), and the unique features of the business operations (the how). If the newcomer is not knowledgeable about those issues, a transition period may be necessary to ease him or her into the job under the guidance of the founder/business owner who initiated the change.

10.3 How to Select an External Successor

One common choice in transition management is to look for an external (a so-called "off-the-street hire") to replace the business leader. There are important advantages and disadvantages to consider when recruiting and selecting an external successor to the GM or other key people in a small or family business.

What are the advantages and disadvantages of an external successor? Consider (in no order of importance) that an outside hire enjoys these advantages for the business:

- Has a fresh perspective.
- May have experience drawn from other organizations that can benefit the business.

- Is not bound by old loyalties to individuals or family members and can take a more objective view of what is needed for the business.
- May have a broader perspective of the local business climate or industry conditions than internal candidates.

But there are disadvantages to an outside hire. They:

- May take longer to become productive because they do not know the unique way the business carries out operations, deals with customers, or handles suppliers and any dealers/distributors.
- Do not know the employees!
- Need to resist the urge to jump in and prove their value by making many changes until they have a better grasp of the history of what led to the business situation or past decisions.
- Are often pressured to satisfy stakeholders quickly and decisively that they are executing on directions given to them by the owner, a Board of Directors, a governing family council, or other groups of relevance.

Perhaps the most important issues to consider are the needs of the business compared to the needs of the owner leaving the business. Business owners may have trouble distinguishing between the two, but the differences can be real. The business owner may be focused on retiring—"getting out of Dodge as quickly as possible"—when that can be harmful to a peaceful transition of the business from one GM to another; likewise, some business owners have trouble wanting to phase out over a long time span.

Most challenging of all: business owners have a nasty habit of selecting people like them—what some call the *like me bias* (Rothwell 2015). When given a selection task, men will pick men, women will pick women, white people will pick white people, engineers will pick engineers, and generally business owners will try to clone themselves. That happens because comfort levels are highest with people like us. (That is also why your choice of friends tells us much about you.)

Cloning can be dangerous to the business. It might be good if external competitive conditions never change. But they do change. What the business needs may not fit with the comfort level of the present owner/operator. A new direction, and thus a leader with different skills and values, may be needed for the business to thrive. Doing more of the same may not be what the business needs, and a fresh—and different—leader may be just what is needed. But owners may have trouble seeing past their own biases for replacing themselves with people they like because those people are like them.

The same problem can plague family businesses. If the founder is a man or woman, he or she may have a bias against picking a family member of the opposite gender. In some nations, the expectation is that the eldest son of the family will inherit a controlling share of the business—even when the youngest daughter may be the one with the better business sense and a superior grasp of the business. In some businesses in America, that same bias persists, stemming from the tradition of *primogeniture* in the European aristocracy (where the eldest male inherits the aristocratic title and all the money and lands associated with it). And it's damaging to businesses because, after the death of the patriarch or matriarch, it may lead to lawsuits among siblings that will force the sale of the business in a contest over fair distribution of business assets among all the children or relatives.

Business owners setting out to hire should exercise due diligence in their choice. They should:

- Review the applicant's resume carefully, looking for experience and industry experience.
- Check references.
- Try to check work history beyond references (what do past co-workers say about this person if you can find such people).
- Check social media history of the applicant.
- Check criminal record.
- Check credit history.

Take care of falling victim to common mistakes when hiring. Do not be overly impressed with an applicant's educational achievements, mode of dress, handshake, personal mannerisms, personal appearance (beauty does not equal competence), or factors that have little to do with job performance (such as race, gender, veteran status, disability, or immigration status if there is a legal right to work in the US). Your ideal candidate is not necessarily a Harvard MBA in a US$3,000 tailor-made silk Armani suit whose suave Oxford accent, handsome demeanor, and highly articulate speaking style impresses everyone. (Such people may be here today and gone tomorrow.) It is better to stick with those applicants with a track record that matches what you want to see happen with your business and whose history of managing people matches up to how you want to see your loyal employees treated after you exit the organization!

Your best interview questions for a prospective job applicant should center on questions like these:

- Why do you want to enter this business?
- What makes you think you are the best choice as my successor?
- What have you heard about this business, and from whom have you heard it?
- How should the transition be handled? How do we go from me running things to you running things? What's the transition plan? Can you put it in writing and show it?
- What obstacles or problems do you envision coming up in transferring the business from me to you? How can we plan to overcome them?
- Do you have any necessary licenses or credentials needed to do this work? (Some industries restrict or limit entry by imposing licensure or registration requirements.)
- What experience have you had in business transitions and how have you handled them?

It is best to have more than one opinion about the suitability of those you think of hiring to be groomed to take over for you. If it is a family business, invite family members to participate in recruiting and selecting a replacement. If it is a small business, consider inviting managers in the organization to participate in the selection process.

Those brought in from outside will typically follow several steps. They include:

- *Step 1*: Experiencing presocialization.
- *Step 2*: Participating in the recruiting and selection process.
- *Step 3*: Giving and receiving initial impressions.
- *Step 4*: Doing a deeper dive by entry socialization and onboarding.
- *Step 5*: Doing an even deeper dive by long-term socialization.
- *Step 6*: Participating in make or break assignments and experience.

These steps are reviewed below.

10.3.1 Step 1: Experiencing Presocialization

Presocialization refers to an individual's life and training before entering a new organization. Individual expectations about work, about the occupation, and about specific organizations are formed during presocialization. Generally, individuals do not apply for jobs with organizations that project a public image antithetical to their beliefs; rather, individuals are inclined to join organizations with a positive reputation as an employer of choice and appear to be at least neutral in the values they project into public life. Some organizations—such as U.S. Army, the CIA, the American Tobacco Company, or firms like Chick-fil-a or Hobby Lobby—may face difficulties when recruiting because they are closely associated with value systems that not all people find acceptable.

Presocialization is also important regarding the reputation of the small or family business and the public reputation of the firm's owner. If business owners project a controversial public image—being outspoken about vaccinations at local school board meetings, as one example—that public image or reputation may complicate efforts to recruit talented people from outside the organization to be successors. One way to address this issue is to work friendship networks and attempt to surface prospective job candidates from outside the business who share the owner's values and beliefs.

10.3.2 Step 2: Participating in the Recruiting and Selection Process

Job applicants who apply from outside an organization begin a process of induction. If they are chosen for the job, the induction progresses to deeper levels; if they are not chosen for the job, they take away impressions from the experience that may shape their understanding for the future. How job applicants are treated during the recruiting and selection process can shape their understanding of the business, its current challenges, the internal politics, the key people and key job incumbents of the organization, the customers, the suppliers, the dealer/distributors, and much more. Great care should be taken in managing just who an applicant meets and what he or she is told during that process. Expectations built during recruitment and selection should not be shattered after job applicants enter the organization, particularly as CEO.

In one small business—which shall remain nameless for this example—the CEO was chosen after an expensive and time-consuming national search. Every employee in the small business participated in the interviewing of CEO candidates from outside the organization. Unfortunately, during this process, the CEO was led to believe that one member of the search committee had a romantic interest in him. Once hired, the CEO acted on that mistaken belief, and you can imagine what were the consequences—legal action for sexual harassment. The CEO was fired, and that prompted yet another lengthy and extended national search! When looking back on the situation, the organization's leaders realized that they had fallen prey to groupthink, the tendency for people in groups to "go along to get along." Critical thinking was suspended when a few key leaders in the business asked about hiring a specific candidate. Care should be taken to avoid groupthink.

Another issue that can arise during recruiting and selection is to have candidates treated to false expectations. In one case a CEO candidate was promised a huge bonus at the year end if the business met specific, measurable sales targets. Once chosen, the CEO candidate exceeded every target. But then she was told that the bonus she was promised was not approved by the full Board of Directors. You can only imagine what happened next—the CEO searched for another organization where people were more truthful, and she exited in short order.

10.3.3 Step 3: Giving and Receiving Initial Impressions

If a new leader enters from outside an organization and is not known to the people of that organization from years of interaction (as is an internal candidate), then the newcomer is greeted with great interest. Everyone watches new leaders to see what they do. The initial impressions they give to others, and the initial impressions others give to them, can be difficult to overcome if they are not intentional.

An example may illustrate the point.

In one organization a new GM entered the scene and promptly announced widespread cost-cutting was needed. She did not seek input from managers but instead acted without pushback on what she had been advised to do by the family owners. She exercised across-the-board budget reductions in everything. The result: disaster. Sales plummeted. Key people quit. Customers expressed extreme dissatisfaction. Competitors swooped in and snapped up market share. The moral to the story: take care when hired from outside as a leader to believe everything you hear without checking yourself. Ultimately the new GM was forced out, victimized by bad advice at the outset and by a bad image created from it.

Someone—perhaps the exiting CEO or GM—should serve as mentor and coach to introduce a newcomer to the people (the who), the business issues (the what), pressing challenges facing the business at the moment (the when), pressing challenges facing different business locations if any (the where), causes of key challenges facing the business (the why), and steps already taken to address key challenges (the how).

10.3.4 Step 4: Doing a Deeper Dive by Entry Socialization and Onboarding

As a hired-from-outside CEO or GM begins, it is wise to plan for the entry socialization process and for onboarding. A tool like Tool 1 at the end of this chapter, tailored to the needs of the organization, can be an excellent starting point for a well-organized onboarding process for the new leader. Care should also be taken to ensure that the new leader is promptly introduced to key people and key job incumbents in the organization. Those introductions should be more than mere cameo appearances at business meetings; rather, it is best to host dinners and visits to homes to get to know people in less formal settings. That approach will yield payoffs later by creating a stronger, more cohesive interpersonal bond among members of the senior executive team.

10.3.5 Step 5: Doing an Even Deeper Dive by Long-Term Socialization

As new leaders enter an organization from outside, they have a predictable impact on perceived priorities. Their stated priorities will prompt new behaviors and new efforts by others in the organization. As a simple example, if a new GM suggests that more time and attention should be devoted to acquiring and using updated technology, then that may well spur efforts to do that.

But how new leaders handle crises will shape the long-term impact of that new leader. For instance, if a new leader authorizes a downsizing, then others will draw conclusions about the leader from how the crises created by the downsizing are managed. Just how does the leader behave in crisis? The answer to that question will often affect the long-term impressions and legacy of new leaders.

10.3.6 Step 6: Participating in Make or Break Assignments and Experiences

As new leaders reach milestone dates like the end of the first year or the departure of a previous leader (like the former business owner leaving the scene), the image they project on their organizations will continue to be shaped by how they manage daily operations and how they manage crises.

Their reputation, important for attracting and retaining talented people, will be shaped by how their behavior is interpreted by others. If that reputation grows troublesome, that may spark another leadership change or else the involvement of an executive coach to facilitate a process of improvement.

10.4 How to Develop an Internal Successor

There are distinct similarities in the transition challenge between recruiting someone from outside the organization to take over for you and developing someone from inside the organization to take over for you. It is always best to follow a systematic, well-planned approach rather than simply ask someone to shadow you ("follow you around"). When people merely shadow you without a plan, the transition can be very chaotic and disconnected. The person who shadows you has no idea how daily challenges fit into a bigger framework or relate to each other. And the preparation may miss reviews of critically important responsibilities, duties, or tasks that come up only infrequently. Preparing a successor bears many similarities to planned on-the-job training (Rothwell and Kazanas 2004) and directive performance coaching (Rothwell and Bakhshandeh 2022).

A practical approach to managing the transition is for the departing leader (business owner or GM) to prepare a very detailed job description. That job description can then be sequenced in order of what is most important for the newcomer to learn—and strategies by which to carry out that training. The tool appearing at the end of this chapter (Tool 2) can guide the process for developing that systematic on-the-job training and coaching.

Over time it may help to work with the new hire to prepare and implement an Individual Development Plan (IDP). An IDP typically addresses such questions as:

- What should the person learn based on organizational/job needs?
- How should the person go about the learning process?
- What resources are needed to support the learning?
- Over what time frame should the learning process occur?
- How should the results of the learning be evaluated?

Examples of IDPs can easily be found by entering the term Individual Development Plan into any browser. Many detailed guides can be found for free online.

10.5 How to Transition When Making a Choice Other Than to Hire from Outside or to Promote from Inside

As Chapter 1 illustrated, many choices exist for business owners who wish to exit their businesses. Among them: an outright sale; a merger with another business; a liquidation/fire sale; or a decision to do nothing until the owner's death. Each alternative to promoting an employee from within to take over the management of the business or else hiring someone from outside the business to take over will create different transition management challenges.

It is important when planning the owner's departure to consider the range of options available. One size does not fit all. The best solution may involve a combination of methods—such as hiring a new leader, changing what role the leader plays, promoting people from within and/ or changing the roles of internal leaders, and considering many other choices.

The challenge is up to you if you are the owner. The authors simply wish to give you ideas on what to consider—and what to watch out for.

10.6 Planning the Exit of the Former Owner

Any manager, including an owner, who exits an organization will go through predictable steps in that process. They may include:

- *Step 1*: Reaching the exit decision: Sudden departure/phased departure/ decision to depart
- *Step 2*: Giving notice of departure to key people
- *Step 3*: Giving notice of departure to staff
- *Step 4*: Giving notice of departure to others (suppliers, customers, dealers)
- *Step 5*: Giving evidence of departure (cleaning out the office/having a final party)
- *Step 6*: Phasing out of duties and responsibilities
- *Step 7*: Formally handing over duties to others
- *Step 8*: Informing people about how to reach you after you leave
- *Step 9*: Remaining involved as you see fit—and as others ask

These steps are reviewed below in more detail.

10.6.1 Step 1: Reaching the Exit Decision: Sudden Departure/Phased Departure/Decision to Depart

Small and/or family business owners face choices on exactly how they will exit from the firm. Usually, their exits will be gradual. But exceptions can occur when the business owner suddenly dies, suddenly grows disabled through a heart attack or stroke, or is suddenly fired. Many business owners admittedly have trouble letting go, particularly when they have devoted their lifetimes to building a business. They may wish to explore phased departures in which they gradually give up their responsibilities to someone else.

Usually, it depends on what you want to do if you are the business owner contemplating an exit.

10.6.2 Step 2: Giving Notice of Departure to Key People

Before you depart voluntarily, plan to communicate with others who depend on you.

That includes key people in the business. It also includes key people in your life—such as your significant other, your children, your relatives, and business acquaintances who may depend on you.

There are two kinds of meetings with key people.

The first kind is *exploratory*. You sound them out about their thoughts when you express a desire to retire, leave the business, or otherwise change your role. That meeting may be lengthy as you think out loud about your personal situation and reasons shaping your decisions. Be prepared to listen carefully to what others tell you, and that is especially true with family members who may have your best interests at heart but also may have a selfish stake in what you decide.

The second kind is *explanatory*. You tell people what you have decided to do and then ask how it may affect them. Be prepared to work through how your decision to leave will be greeted. Focus attention on problem-solving in the transition process.

10.6.3 Step 3: Giving Notice of Departure to Staff

Consider how you will make an announcement of your departure to the organization's workers. Expect that word will get out fast if you share word of your decision with anyone.

It may be best to limit conversations initially to key people and key job incumbents and then move on to "town hall meetings" in which you announce your departure to everyone at once.

If your organization has multiple locations, be prepared to share the first town hall meeting by zoom with all the business locations. If you do not do that, then there will be different interpretations of the meeting circulating to the locations in which you did not meet.

Clarify who will be assuming your responsibilities and when that transition will occur. Address who is affected, what will happen, when it will happen, where it will happen, how it will happen, and why it is happening. Share a willingness to meet with anyone who wants to ask you questions about the transition—which may center on how your departure will influence their jobs, their career prospects, and their departments.

10.6.4 Step 4: Giving Notice of Departure to Others (Suppliers, Customers, Dealers)

The minute you announce to your employees you are planning to exit the business, you will find that word travels fast.

Be ready with a press release and take steps quickly to contact your company's key investors, suppliers, customers, dealers/distributors, and others who may feel that your departure signals a change of importance to them. Be prepared to answer difficult questions. As with employees, address who is affected, what will happen, when it will happen, where it will happen, how it will happen, and why it is happening. Share a willingness to meet with anyone who wants to ask you questions about the transition—which may center on how your departure will directly and immediately influence them.

10.6.5 Step 5: Giving Evidence of Departure (Cleaning Out the Office/Having a Final Party)

As you prepare for your ultimate departure from the organization, brainstorm everything that you must do. Try to task it out.

When will you:

- Clean out your office?
- Return keys?
- Give up passwords and entry codes to the business facilities and, when appropriate, bank accounts or other important access?
- Return any company equipment you have at home?
- Turn in the company car, if you have one?
- Say goodbye to your friends?

Someone might get the idea of giving you a party. If they do, such parties usually center on achieving three goals: (1) *grieving*: people will feel loss at your departure if they have known you for a long time, and so be prepared to reassure them and clarify how and when you will stay in touch with them; (2) *celebrating*: people will want to look back on their relationship with you and celebrate the mutual successes and challenges you have shared; and (3) *clarifying who is taking on your duties*: make it clear when the formal transition will occur and who will be taking over all of your duties.

10.6.6 *Step 6: Phasing Out of Duties and Responsibilities*

If you phase out gradually rather than make a clean break with the business, then a phase-out plan should be clear. That may be required if you sold the business. New owners will want to give you a contract to clarify what you do, when you do it, and how you are compensated for that work. Try to have that phase-out contract prepared and executed before the formal business sale occurs.

10.6.7 *Step 7: Formally Handing Over Duties to Others*

Make sure everyone is clear when your duties are handed over to others. That is important if you are gradually phasing out, since many people will be confused about your new role if you are gradually pursuing a "phased retirement" or similar incremental departure.

One way to handle it is to prepare a table. In the left column, list out every item from a detailed job description for you before you give up your job. Then in the next column indicate who will carry out that duty as you leave or after you left, and then in the right column indicate a specific date certain when the responsibility will be transferred to the new person. That can help clarify who does what when. This approach is called *responsibility charting*.

10.6.8 *Step 8: Informing People about How to Reach You after You Leave*

Be clear in communicating to other people how to reach you after you leave the organization. If you do not want to be bothered, say so politely. If you do wish to be contacted, clarify the conditions in which you would welcome such communication.

Sometimes, a departing manager is needed to provide information about the reasons for past decisions or to offer help in dealing with a customer, supplier, dealer/distributor, or an employee. Indicate if you will do that after you leave.

10.6.9 Step 9: Remaining Involved as You See Fit—and as Others Ask

Business owners who have devoted their lives to a business may have trouble divorcing themselves from involvement with that business. That is likely in a family business in which it may be difficult to separate family from business. It is up to you to contact those in the business after you leave to "check in"—and perhaps to ask how things are going. Some business owners will not want to do that because they want to enjoy retirement or else push on to new challenges and leave the past in the past.

But try to clarify to your former employees, managers, customers, and others on what basis you might welcome word from them.

10.7 Chapter Summary

This chapter presented compelling vignettes to illustrate different situations that might occur when a business transitions from one owner or manager to others. Key definitions were provided for such terms as Individual Development Plan (IDP), execution, and transition management. The chapter offered coaching tips on how to plan for transition. The chapter also reviewed common approaches and issues involved with hiring a successor from outside the business, promoting a successor from inside the business, and choosing one of many alternatives to an external hire or internal promotion. The chapter offered step-by-step guidance on how to handle the selection of a new CEO, GM, or business owner from outside, promotion from inside, or some other choice.

10.8 Chapter Tools

Tables 10.1 and 10.2.

Table 10.1   A Checksheet to Guide Executive Onboarding

Executive's Name	Today's Date
Coach's Name	
Onboarding Plan	

Notes on the Onboarding Plan (*Make notes here about special issues for the onboarding*):

(*Continued*)

Table 10.1 (Continued) A Checksheet to Guide Executive Onboarding

Needed?		Questions to Answer in the Onboarding		What Instructional Objectives, Activities, and Timetables Should Be Worked Out to Address These Questions?
Yes ✓	No ✓	Should the Executive:		
☐	☐	1	Tour company facilities, including:	
☐	☐		A	All departments?	
☐	☐		B	His/her office?	
Needed?		**Questions to Answer in the Onboarding**		**What Instructional Objectives, Activities, and Timetables Should Be Worked Out to Address These Questions?**
Yes ✓	No ✓	Should the Executive:		
☐	☐		C	Cafeteria?	
☐	☐	2	Receive a standard onboarding like that given for all new Organization employees, including a description of	
☐	☐		A	Employee benefits?	
☐	☐		B	Vacation time policies and scheduling?	
☐	☐		C	Holidays?	
☐	☐		D	A probationary period (if applicable)?	
☐	☐		E	Company tuition refund policy?	
☐	☐		F	Company-sponsored in-house training for staff members?	
☐	☐		G	Retirement benefits?	
☐	☐		H	Credit union?	
☐	☐		I	Off-the-job, company-sponsored social activities?	
☐	☐		J	Hours of work (starting time, lunch period, quitting time?)	
☐	☐		K	Pay periods?	

(Continued)

Table 10.1 (Continued)   A Checksheet to Guide Executive Onboarding

□	□		L	Parking arrangements?	
□	□		M	Other matters? (List them below.)	
□	□	3		Receive an onboarding to the company, including discussion about its:	
□	□		A	Purpose (What is the business?)	
Needed?			**Questions to Answer in the Onboarding**		**What Instructional Objectives, Activities, and Timetables Should Be Worked Out to Address These Questions?**
Yes ✓	**No** ✓		**Should the Executive:**		
□	□		B	Goals/objectives (What is the company trying to achieve over the next five years? One year?)	
□	□		C	Structure (What are the departments and work units in the company? What do they do? An organization chart would be helpful for this.)	
□	□		D	History (How did the company get where it is today?)	
□	□		E	Top management team (Who are they? What do they consider important?)	
□	□		F	Other matters (List below.)	
□	□	4		Receive an onboarding to the department, including discussions about:	
□	□		A	The staff member's unit within the structure of the department?	
□	□		B	The department's place in the organization?	
□	□		C	Department goals/objectives?	
□	□		D	Department history?	
□	□		E	Other units and staff members in the department and what they do?	

(Continued)

Table 10.1 (Continued) A Checksheet to Guide Executive Onboarding

☐	☐		F	The department manager's expectations for all staff members?	
☐	☐		G	What kinds of problems to bring to the department manager's attention?	
☐	☐		H	Other matters (List them below.)	
Needed?		**Questions to Answer in the Onboarding**			**What Instructional Objectives, Activities, and Timetables Should Be Worked Out to Address These Questions?**
Yes ✓	No ✓	**Should the Executive:**			
☐	☐	5		Receive a special onboarding to the new work unit, including	
☐	☐		A	A tour of the unit, with emphasis on	
☐	☐			1 The executive's office and work area?	
☐	☐			2 Washrooms?	
☐	☐			3 Copy machines?	
☐	☐			4 Vending machines?	
☐	☐			5 Computers and computer systems?	
☐	☐			6 Work stations of direct reports?	
☐	☐		B	Introductions to many people?	
☐	☐		C	A review of each direct report's HR records?	
☐	☐		D	Overview of work unit activities, tasks, and procedures?	
☐	☐		E	Overview of equipment used in the work unit?	

(Continued)

Table 10.1 (Continued) A Checksheet to Guide Executive Onboarding

□	□		F	Overview of work processes and special procedures applicable to the work units reporting to the executive?	
□	□		G	A description of the work unit's purpose and other work units that depend on it?	
□	□		H	Goals/objectives of the work unit?	
□	□		I	History of the work unit, including special problems unique to it?	
□	□		J	Other matters (List below.)	
Needed?			**Questions to Answer in the Onboarding**		**What Instructional Objectives, Activities, and Timetables Should Be Worked Out to Address These Questions?**
Yes ✓	**No** ✓		**Should the executive:**		
□	□	6	Receive a special onboarding to the job, including		
□	□		A	A description of the executive's role?	
□	□		B	A description of what executives are expected to do in this company in particular?	
□	□		C	A review of the executive's job description with the organization's owner or Board of Directors?	
□	□		D	A review of the executive's performance targets and bonus plan with owner(s) and/or Board of Directors?	
□	□		E	Other matters (List them below.)	
□	□	7	Receive a special review of important industry issues, including		
□	□		A	A discussion of what industry issues have been important in the past? Are very important? Are likely to become more important?	

(Continued)

Table 10.1 (Continued)   A Checksheet to Guide Executive Onboarding

					What Instructional Objectives, Activities, and Timetables Should Be Worked Out to Address These Questions?
☐	☐		B	A discussion of what industry issues are likely to affect the organization?	
Needed?		**Questions to Answer in the Onboarding**			**What Instructional Objectives, Activities, and Timetables Should Be Worked Out to Address These Questions?**
Yes ✓	**No** ✓	**Should the Executive:**			
☐	☐		C	Have a discussion of what industry issues are likely to affect the department?	
☐	☐		D	Have a discussion of what industry issues are likely to affect the executive's work unit--and why?	
☐	☐		E	Have a discussion of what industry issues are likely to affect the executive's job? The jobs of subordinates?	
☐	☐		F	Discuss other matters with someone in the organization?	
☐	☐	8		Receive details about company policies and procedures affecting the executive's job, including hands-on briefings about the	
☐	☐		A	Organization and department planning activities?	
☐	☐		B	Organization and department budgeting activities?	
☐	☐		C	Travel policies/procedures?	
☐	☐		D	Purchasing?	
☐	☐		E	Contracting for assistance?	
☐	☐		F	Organization accounting methods?	
☐	☐		G	Organization production control and scheduling?	
☐	☐		H	Organization production reporting?	

(Continued)

Table 10.1 (Continued)   A Checksheet to Guide Executive Onboarding

☐	☐		I	Property control and inventory?	
☐	☐		J	Computer/IT systems?	
Needed?				**Questions to Answer in the Onboarding**	**What Instructional Objectives, Activities, and Timetables Should Be Worked Out to Address These Questions?**
Yes ✓	**No** ✓			**Should the Executive:**	
☐	☐		K	Security?	
☐	☐		L	Personnel matters—including hiring, evaluating, disciplining, and terminating direct reports?	
☐	☐		M	Attendance records on direct reports?	
☐	☐		N	Phones?	
☐	☐		O	Other important organization policies? (List them in the space below.)	
☐	☐	9		Receive information about federal, state, and local laws, rules, and regulations affecting	
☐	☐		A	The industry? (for instance, regulatory bodies dealing with industry)	
☐	☐		B	The company? (for instance, OSHA, EEOC, and state government counterparts)	
☐	☐		C	The facility? (local plant or office as opposed to the entire firm)	
☐	☐		D	The department?	
☐	☐		E	The work unit?	
☐	☐		F	The staff member's job?	
☐	☐		G	Other matters (List them below.)	

(Continued)

Table 10.1 (Continued)   A Checksheet to Guide Executive Onboarding

10	*Summarize on a separate sheet the instructional objectives for the executive's onboarding. When he or she finishes the onboarding, he or she should be able to:*
11	*Summarize below the activities that need to be carried out to meet each onboarding objective established in question 10 above. Also, indicate what else the executive wants to do to cut the unproductive onboarding period and make it more productive—such as hold town hall meetings, meet individually with key people, invite people to the executive's home for dinner to create closer bonds, and so forth.*
12	*Summarize below the timetable for meeting the objectives and carrying out the onboarding activities you decided on.*

Table 10.2   A Worksheet for Transition Planning

A Worksheet for Transition Planning											
Directions: Under column 1 below, list all of your work duties, responsibilities or work activities. Be as comprehensive as possible. If there are not enough numbered items, add more paper and continue. Then, under column 2, pick ONE key report (that is, one person who reports to you) and **rate how well-prepared that person is to carry out each work activity you listed under column.** Use this scale: **1 = Not at all prepared; 2 = Somewhat prepared; 3 = Prepared; 4 = Well Prepared; and 5 = Very well prepared.** Then under column 3, **rate how important that development need is.** Use this scale: **1 = Not at all important; 2 = Not important; 3 = Somewhat important; 4 = Important; and 5 = Very important.** Under column 4, **list what to do to develop the key report for each high priority activity on which he or she is rated 1 or 2.** There are no right or wrong answers to this activity, but some answers are better than others.											
Column 1	*Column 2*					*Column 3*					*Column 4*
List Your Work Duties, Activities, and Responsibilities	Rate how well prepared one of your key reports is to carry out the work effort listed under column 1					Rate how important it is to carry out the work duty listed under column 1					List what to do to develop the key report for each high priority activity listed under column 1
	1	2	3	4	5	1	2	3	4	5	
1	1	2	3	4	5	1	2	3	4	5	
2	1	2	3	4	5	1	2	3	4	5	
3	1	2	3	4	5	1	2	3	4	5	
4	1	2	3	4	5	1	2	3	4	5	
5	1	2	3	4	5	1	2	3	4	5	
6	1	2	3	4	5	1	2	3	4	5	
7	1	2	3	4	5	1	2	3	4	5	
8	1	2	3	4	5	1	2	3	4	5	

Works Cited

Coffee, Adam. 2021. *The Exit-Strategy Playbook: The Definitive Guide to Selling Your Business.* Carson City, NV: Lioncrest Publishing.

Dowdy, Naomi. 2011. *Moving On And Moving Up From Succession to Significance: Practical Principles For Legacy Management And Leadership Transition.* Altamonte Springs, FL: Creation House.

France, Bradley. 2019. *The Succession Solution: The Strategic Guide to Business Transition.* Self-published eBook.

Gust, Gerard. 2019. *Secrets to Succession: The PIE Method to Transitioning Your Family Business*. eBook.

Keyes, Julia. 2020. *Poised For Exit: A Woman Entrepreneur's Guide to Business Transition*. Oceanside, CA: Indie Books International.

Muehlhausen, Jim. 2020. *Half-Retire: Keep Your Business, Ditch The Stress*. New York: Savio Republic.

Rothwell, William and Bakhshandeh Behnam. 2022. *High Performance Coaching*. New York: Routledge.

Rothwell, William. 2015. *Effective Succession Planning: Ensuring Leadership Continuity and Building Talent From Within*. 5th ed. New York: AMACOM.

Rothwell, William and Hercules Kazanas. 2004. *Improving On The Job Training*. 2nd ed. San Francisco, CA: Pfeiffer.

Sleger, Johnathon. 2021. *Contracting Exit Strategy: Help Business Owners With The Arduous Task Of Exiting Their Business: Retirement Strategies*. eBook.

Stern, Sara. 2019. *Start here: A Guide for Family Business Succession*. eBook.

Tepper, Mark M. 2014. *Walk Away Wealthy: The Entrepreneur's Exit-Planning Playbook*. Austin, TX: Greenleaf Book Group.

Woflred, Tim. 2009. *Managing Executive Transitions: A guide for nonprofits*. St. Paul, MN: Fieldstone Alliance.

Appendix I: Frequently Asked Questions (FAQs)

William J. Rothwell and Robert K. Prescott

Question 1: When should you begin succession planning for your small or family business?

You need to decide what you, as the owner of the business, want to do with the rest of your life. If you do not know that, then it will be difficult to decide what to do or when to do it. You need to get your own desires clear first.

Then talk to your significant others. What do your family members say about succession? Do you want to sell the business? What do they say about that? Do you want to hire someone to take over for you? Do you want to promote someone—an employee or a family member—to take over for you? Can you find a good, well-qualified external or internal succession candidate?

Then talk to your lawyer, accountant or bookkeeper, financial advisor, human resources specialist, or consultant and perhaps (if a family business) to a counselor, family therapist, or psychologist. See what advice they may give you. If they refer you to competent colleagues who know more than they do about succession planning or business transfer, then follow up with meeting who they refer you to.

Question 2: Who should be the focus of attention in succession planning?

You need to identify key people and key position incumbents. If you are the owner or the General Manager/CEO, then you are the starting point. But there are also other key people whose loss might be devastating to your business. Who are they?

Key people meet three criteria. The first is these people have an immediate and important impact on business operations. They have a high impact on making sales, dealing with customers, suppliers and dealers/distributors, and other business processes. The second is that they are difficult, and perhaps impossible, to replace. Perhaps they have unique knowledge and skills. Perhaps they have important relationships with key customers or other key business stakeholders. Third, they have roles to play in bringing future strategic plans into reality. Without them, it is less likely those plans are realistic.

Key position incumbents are those whose placement on the organization chart makes them critically important for business operations. The leaders of the organization and his or her direct reports are key position incumbents. Often department heads can be.

First think about successors for your own job as owner or leader of the organization. Then think about your most important direct reports and, beyond them, the most important people in your organization. With these people, succession planning should start.

Question 3: What should be the focus of attention in succession planning?

There are three key issues to consider in succession planning. First is business continuity. Who can ensure that the organization survives and thrives? Typically these people are management workers occupying positions on the organization chart. Second is technical expertise. Who has the know-how to make the business succeed? That may involve any specialized knowledge needed for the business to survive. What are the toughest-to-learn skills in the organization, and who has them? What is the criticality of knowledge of different groups in the organization?

Third are social relationships. Who has the best relationships with those who matter most to the organization? Who is best with key customers? Key suppliers? Key dealers/distributors? Key members of the communities in which the business operates? What other groups are critical to business operations, and who has the best relationships with them? How can social relationships and professional contacts be passed on from the present generation of managers/employees to the next generations?

Question 4: Where should succession planning be carried out?
There should be a succession plan for every location in which the business operates. What will you do if you lose the city to a natural or manmade disaster? Can the organization continue to function? There should be a replacement plan for each facility.

Most businesses have risk management/business continuity plans for dealing with the effects of a hurricane, tornado, fire, or other disasters. Many have similar plans for any devastating loss of money, data, or physical facilities. But businesses should also have replacement plans for humans if a disaster occurs.

Question 5: Why is succession planning important to a small or family business?
You need succession planning to safeguard your employees and your family. It is not responsible to allow events to unfold on their own after your sudden demise or disability. Think about other people even if you will be gone and may not care what happens after you are gone.

Question 6: How should succession planning be carried out in a small or family business?
You can recruit from outside, promote from inside, or do something else. The range of options in Chapter 1 of this book is extensive. Consider your priorities. Once you have identified what you want to do with your own life after the organization, or what you want to do after your departure, then consider how the business will continue to thrive. Consider first the management issues. Then consider the legal, accounting, and other relevant issues.

Question 7: How much time should be invested in succession planning for a small or family business?
The time needed depends on what you do.

If you promote someone from within and you have nobody already who is qualified, you must develop them. That could take a while—perhaps a few years. If you hire someone from outside, the time it will take to develop the person to take over will depend on how experienced the candidate is and how thoroughly the business leader wishes to plan the development.

Other choices will change how much time and effort is required.

Question 8: How much money should be invested in succession planning for a small or family business?
The investment in succession planning depends on the choices the leader makes about the future.

Question 9: What prompts a small or family business to begin succession planning?
Many succession planning efforts begin after a "close call."
Examples of close calls include:

■ A sudden illness by the business owner or General Manager.
■ A disability by the business owner or General Manager (lying in a hospital bed will make the issue cogent).
■ The sudden, unexpected loss of a key person or a key job incumbent to death, disability, or resignation.

There may be other issues that can build the importance of succession. Glancing around the table of the executive team and realizing that every member is past retirement age may be all it takes.

Question 10: What are the key obstacles to succession planning for small or family businesses?
The biggest obstacle to succession planning centers on the mindset of the business owner.

Some business owners associate succession planning with their own mortality. Since they do not want to contemplate their own deaths, they do not want to think about succession planning. Another common obstacle is that business owners have no intention of retiring or of ever phasing out of the business. They want to hang around forever—even when the business would benefit from their departures!

In family businesses, a major obstacle to succession planning may center on issues of family fairness and unresolved family conflicts. If the founding entrepreneur follows an expectation common in many national cultures to leave a controlling share of the business to the oldest male child despite the wishes of the family or the competence of other children, it can spark anger among family members after the death or departure of the business owner. That can lead to legal fights among children to "get their fair shares of the business value."

There are many other obstacles to succession. But the ones mentioned above are some of the most important.

Question 11: What should be done about a successor in an emergency?

You would be well advised, if you are a business owner, to have an emergency backup for yourself, your key people, and your key job incumbents. Go through an annual replacement planning exercise to see if you have backups for all key spots. If you do not, take steps so you do. It is the wise and prudent course of action.

Question 12: What key issues come up in succession planning for small or family businesses?

Remember to cover the key bases of succession planning:

- What does good management require to discover a successor for every key person and every key job incumbent in the organization?
- What legal issues will result from any choices made about successor decisions? How should business transfer or gifting be handled legally?
- What accounting and tax issues will result from any choices made about succession? What is the least costly option, and how can you pursue it so it preserves business assets from excessive taxation by local, state, and federal bodies?
- What psychological issues will result from any choices made about succession? If you pick one person, will others be alienated and think of leaving the organization? What will happen if they do leave, and how can you avert the loss of critically important talent?

Appendix II: Resources about Small and Family Business Succession Planning

Farhan Sadique

Articles

Argote, Linda and Henrich R. Greve. "A Behavioral Theory of the Firm: 40 Years and Counting: Introduction and Impact." *Organization Science*, 18, no. 3 (2007). https://doi.org/10.1287/orsc.1070.0280

Akhter, Naveed, and Francesco Chirico. "How To Understand Exit In Family Firm Portfolios: PDF Free Download." *Transeo Academic Awards* (2013). https://docplayer.net/2731931-Entrepreneurial-exit-in-family-firm-portfolios-naveed-akhter-doctoral-candidate-francesco-chirico-associate-professor.html

Akhter, Naveed, Philipp Sieger, and Francesco Chirico. "If We Can't Have It, Then No One Should: Shutting Down Versus Selling in Family Business Portfolios." *Strategic Entrepreneurship Journal*, 10, no. 4 (2016): 371–94. https://doi.org/10.1002/sej.1237.

Ali, Ashiq, Tai-Yuan Chen, and Suresh Radhakrishnan. "Corporate Disclosures by Family Firms." *Journal of Accounting and Economics, Conference Issue on Corporate Governance: Financial Reporting, Internal Control, and Auditing*, 44, no. 1 (September 1, 2007): 238–86. https://doi.org/10.1016/j.jacceco.2007.01.006.

Almlöf, Hanna, and Hans Sjögren. "Owner-Manager When Death Do Us Part: Roles of a Widow in Sudden Succession in Family Firms." *Journal of Family Business Management* ahead-of-print. (January 1, 2021). https://doi.org/10.1108/JFBM-01-2021-0006.

Anderson, Ronald C., Sattar A. Mansi, and David M. Reeb. "Founding Family Ownership and the Agency Cost of Debt." *Journal of Financial Economics*, 68, no. 2 (May 1, 2003): 263–85. https://doi.org/10.1016/S0304-405X(03)00067-9.

Ayres, Glenn R. "Rough Family Justice: Equity in Family Business Succession Planning." *Family Business Review*, 3, no. 1 (March 1, 1990): 3–22. https://doi.org/10.1111/j.1741-6248.1990.00003.x.

Balcaen, Sofie, Jozefien Buyze, and Hubert Ooghe. "Financial Distress and Firm Exit: Determinants of Involuntary Exits, Voluntary Liquidations and Restructuring Exits." *SSRN Scholarly Paper*. Rochester: Social Science Research Network (July 9, 2009). https://doi.org/10.2139/ssrn.1431835.

Barach, Jeffrey A., Joseph Gantisky, James A. Carson, and Benjamin A. Doochin. "Entry of the Next Generation: Strategic Challenge for Family Business." *Undefined* (1988). https://www.semanticscholar.org/paper/Entry-of-the-Next-Generation%3A-Strategic-Challenge-Barach-Gantisky/c90a8a0ba939ec071605ff01010146df02f83048.

Barnes, L. B., and Simon A. Harshon. "Transferring Power in The Family Business." *Change Management* (1976) https://hbr.org/1976/07/transferring-power-in-the-family-business.

Basco, Rodrigo, Thomas Bassetti, Lorenzo Dal Maso, and Nicola Lattanzi. "Why and When Do Family Firms Invest Less in Talent Management? The Suppressor Effect of Risk Aversion." *Journal of Management and Governance* (September 25, 2021). https://doi.org/10.1007/s10997-021-09599-1.

Battisti, Martina, and Hiroyuki Okamuro. "Selling, Passing on or Closing? Determinants of Entrepreneurial Intentions on Exit Modes." *SSRN Scholarly Paper*. Rochester, NY: Social Science Research Network (November 18, 2010). https://doi.org/10.2139/ssrn.1711336.

Beckhard, R. "Managing Change in the Family Firm—Issues and Strategies." *Sloan Management Review*, 24 (1983): 59.

Bennedsen, Morten, Kasper Meisner Nielsen, Francisco Perez-Gonzalez, and Daniel Wolfenzon. "Inside the Family Firm: The Role of Families in Succession Decisions and Performance." *Quarterly Journal of Economics*, 122, no. 2 (May 1, 2007): 647–691. https://doi.org/10.1162/qjec.122.2.647

Bernhard, Fabian, and Rania Labaki. "To Sell or Not to Sell? The Financial and Socio-Emotional Dilemma of the Ownership Decision in the Family Business." *International Fragmentation* (2016): 141–151. https://doi.org/10.1007/978-3-319-33846-0_8.

Bocatto, Eduardo, Carles Gispert, and Josep Rialp. "Family-Owned Business Succession: The Influence of Pre-performance in the Nomination of Family and Nonfamily Members: Evidence from Spanish Firms." *Journal of Small Business Management*, 48, no. 4 (October 1, 2010): 497–523. https://doi.org/10.1111/j.1540-627X.2010.00306.x.

Bruce, Doug, and Derek Picard. "Making Succession a Success: Perspectives from Canadian Small and Medium-Sized Enterprises." *Journal of Small Business Management*, 44, no. 2 (April 1, 2006): 306–9. https://doi.org/10.1111/j.1540-627X.2006.00171.x.

Cesaroni, Francesca Maria, and Annalisa Sentuti. "Family Business Succession and External Advisors: The Relevance of "Soft" Issues." *Small Enterprise Research*, 24, no. 2 (May 4, 2017): 167–88. https://doi.org/10.1080/13215906.2017.1338193.

Chen, Shuping, Xia Chen, Qiang Cheng, and Terry Shevlin. "Are Family Firms More Tax Aggressive than Non-Family Firms?" *Journal of Financial Economics*, 95, no. 1 (January 1, 2010): 41–61. https://doi.org/10.1016/j.jfineco.2009.02.003.

Chirico, F., L. Gomez-Mejia, Karin Hellerstedt, M. Withers, and M. Nordqvist. "To Merge, Sell, or Liquidate? Socioemotional Wealth, Family Control, and the Choice of Business Exit." *Journal of Management* (2019). https://doi.org/10.1177/0149206318818723.

Chrisman, James J., Jess H. Chua, and Pramodita Sharma. "Important Attributes of Successors in Family Businesses: An Exploratory Study." *Family Business Review*, 11, no. 1 (1998): 19–34. https://doi.org/10.1111/j.1741-6248.1998.00019.x.

Curimbaba, Florence. "The Dynamics of Women's Roles as Family Business Managers." (2002). https://journals.sagepub.com/doi/10.1111/j.1741-6248.2002.00239.x.

Daspit, Joshua J., Daniel T. Holt, James J. Chrisman, and Rebecca G. Long. "Examining Family Firm Succession From a Social Exchange Perspective: A Multiphase, Multistakeholder Review." *Family Business Review*, 29, no. 1 (March 1, 2016): 44–64. https://doi.org/10.1177/0894486515599688.

De Massis, Alfredo, Jess H. Chua, and James J. Chrisman. "Factors Preventing Intra-Family Succession." *Family Business Review*, 21, no. 2 (June 1, 2008): 183–99. https://doi.org/10.1111/j.1741-6248.2008.00118.x.

De Massis, Alfredo, Josip Kotlar, Giovanna Campopiano, and Lucio Cassia. "Dispersion of Family Ownership and the Performance of Small-to-Medium Size Private Family Firms." *Journal of Family Business Strategy*, 4, no. 3 (September 1, 2013): 166–75. https://doi.org/10.1016/j.jfbs.2013.05.001.

DeTienne, Dawn R., and Francesco Chirico. "Exit Strategies in Family Firms: How Socioemotional Wealth Drives the Threshold of Performance." *Entrepreneurship Theory and Practice*, 37, no. 6 (November 1, 2013): 1297–1318. https://doi.org/10.1111/etap.12067.

DeTienne, Dawn R., Alexander McKelvie, and Gaylen N. Chandler. "Making Sense of Entrepreneurial Exit Strategies: A Typology and Test." *Journal of Business Venturing*, 30, no. 2 (March 1, 2015): 255–272. https://doi.org/10.1016/j.jbusvent.2014.07.007.

Duhaime, Irene M., and John H. Grant. "Factors Influencing Divestment Decision-Making: Evidence from a Field Study." *Strategic Management Journal*, 5, no. 4 (1984): 301–18. https://doi.org/10.1002/smj.4250050402.

Emami, Amir, Dianne H. B. Welsh, Veland Ramadani, and Ali Davari. "The Impact of Judgment and Framing on Entrepreneurs' Decision-Making." *Journal of Small Business & Entrepreneurship*, 32, no. 1 (January 2, 2020): 79–100. https://doi.org/10.1080/08276331.2018.1551461.

Feldman, Emilie R., Raphael (Raffi) Amit, and Belén Villalonga. "Corporate Divestitures and Family Control." *Strategic Management Journal*, 37, no. 3 (2016): 429–46. https://doi.org/10.1002/smj.2329.

Ferrari, Filippo. "In the Mother's Shadow: Exploring Power Dynamics in Family Business Succession." *Gender in Management: An International Journal*, 34, no. 2 (January 1, 2019): 121–39. https://doi.org/10.1108/GM-07-2017-0091.

Filser, Matthias, Sascha Kraus, and Stefan Märk. "Psychological Aspects of Succession in Family Business Management." *Management Research Review*, 36 (March 22, 2013): 256–77. https://doi.org/10.1108/01409171311306409.

Flamini, Giulia, Paola Vola, Lucrezia Songini, and Luca Gnan. "The Determinants of Tax Aggressiveness in Family Firms: An Investigation of Italian Private Family Firms." *Sustainability*, 13, no. 14 (January 2021): 7654. https://doi.org/10.3390/su13147654.

Gallucci, Carmen, Rosalia Santulli, Michele Modina, and Michela De Rosa. "The Role of Family Governance beyond Financial Ratios: An Integrated Perspective on Family Firms' Survival." *Journal of Financial Management, Markets and Institutions*. 8, no. 2 (December 1, 2020): 2050006. https://doi.org/10.1142/S2282717X20500061.

García-Álvarez, Ercilia, and Jordi López-Sintas. "A Taxonomy of Founders Based on Values: The Root of Family Business Heterogeneity." *Family Business Review*, 14, no. 3 (September 1, 2001): 209–30. https://doi.org/10.1111/j.1741-6248.2001.00209.x.

Ghee, Wee Yu, Mohamed Dahlan Ibrahim, and Hasliza Abdul-Halim. "Family Business Succession Planning: Unleashing the Key Factors of Business Performance." *Asian Academy of Management Journal*, 20, no. 2 (2015): 103–126.

Gilding, Michael, Sheree Gregory, and Barbara Cosson. "Motives and Outcomes in Family Business Succession Planning." *Entrepreneurship Theory and Practice*, 39, no. 2 (March 1, 2015): 299–312. https://doi.org/10.1111/etap.12040.

Gomez-Mejia, L., K. T. Haynes, Manuel Núñez-Nickel, Kathy Jacobson, and J. Moyano-Fuentes. "Socioemotional Wealth and Business Risks in Family-Controlled Firms: Evidence from Spanish Olive Oil Mills." (2007). https://doi.org/10.2189/asqu.52.1.106.

Gorin, Steve. "Highlights from the Simply Tax Podcast: How to Choose an Entity for a Family Business." Accessed December 16, 2021. https://www.thompsoncoburn.com/insights/blogs/business-succession-solutions/post/2019-01-18/highlights-from-the-simply-tax-podcast-how-to-choose-an-entity-for-a-family-business.

Handler, Wendy C. "Succession in Family Firms: A Mutual Role Adjustment between Entrepreneur and Next-Generation Family Members." *Entrepreneurship Theory and Practice*, 15, no. 1 (October 1, 1990): 37–52. https://doi.org/10.1177/104225879001500105.

Handler, Wendy C. "The Succession Experience of the Next Generation." *Family Business Review*, 5, no. 3 (September 1, 1992): 283–307. https://doi.org/10.1111/j.1741-6248.1992.00283.x.

Handler, Wendy C., and Kathy E. Kram. "Succession in Family Firms: The Problem of Resistance." *Family Business Review*, 1, no. 4 (1988): 361–81. https://doi.org/10.1111/j.1741-6248.1988.00361.x.

Härtel, Charmine E. J., Gil Bozer, and Leon Levin. "Family Business Leadership Transition: How an Adaptation of Executive Coaching May Help." *Journal of Management & Organization*, 15, no. 3 (July 2009): 378–91. http://dx.doi.org/10.5172/jmo.2009.15.3.378.

Harveston, Paula D., Peter S. Davis, and Julie A. Lyden. "Succession Planning in Family Business: The Impact of Owner Gender." *Family Business Review*, 10, no. 4 (December 1, 1997): 373–96. https://doi.org/10.1111/j.1741-6248.1997.00373.x.

Hernández-Linares, Remedios, Soumodip Sarkar, and Manuel J. Cobo. "Inspecting the Achilles Heel: A Quantitative Analysis of 50 Years of Family Business Definitions." *Scientometrics*, 115, no. 2 (May 1, 2018): 929–51. https://doi.org/10.1007/s11192-018-2702-1.

Hobbs, Steven H, and Fay Wilson Hobbs. "Family Businesses and the Business of Families: A Consideration of the Role of the Lawyer Symposium - The Intersecting Institutions of Marriage: Conflicts and Consequences" *AlabamaLaw*, 153 (1997).

Hoffman, James, Ritch Sorenson, and Keith Brigham. "Surprising Reasons Owners Exit Family Businesses." *Entrepreneur & Innovation Exchange* (January 15, 2020). https://doi.org/10.32617/423-5e1f1e28f22a5.

Hubler, Thomas. "Ten Most Prevalent Obstacles to Family-Business Succession Planning." *Family Business Review*, 12, no. 2 (June 1, 1999): 117–21. https://doi.org/10.1111/j.1741-6248.1999.00117.x.

Kansikas, Juha, and Tuomas Kuhmonen. "Family Business Succession: Evolutionary Economics Approach." *Journal of Enterprising Culture*, 16, no. 3 (September 1, 2008): 279–98. https://doi.org/10.1142/S0218495808000156.

Karim, Tarana. "Succession Management and Its Impact on Family Business." *European Journal of Business and Management*, 6, no 37 (2014): 315–320.

Labaki, Rania, and Gérard Hirigoyen. "The Strategic Divestment Decision in the Family Business Through the Real Options and Emotional Lenses." (2020). https://doi.org/10.4018/978-1-7998-2269-1.ch012.

Lansberg, Ivan. "The Succession Conspiracy." *Family Business Review*, 1, no. 2 (June 1, 1988): 119–43. https://doi.org/10.1111/j.1741-6248.1988.00119.x.

Lauto, Giancarlo, Daniel Pittino, and Francesca Visintin. "Satisfaction of Entrepreneurs: A Comparison between Founders and Family Business Successors." *Journal of Small Business Management*, 58, no. 3 (May 3, 2020): 474–510. https://doi.org/10.1080/00472778.2019.1660937.

LeCounte, John F. "Founder-CEOs: Succession Planning for the Success, Growth, and Legacy of Family Firms." *Journal of Small Business Management* (March 19, 2020): 1–18. https://doi.org/10.1080/00472778.2020.1725814.

Lee, Yoon G., Cynthia R. Jasper, and Karen P. Goebel. "A Profile of Succession Planning among Family Business Owners." *Journal of Financial Counseling and Planning*, 14, no. 2 (2003): 31–41. https://ezaccess.libraries.psu.edu/login?url=https://www.proquest.com/scholarly-journals/profile-succession-planning-among-family-business/docview/1355867058/se-2?accountid=13158.

Marler, Laura E., Isabel C. Botero, and Alfredo De Massis. "Succession-Related Role Transitions in Family Firms: The Impact of Proactive Personality." *Journal of Managerial Issues*, 29, no. 1 (2017): 57–81.

Massis, Alfredo De. "Factors Preventing Intra-Family Succession." *Family Business Review* (2012). https://docplayer.net/14797187-Factors-preventing-intra-family-succession.html.

Matser, Ilse, Jelle Bouma, and Erik Veldhuizen. "No Hard Feelings? Non-Succeeding Siblings and Their Perceptions of Justice in Family Firms." *Journal of Family Business Management*, ahead-of-print (January 1, 2020). https://doi.org/10.1108/JFBM-09-2018-0048.

Mitter, Christine, Michaela Walcher, Stefan Mayr, and Christine Duller. "Bankruptcy at Family and Non-Family Firms: Do They Fail Differently?" *Journal of Family Business Management*, ahead-of-print (January 1, 2021). https://doi.org/10.1108/JFBM-08-2021-0081.

Mokhber, Mozhdeh, Tan Gi Gi, Siti Zaleha Abdul Rasid, Amin Vakilbashi, Noraiza Mohd Zamil, and Yee Woon Seng. "Succession Planning and Family Business Performance in SMEs." *Journal of Management Development*, 36, no. 3 (January 1, 2017): 330–47. https://doi.org/10.1108/JMD-12-2015-0171.

Nguyen, Minh-Hoang, Huyen Thanh Thanh Nguyen, Tam-Tri Le, Anh-Phuong Luong, and Quan-Hoang Vuong. "Gender Issues in Family Business Research: A Bibliometric Scoping Review." *Journal of Asian Business and Economic Studies*, ahead-of-print (January 1, 2021). https://doi.org/10.1108/JABES-01-2021-0014.

Pérez-González, Francisco. "Inherited Control and Firm Performance." *American Economic Review*, 96, no. 5 (December 2006): 1559–88. https://doi.org/10.1257/aer.96.5.1559.

Ramadani, Veland, Léo-Paul Dana, Nora Sadiku-Dushi, Vanessa Ratten, and Dianne H. B. Welsh. "Decision-Making Challenges of Women Entrepreneurship in Family Business Succession Process." *Journal of Enterprising Culture*, 25, no. 4 (December 1, 2017): 411–39. https://doi.org/10.1142/S0218495817500157.

Saymaz, Savas. "Family Business Succession Planning Opportunities." *The CPA Journal* (2019). https://www.cpajournal.com/2020/01/08/family-business-succession-planning-opportunities/.

Sharma, Pramodita, James J. Chrisman, and Jess H. Chua. "Strategic Management of the Family Business: Past Research and Future Challenges." *Family Business Review*, 10, no. 1 (March 1, 1997): 1–35. https://doi.org/10.1111/j.1741-6248.1997.00001.x.

Shen, Na. "Family Business, Transgenerational Succession and Diversification Strategy: Implication from a Dynamic Socioemotional Wealth Model." *Cross Cultural & Strategic Management*, 25, no. 4 (January 1, 2018): 628–41. https://doi.org/10.1108/CCSM-06-2017-0074.

Siehl, Caren, John Davis, and W. Gibb Dyer. "Review of Cultural Change in Family Firms: Anticipating and Managing Business and Family Transitions., W. Gibb Dyer, Jr." *Administrative Science Quarterly*, 32, no. 4 (1987): 635–37. https://doi.org/10.2307/2392903.

Songini, Lucrezia, Luca Gnan, and Teemu Malmi. "The Role and Impact of Accounting in Family Business." *Journal of Family Business Strategy, The Role and Impact of Accounting in Family Business*, 4, no. 2 (June 1, 2013): 71–83. https://doi.org/10.1016/j.jfbs.2013.04.002.

Stavrou, Eleni T. "Succession in Family Businesses: Exploring the Effects of Demographic Factors on Offspring Intentions to Join and Take over the Business." *Journal of Small Business Management*, 37, no. 3 (July 1999): 43–61.

Symeonidou, Noni, Dawn R. DeTienne, and Francesco Chirico. "The Persistence of Family Firms: How Does Performance Threshold Affect Family Firm Exit?" *Small Business Economics*, May 10, 2021. https://doi.org/10.1007/s11187-021-00482-9.

Tabor, Will, and James Vardaman. "The Key to Successful Succession Planning for Family Businesses." *Harvard Business Review* (May 15, 2020). https://hbr.org/2020/05/the-key-to-successful-succession-planning-for-family-businesses.

Tang, Joseph Kie Kuong, and Wan Sabri Hussin. "Next-Generation Leadership Development: A Management Succession Perspective." *Journal of Family Business Management*, ahead-of-print (January 1, 2020). https://doi.org/10.1108/JFBM-04-2019-0024.

Thomas, Jill. "Freeing the Shackles of Family Business Ownership." *Family Business Review*, 15, no. 4 (2002): 321–36. https://doi.org/10.1111/j.1741-6248.2002.00321.x. 108.

Villalonga, Belen, and Raphael Amit. "How Do Family Ownership, Control and Management Affect Firm Value?" *Journal of Financial Economics*, 80, no. 2 (May 1, 2006): 385–417. https://doi.org/10.1016/j.jfineco.2004.12.005.

Wang, Calvin. "Daughter Exclusion in Family Business Succession: A Review of the Literature." *Journal of Family and Economic Issues*, 31, no. 4 (December 2010): 475–84. https://doi.org/10.1007/s10834-010-9230-3.

Ward, John L. "Growing the Family Business: Special Challenges and Best Practices." *Family Business Review*, 10, no. 4 (December 1, 1997): 323–37. https://doi.org/10.1111/j.1741-6248.1997.00323.x.

Yedder, Moez Ben. "Human Resource Management in Family Business Succession: Victim or Saviour?" *Journal of Enterprising Culture*, 26, no. 4 (December 1, 2018): 401–21. https://doi.org/10.1142/S0218495818500152.

Book

Aronoff, C. *Letting Go: Preparing Yourself to Relinquish Control of the Family Business*. New York: Palgrave Macmillan. 2011.

Baron, Josh, and Rob Lachenauer. *Harvard Business Review Family Business Handbook: How to Build and Sustain a Successful, Enduring Enterprise*. Boston: Harvard Business Review Press, 2021.

Blau, Peter M. *Exchange and Power in Social Life*. New York: Routledge, 2017. https://doi.org/10.4324/9780203792643.

Colli, Andrea. *The History of Family Business, 1850–2000*. New York: Cambridge University Press, 2003.

Gordon, Grant, and Nigel Nicholson. *Family Wars: Stories and Insights from Famous Family Business Feuds*. London: Kogan Page Publishers, 2010.

Gust, Gerard. *Secrets to Succession: The PIE Method to Transitioning Your Family Business*. Gust Publishing. 2019.

Isaac, George A. *Your Business, Your Family, Your Legacy: Building a Multigenerational Family Business That Lasts*. S.l.: CreateSpace Independent Publishing Platform, 2020.

Jurinski, James, and Gary A. Zwick. *Transferring Interests in the Closely Held Family Business.* ALI-ABA, 2002.

Kenyon-Rouvinez, D., G. Adler, G. Corbetta, and Gianfilippo Cuneo. *Sharing Wisdom, Building Values: Letters from Family Business Owners to Their Successors. 2011 edition.* London: Palgrave Macmillan, 2016.

LeCouvie, K., and J. Pendergast. *Family Business Succession: Your Roadmap to Continuity. 2014 edition.* New York: Springer, 2014.

Sonnenfeld, Jeffrey. *The Hero's Farewell: What Happens When CEOs Retire.* New York: Oxford University Press, 1991.

Ward, J. *Keeping the Family Business Healthy: How to Plan for Continuing Growth, Profitability, and Family Leadership.* 2011th edition. New York: Springer, 2011.

Webpages/Blog

Alshaikh, Alaa. "Solving Succession Problems in Family-Owned Businesses." *Gallup.com*, April 8, 2019. https://www.gallup.com/workplace/248297/solving-succession-problems-family-owned-businesses.aspx.

Ames, Ella. "How to Create an Exit Strategy for Your Small Business." *The Balance Small Business.* Accessed December 16, 2021. https://www.thebalancesmb.com/small-business-exit-strategies-2947988.

Arnonoff, Craig E. "How to Transition from a Family-Run to a Family-Owned Business." *The Family Business Consulting Group.* Accessed December 16, 2021. https://www.thefbcg.com/resource/how-to-transition-from-a-family-run-to-a-family-owned-business/.

Arthur Andersen/MassMutual. "American Family Business Survey." https://www.massmutual.com/mmfg/pdf/afbs.pdf.

Austin, Marc E. "The Major Do's and Don'ts of Family Business Succession." *Private Capital Group, LLC*, 2020. https://www.pcgct.com/blog/the-major-dos-and-donts-of-family-business-succession.

Bankler, Steven. "6 Family Business Succession Tips." *San Antonio CPA | Forensic Investigative Accounting | Litigation Support* (blog), June 22, 2021. https://bankler.com/6-family-business-succession-tips/.

Banks, Morris, and Kelly, O'Donnell. "Succession Planning for the Successful Family Business in 2020." *JD Supra*, October 15, 2020. https://www.jdsupra.com/legalnews/succession-planning-for-the-successful-45239/.

Baron, Josh, and Rob, Lachenauer. "Surviving in a Family Business When You're Not Part of the Family." *Harvard Business Review*, January 15, 2015. https://hbr.org/2015/01/surviving-in-a-family-business-when-youre-not-part-of-the-family.

Benedictine University. "Leadership Transition within Family Businesses | Dynamic Language." *Benedictine University CVDL* (blog), July 13, 2016. https://cvdl.ben.edu/blog/family-business-transitioning-leaders/.

Bennedsen, Morten. "Family Business Longevity Requires Owners to Step Back." *INSEAD Knowledge*, May 29, 2018. https://knowledge.insead.edu/blog/insead -blog/family-business-longevity-requires-owners-to-step-back-9251.

Bhalla, Vikram, and Nicolas, Kachaner. "Succeeding with Succession Planning in Family Businesses." *BCG Global*, January 8, 2021. https://www.bcg.com/publi- cations/2015/leadership_talent_growth_succeeding_with_succession_planning _family_businesses.

Bochnewich Law Offices. "Your Guide to Family Business Succession Planning." *Palm Desert Law Firm, Bochnewich Law Offices* (blog), June 5, 2020. https:// www.btrustlaw.com/blog/a-simple-guide-for-family-business-succession -planning/.

Business News Daily. "Businesses Suffer When Their Founders Die - Businessnewsdaily.Com." October 28, 2021. https://www.businessnewsdaily .com/4016-founder-death-spurs-business-decline.html.

City National Bank. "Lessons from the Family Business: How to Transfer Your Company and Legacy." Accessed December 16, 2021. https://newsroom.cnb .com/content/news-and-insights/en/business/exit-strategy/how-to-transfer-you -family-business-and-legacy.html.

City National Bank. "Preparing to Transition the Family Business to the Next Generation." *City National Bank*. Accessed December 16, 2021. https://news- room.cnb.com/content/news-and-insights/en/business/exit-strategy/transition -the-family-business.html.

City National Bank. "Succession Planning: How to Transition Your Business to Multiple Owners." Accessed December 16, 2021. https://newsroom.cnb.com/ content/news-and-insights/en/business/exit-strategy/business-succession-plan -multiple-owners.html.

Cockrell, Clay. "I'm a Therapist to the Super-Rich: They Are as Miserable as Succession Makes Out." *The Guardian*, November 22, 2021, sec. Opinion. https://www.theguardian.com/commentisfree/2021/nov/22/therapist-super-rich -succession-billionaires.

Collins, Jim. "Good to Great." 2001. https://www.jimcollins.com/article_topics/ articles/good-to-great.html#articletop.

Deloitte. "Business Succession Planning." 72(n.d.) https://www2.deloitte.com/con- tent/dam/Deloitte/us/Documents/deloitte-private/us-dges-business-succession -planning-collection.pdf

Deprez Leadership. "Succession When A Business Owner Dies." *Deprez Leadership* (blog), September 5, 2019. https://www.deprezleadership.com/blogs/succession -when-a-business-owner-dies/.

"Developing Leadership Talent: A Guide to Succession Planning and Leadership Development." 67 (2020).

DiPietro, Janice. "How to Handle Family Business Succession With Zero Drama." 2018. https://www.familybusinessmagazine.com/succession-no-drama -approach.

Eisenberg, Richard. "How To Make Family Business Succession Successful." *Forbes*, January 22, 2019. https://www.forbes.com/sites/nextavenue/2019/01/22/how-to-make-family-business-succession-successful/.

Estate Plan Review: COVID-19 Could Change Everything - Moulton Law Offices. "Succession Planning Tips for Family Owned Businesses - Moulton Law Offices." December 7, 2019. https://moultonlaw.com/succession-planning-tips-for-family-owned-business/.

Family Business Consulting by HRB. "Succession Planning | Family Business | Process Management." November 5, 2013. https://hrb-family-business-consulting.com/how-to-properly-manage-succession-planning-in-small-business-and-family-business/succession-planning/.

"Family Business Law Is Not Family Law: Handling Management and Legal Challenges in a Family Business." Accessed December 16, 2021. https://maspons.com/family-business-law-is-not-family-law-handling-management-and-legal-challenges-in-a-family-business/.

"Family Business Succession and Planning | Wolf, Baldwin & Associates, P.C. | Pottstown Pennsylvania." Accessed December 16, 2021. https://www.wolf-baldwin.com/articles/estate-planning-articles/family-business-succession-and-planning/.

Fellhauer, Thomas. "Business Succession Planning Part 1: What Happens When The Founder Dies? - Pushor Mitchell LLP." February 24, 2011. https://www.pushor-mitchell.com/2011/02/business-succession-planning-part-1-what-happens-when-founder-dies/.

Findlaw. "Succession Planning for Small Businesses." Accessed December 16, 2021. https://www.findlaw.com/smallbusiness/closing-a-business/succession-planning-for-small-businesses.html.

Forbes Coaches Council. "Council Post: 15 Tips For Navigating Family Business Challenges." *Forbes*. Accessed December 16, 2021. https://www.forbes.com/sites/forbescoachescouncil/2020/01/17/15-tips-for-navigating-family-business-challenges/.

Generational Equity. "Succession Planning | Definition, Importance, Process & Challenges." *Generational Equity*. Accessed December 16, 2021. https://www.genequityco.com/insights/succession-planning.

George, Chris. "Five Steps To Successfully Transition Your Family Business To The Next Generation by Chris George | Sponsored Insights." *WilmingtonBiz*, October 1, 2014. http://www.wilmingtonbiz.com/insights/chris_george/five_steps_to_successfully_transition_your_family_business_to_the_next_generation/326.

Gomez, Evangeline. "Identifying a Successor for Your Family-Owned Business." *Forbes*. Accessed December 15, 2021. https://www.forbes.com/sites/evangeline-gomez/2011/10/12/identifying-a-successor-for-your-family-owned-business/.

Guin, David, and Mark, Haranzo. "How to Transition Business to a Non-Family Executive?" *Sarah*, 2015. https://www.familybusinessmagazine.com/preparing-transition-your-business-leader-outside-family-0.

Horowitz, Shel. "Power, Politics, Policies, and Purpose: Focal Points of the Family/ Business Dynamic." Accessed December 16, 2021. https://www.frugalmarketing.com/dtb/johnward.shtml.

"How to Transition Your Family Business to a New Generation." Accessed December 16, 2021. https://www.pnc.com/insights/small-business/business-planning/how-to-transition-your-family-business-to-a-new-generation.html.

Ip, C. "Lessons From "Succession" for Non-Billionaire Families." *The Atlantic*, December 10, 2021. https://www.theatlantic.com/family/archive/2021/12/lessons-from-succession-for-non-billionaire-families/620965/.

KatzAbosch. "Family Business Owners: Succession & Estate Planning." *KatzAbosch*, March 24, 2021. https://www.katzabosch.com/thought-leadership/family-business-owners-must-weave-together-succession-and-estate-planning/.

KCoe Editorial. "Why Do Family Businesses Fail at Succession Planning?" *KCoe Isom* (blog), July 27, 2016. https://www.kcoe.com/why-do-family-businesses-fail-at-succession-planning/.

Kennedy, C. "Succession Planning for Family Businesses." *Riker Danzig*, July 8, 2021. http://riker.com/. http://riker.com/publications/succession-planning-for-family-businesses.

Lansberg, I. "Twelve Tasks in Succession." 7 (1993). https://www.northwoodfamily office.com/wp-content/uploads/2018/02/1993-Twelve-Tasks-in-Succession-Planning-Lansberg.pdf

Law Office of Stimmel, Stimmel, and Roeser. "Chapter One: Power in the Family Business: Structural and Emotional | Stimmel Law." Accessed December 16, 2021. https://www.stimmel-law.com/en/articles/chapter-one-power-family-business-structural-and-emotional.

Malis, J. "Tips for a Successful Family Business Succession." Accessed December 16, 2021. https://www.sbelderlaw.com/tips-for-a-successful-family-business-succession.

Massimo, C. "Council Post: Business Owners, What's Your Succession Plan?" *Forbes*. Accessed December 16, 2021. https://www.forbes.com/sites/forbesnycouncil/2019/06/05/business-owners-whats-your-succession-plan/.

Mejía, J. "8 Tips for Successful Family Business Transitions." *AARP*. Accessed December 16, 2021. https://www.aarp.org/work/self-employment/info-2017/family-business-transitions.html.

Michuad, P., C. Collette, and J. Davis. "CEO Succession in the Family Business | A Better Plan for Success." Accessed December 15, 2021. https://cfeg.com/insights _research/CEO-Succession-in-the-Family-Business.

Monday, G. "A Blueprint for Family Business Succession Planning | Blt." *Business Law Today from ABA*, January 16, 2018. https://businesslawtoday.org/2018/01/a-blueprint-for-family-business-succession-planning/.

Monday, G. "Information about This Family Business Blog in 2021." *Monday's Family Business Law*, January 4, 2021. https://www.mondaybusinesslaw.com/information-about-this-family-business-blog-in-2021/.

Monte, J. "Identifying Successors to Run Your Company: Family Vs....." *EDSI*. Accessed December 15, 2021. https://www.edsisolutions.com/blog/identifying -successors-to-run-your-company-family-vs-non-family.

Nelson, N. "Planning for Business Succession." February 7, 2021. https://www.wolt- erskluwer.com/en/expert-insights/planning-for-business-succession.

Panay News. "Founder's Dilemma: Is It Power or Legacy?" *Panay News*, December 15, 2021. https://www.panaynews.net/founders-dilemma-is-it-power-or -legacy/.

PNC Private Bank. "Family Business Transfer: Understanding the Challenges." Accessed December 16, 2021. https://www.pnc.com/insights/wealth-manage- ment/business-continuity-and-succession-planning/lowering-the-hurdles-to-a -successful-family-business-transfer.html.

Pofeldt, E. "Many Firms Don't Survive After Owners Die." *Forbes*, October 28, 2021. https://www.forbes.com/sites/elainepofeldt/2013/02/26/many-firms-dont -bounce-back-after-owners-die/.

Reddal, Per Stenius. "Importance of Succession Planning in Family Owned Businesses." *Reddal*, 2016. http://www.reddal.com/insights/succession -planning-in-the-context-of-a-family-business-and-why-you-need-outside -help/.

Rivers, W. "Death Statistics and Family Business Succession Planning." Family Business Institute (blog), October 7, 2014. https://www.familybusinessinstitute .com/death-statistics-family-business-succession-planning/.

Rivers, W. "Guidelines for Successful Family Transition in Construction (and Most Other Industries Too!)." *Family Business Institute* (blog), October 12, 2021. https://www.familybusinessinstitute.com/guidelines-for-successful-family-transi- tion-in-construction-and-most-other-industries-too/.

Rivers, W. "What Percentage of Family Businesses Have Succession Plans in Place?" *Family Business Institute* (blog), July 30, 2019. https://www.familybusinessi nstitute.com/percentage-of-family-businesses-with-succession-plan/.

Robaton, A. "Dealing with Family Firms: A Love-Hate Relationship for Advisors." *CNBC*, October 21, 2014. https://www.cnbc.com/2014/10/20/dealing-with-fam- ily-firms-a-love-hate-relationship-for-advisors.html.

Roberts, D. "Who Will Run Your Family Business after You? | News | Floor Covering Weekly." February 19, 2015. https://www.floorcoveringweekly.com/ main/topnews/who-will-run-your-family-business-after-you--9687.

Romanowski, Dallas. "Is A Family Transfer Right For Your Business? By Dallas Romanowski | Sponsored Insights." *WilmingtonBiz*, January 14, 2021. http:// www.wilmingtonbiz.com/insights/dallas__romanowski/is_a_family_transfer _right_for_your_business/2913.

Rosenbaum, E. "The Real-Life Family Business Drama You Don't See on HBO's "Succession."" *CNBC*, November 14, 2021. https://www.cnbc.com/2021/11/14/ the-real-life-family-business-drama-not-on-hbos-succession.html.

RSM. "Family Business Transition." Accessed December 16, 2021. https://rsmus.com /what-we-do/services/tax/private-client/business-transition-planning/family -transition.html.

Schleckser, J. "5 Simple Rules For Transitioning a Family Business to the Next Generation." *Inc.com*, July 3, 2018. https://www.inc.com/jim-schleckser/5 -simple-rules-for-transitioning-a-family-business-to-next-generation.html.

Sekulich, T. "The Walmart Family Business Success – Lessons from Sam Walton." *Tharawat Magazine* (blog), September 25, 2016. https://www.tharawat-maga-zine.com/grow/walmart-family-business-success-secret/.

Shrivastava, A. "3 Family Business Legal Challenges and What Can You Do about It." *IPleaders* (blog), April 2, 2018. https://blog.ipleaders.in/family-business -legal-challenges/.

Stimmel Law. "Family Property Co-Ownership - Recipe for Disasters, Prescription for Cures." Accessed December 16, 2021. https://www.stimmel -law.com/en/articles/family-property-co-ownership-recipe-disasters-prescrip-tion-cures.

Strauss, S. "The Do's and Don'ts of Working with Family: How to Successfully Work with Your Relatives." *USA TODAY*. Accessed December 15, 2021. https://www .usatoday.com/story/money/usaandmain/2021/11/04/family-businesses-how -work-your-relatives-and-how-not/6254223001/.

Thienel, S. "Business Succession Planning Tips for 2020 | Thienel Law." *Thienel Law - Columbia, Maryland Business Attorney*, 2020. https://www.thienel-law .com/blog/2020/6/19/death-business-in-2020-succession-planning-tips-for-small -business-owner.

Trust, W. "The Struggles of Succession Planning Without A Successor." Accessed December 15, 2021. https://www.familybusinessmagazine.com/succession -planning-without-successor.

Vance, B. "Developing Effective Successors for Family Businesses | P&N." Accessed December 15, 2021. https://www.pncpa.com/insights/developing-effective-suc-cessors-part-1/.

Walmart. "From Humble Beginnings. To Redefining Retail." *Corporate - US*. Accessed December 15, 2021. https://corporate.walmart.com/about/history.

Walsack, J. "How to Write a Family Business Succession Plan." September 14, 2020. https://www.uschamber.com/co/co/start/strategy/family-business-succession -plan.

Ward, J. "Family Business Succession: 15 Guidelines." *The Family Business Consulting Group*. Accessed December 15, 2021. https://www.thefbcg.com/ resource/family-business-succession-15-guidelines/.

Ward, S. "6 Tips to Make Succession Planning a Snap for Your Family Business." *The Balance Small Business*. Accessed December 16, 2021. https://www .thebalancesmb.com/tips-for-successful-family-business-succession-planning -2947038.

Wasserman, E. "Guide to Business Ownership: How to Choose a Successor." *Inc .com*, February 1, 2010. https://www.inc.com/guides/choose-your-successor .html.

Wells Fargo. "8 Best Practices to Prepare the next Generation for the Family Business | The Private Bank." *September* 2021. https://www.wellsfargo.com/ the-private-bank/insights/wpu-8-best-practices/.

Yuille, B. "7 Steps to Selling Your Small Business." *Investopedia*, 2021. https://www.investopedia.com/articles/pf/08/sell-small-business.asp.

Zahrt, M. C. "How to Talk to Your Family About Succession Planning." 2020. https://www.fosterswift.com/communications-Talk-Family-Business-Succession-Planning.html.

Videos

AALU. *Succession Planning for Family Businesses*, 2016. https://www.youtube.com/watch?v=Y6Bgf5QCxvo.

"Barriers to Succession - The Family Business Podcast." November 20, 2020. https://fambizpodcast.com/barriers-to-succession/.

BDO Unibank. *Family Business IV: Preparing Your Family Business for Succession*, 2018. https://www.youtube.com/watch?v=6YblBXEawOw.

BKD CPAs & Advisors. *Choice of Entity for Family Businesses - Part II #052*, 2019. https://www.youtube.com/watch?v=MCXK28NNNEs.

Bloomington, MN Noon Rotary. *Family Business Succession Planning*, 2015. https://www.youtube.com/watch?v=qR-YJlamdj0.

Boughton Law. *Seminar Presentation: Succession Planning for Family Owned Businesses*, 2014. https://www.youtube.com/watch?v=z5XeZpqfpfU.

BrokersAlliance. *The Basics of Business Succession Planning*, 2012. https://www.youtube.com/watch?v=FzhnEbGr1xI.

Business RadioX. *Transitioning a Family Business from One Generation to Another (Part 1 of 2)*. Accessed December 16, 2021. https://www.youtube.com/watch?v=ouhRnijtqVE.

Cambridge Family Enterprise Group. *Three-Circle Model: Building Effective Groups in the Family Business System*, 2018. https://www.youtube.com/watch?v=lanT-HQha28.

Cambridge Family Enterprise Group. *Will Family Businesses Survive. Hear More from John Davis*, 2018. https://www.youtube.com/watch?v=ZaVxMveDso4.

CaronTreatment. *Family Business Dynamics: The Intersection of Psychology and Strategy*, 2021. https://www.youtube.com/watch?v=l-4LXBmzctE.

Cherry Bekaert LLP. *Webinar: Succession Planning for Family Businesses*, 2020. https://www.youtube.com/watch?v=HGlX9DAzhjo.

Continuity Family Business Consulting. *How Is Conflict Different in Family Business?*, 2016. https://www.youtube.com/watch?v=tjwUens3aZ8.

Dalton & Tomich, PLC. *Family Business Succession Plans: 5 Things You Need to Know*, 2019. https://www.youtube.com/watch?v=MbyZ3hoTeUQ.

Davis, John. "Family Talent: Develop the Next Generation Wealth Creator | John Davis." *John A. Davis* (blog), December 21, 2016. https://johndavis.com/family-talent-develop-the-next-generation-wealth-creator/.

DocstocTV. *10 Red Flags That Can Cause a Tax Audit*, 2015. https://www.youtube.com/watch?v=q5vazrS6lOs.

Family Enterprise Canada. *Lessons Learned from a Catastrophic Family Business Sale*, 2016. https://www.youtube.com/watch?v=qrVlblbu7cM.

Financialinsiderweek. *Succession Planning Issues of Family Businesses*, 2016. https://www.youtube.com/watch?v=DBOFG2Clxwo.

Grubman, Jim. *Successful Transitions in Your Family Business*. Accessed December 16, 2021. http://fambizpodcast.com/jim-grubman/.

Inc. CEO Project. *5 Rules to Transition a Family Business*, 2019. https://www.youtube.com/watch?v=xW6bshbCQsA.

INSEAD. *Family Business: Power, Politics & Emotional Dynamics*, 2020. https://www.youtube.com/watch?v=tQg_oh7N7us.

INSEAD. *How Family Businesses Can Plan for the Long Term: Morten Bennedsen*, 2014. https://www.youtube.com/watch?v=-utodVnVwLM.

Institute for Family Business. *Conflict in Family Business*, 2019. https://www.youtube.com/watch?v=QjR7aEy0FSQ.

Institute for Family Business. *Mindfulness in Family Business*, 2020. https://www.youtube.com/watch?v=fJWF7Rdqr1k.

Institute for Family Business. *Nurturing Leadership Talent in the Family*, 2020. https://www.youtube.com/watch?v=Y7o1CtFTqfs.

Institute for Family Business. *TEDx Institute For Family Business: Family Business Force for Good Live Panel*, 2020. https://www.youtube.com/watch?v=f6PYepU_BpQ.

Integris. *Navigating The Dynamics Of Your Family Owned Business*, 2020. https://www.youtube.com/watch?v=aJoz-i69cG8.

Journey to CEO. *Family Business Succession*, 2020. https://www.youtube.com/watch?v=wHBygPg7JLI.

Law Sessions with Jennifer Housen. *Succession Law - Intestacy Part 2*, 2021. https://www.youtube.com/watch?v=n3ty8nDvPxI.

MIT Sloan Executive Education. *Family Business Success Today: Beyond Operations, To Ownership*, 2021. https://www.youtube.com/watch?v=Hr-ARnT-cyc.

NCUAchannel. *BOD 4–2 Succession: How To Develop a Plan*, 2016. https://www.youtube.com/watch?v=93mxwUN3_xc.

Pearl Initiative. *Webinar | Understanding Family Dynamics & Conflict in Family Business*, 2020. https://www.youtube.com/watch?v=d4F2rqZneS0.

Ruisi, Chris. *Five Key Steps To A Successful Business Succession Plan*. 2010. https://www.youtube.com/watch?v=o-4r69KMWuI.

Sigma Assessment Systems. *Succession Planning in Family Businesses*, 2019. https://www.youtube.com/watch?v=vrqH7d-oTf8.

Strathmore University. *Family Business Management and Succession Planning – Dr David Wangombe (Part 1)*, 2015. https://www.youtube.com/watch?v=x-OybBf4tvI.

Succession Stories Podcast with Laurie Barkman. *ESOP Management Buyout as a Succession Plan, Darren Gleeman | Succession Stories E71 Laurie Barkman*, 2021. https://www.youtube.com/watch?v=zrr0c6DMcBg.

Succession Stories Podcast with Laurie Barkman. *Making Your Business Sellable for Succession - Miche Jean | Succession Stories E67 Laurie Barkman*, 2021. https://www.youtube.com/watch?v=UullZN4ZGwk.

Succession Stories Podcast with Laurie Barkman. *Moving Succession and Innovation Forward - Tricia Staible, Robinson Fans | Succession Stories E65*, 2021. https://www.youtube.com/watch?v=LctY5KAVSKo.

Tetrault, Rob. *Family Business Succession Planning Model*, 2020. https://www.youtube.com/watch?v=t5SktMLNocQ.

The Family Business Institute. *What Percentage of Family Businesses Have Succession Plans in Place?*, 2019. https://www.youtube.com/watch?v=nno7CZNr8EM.

The Lynch Law Group LLC. *Planning to Transition Your Family Business*, 2021. https://www.youtube.com/watch?v=oiIUqeWNW1k.

The Lynch Law Group LLC. *Steps in Selling a Business: CWE Training Webinar*, 2021. https://www.youtube.com/watch?v=5bT4CD6hI6A.

TheRawlsGroup. *Family Business Succession Planning - What Are the Critical Factors*, 2010. https://www.youtube.com/watch?v=OUs004-ZJR0.

Trout CPA. *Exit Planning: 5 Key Questions Owners Should Contemplate*, 2018. https://www.youtube.com/watch?v=kDgT2bGfEhI.

Valuetainment. *How to Work with Family in Business*, 2016. https://www.youtube.com/watch?v=uXEtw_XgpAw.

Westcott, Mark. *Primary Issues Facing Family Succession Planning*, 2021. https://www.youtube.com/watch?v=ZNM3Mm_fMLw.

Tools

"Business Succession Planning Checklist." https://docplayer.net/13440217-Life-s-brighter-under the-sun-business-succession-planning-checklist.html

Gallie, Brandon. "Business Succession Planning Checklist - BrandonGaille.Com." 2013. https://brandongaille.com/business-succession-planning-checklist/.

The Family Business Podcast. "Successful Transitions in Your Family Business." July 24, 2020. http://fambizpodcast.com/jim-grubman/.

Index

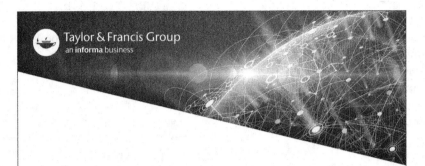

Printed in the United States
by Baker & Taylor Publisher Services